Fourth Amendment Practice and Procedure

Fourth Amendment Practice and Procedure

Inga L. Parsons
Attorney at Law
Law Offices of Inga L. Parsons

National Institute for Trial Advocacy

Anthony J. Bocchino, Editor in Chief
Temple University Beasley School of Law

Zelda Harris, Associate Editor
University of Arizona College of Law

Reproduction Permission
National Institute for Trial Advocacy
53550 Generations Dr
South Bend, IN 46635
(800) 225-6482   FAX (574) 271-8375
E-mail: nita.1@nd.edu Web site: www.nita.org

Parsons, Inga L., *Fourth Amendment Practice and Procedure*
(NITA 2005)
ISBN 1-55681-863-7

Library of Congress Cataloging-in-Publication Data
Parsons, Inga L., 1962-
    Fourth Amendment practice and procedure/ Inga L. Par-
sons.--1st ed.
        p. cm.
    Includes index.
        ISBN 1-55681-863-7
        1. Searches and seizures--United States. 2. United States.
Constitution. 4th Amendment.
    I. Title.

KF9630.P37 2004
345.73'0522--dc22
                          2004065557

Table of Contents

ix

Acknowledgments

These commentaries benefited greatly from the input and advice from my many colleagues at New York University School of Law, in particular the intellectual and moral support provided by Professors Chester L. Mirsky, James Jacobs and Harry Subin. I am grateful for the funding and support of the Filomen D'Agostino and Max E. Greenberg Faculty Research Fund which made the extensive research and availability of interns possible.

I could not have completed the book without Susan E. Wolfe, Esq., a partner at Hoffman & Pollok in New York City and one of my co-authors on *Practice Commentaries to the Federal Rules of Criminal Procedure*. Sue not only provided invaluable assistance in co-writing Chapter Sixteen on Wire Taps and Electronic Surveillance, but gave much of her time as sounding board on numerous issues.

The editing and review by members of the NITA team was a key part of the process especially the efforts by Frank Alan and Megan Anne Julian. I would also like to thank the many students at the Federal Defender Clinic and my summer interns at New York University School of Law who assisted in these commentaries, especially Alison Stang and Jennifer Morales whose editing skills and commitment were instrumental.

Finally, I am forever grateful to my family: Roger, Ara and Ethan Talkov and Charles and Marcia Parsons who not only endured the opening of my own law practice after seven years of teaching, but also withstood all the extra hours I have had to devote to the commentary project over the past years.

INGA L. PARSONS
Attorney at Law

INTRODUCTION

Unlike many other constitutional amendments and rules of procedure that are directly related to the criminal process and criminal rights, the Fourth Amendment touches us all by protecting the fundamental right to be secure in our home and person. As Justice Brennan so eloquently observed:

> There is no gainsaying that arriving at the truth is a fundamental goal of our legal system. But various constitutional rules limit the means by which government may conduct this search for truth in order to promote other values embraced by the Framers and cherished throughout our Nation's history. Ever since its inception, the rule excluding evidence seized in violation of the Fourth Amendment has been recognized as a principal mode of discouraging lawless police conduct. Without the constitutional guarantee against unreasonable searches and seizures would be a mere 'form of words.' The occasional suppression of illegally obtained yet probative evidence has long been considered a necessary cost of preserving overriding constitutional values: There is nothing new in the realization that the Constitution sometimes insulates the criminality of a few in order to protect the privacy of us all.

James v. Illinois, 493 U.S. 307, 311 (1990) (citations and quotations omitted).

The Fourth Amendment protections are being eroded as the pendulum of jurisprudence has swung from providing a barrier between overzealous cops and privacy to balancing the reasonableness of law enforcement in procuring incriminating evidence.

This book is written to assist the practicing lawyer, primarily defense lawyers, in litigating Fourth Amendment issues in this political post-9/11 climate. There are dozens, nay hundreds, of books cataloging the seminal Supreme Court decisions involving the Fourth Amendment. This book offers no competition to such academic tomes. Instead, it is intended to provide accessible, practical advice to supplement an attorney's research skills, legal analysis and common sense. This book also offers encouragement to criminal defense practitioners to keep up the good fight for the rights of people to be secure in their persons, houses, papers, and effects.

Most of the cases and statutes are federal since state laws vary, although many pattern themselves on the federal rules and procedures. However, the precepts are universal and are designed to assist the emerging law student, and the new associate, as well as the veteran practitioner.

CHAPTER ONE
OVERVIEW OF THE
FOURTH AMENDMENT

The Fourth Amendment to the Constitution of the United States of America is relatively succinct. The amendment itself says simply:

> The right of the people to be secure in their persons, houses, papers, and effects, against unreasonable searches and seizures, shall not be violated, and no Warrants shall issue, but upon probable cause, supported by Oath or affirmation, and particularly describing the place to be searched, and the persons or things to be seized.

As an initial matter, it is a good idea for the criminal practitioner to know what the Fourth Amendment says and what it does not say. Assumptions are made about what is contained in its single sentence. Even veteran criminal law practitioners can benefit from rereading the actual text of the Fourth Amendment on which they might not have laid eyes since their first year of law school. Indeed, an oft-repeated anecdote is that the text of the amendment has been perennially offered before congressional committees and soundly rejected.

Despite its brevity, and in part because of it, the Fourth Amendment has spawned (and continues to spawn) an enormous amount of litigation and case law. A recent Lexis check revealed 10,000 opinions since 1945 involving the Fourth Amendment. The critical language that has compelled much of the litigation is what constitutes an unreseasonable search or seizure, when are warrants required, and what amounts to probable cause.

Furthermore, because the remedy for violating the amendment's provisions is the judicially created penalty of exclusion of the evidence, the amount of litigation on both sides has been especially massive since the decision on whether to suppress the evidence could ultimately determine if the case can be prosecuted at all, regardless of the guilt of the defendant. As Justice Scalia observed in his concurrence in *California v. Acevedo*, there was an "explosion" of Fourth Amendment litigation after the exclusionary rule was adopted in 1914. *See Acevedo*, 500 U.S. 565, 582, 111 S. Ct. 1982, 1992, 114 L. Ed. 2d 619, 635 (1991) (Scalia, J., concurring).

The Fourth Amendment's Plain Language

The Fourth Amendment essentially provides that particularized warrants shall issue only upon probable cause supported by oath or affirmation, and protects against unreasonable searches and seizures. The amendment does not require that searches and seizures be preceded by a warrant. Nor does it provide that all searches and seizures require probable cause. The Fourth Amendment dictates that people and their effects, etc., are secure only as against unreasonable searches and seizures although the term "unreasonable" is not defined in the amendment. Moreover, nowhere does the amendment contain the words "legitimate expectation of privacy" or "exclusion of evidence."

The Fourth Amendment is silent on the appropriate remedy for a violation of its mandates. The exclusionary rule, under which the evidence is not allowed to be used in the prosecution's case against the defendant, is a judicial construct created to give teeth to the amendment. Ironically, the erosion of Fourth Amendment protections is directly related to the fact that the exclusionary remedy has made judges reluctant to enforce search and seizure rights in order to avoid the criminal going free because the constable blundered.

Criminal lawyers should know which Fourth Amendment arguments have constitutional legitimacy, such as the need for probable cause for a warrant or that the warrant be particularized, and which arguments are the result of judicial interpretation. The latter derive from case law that is subject to change and might differ from jurisdiction to jurisdiction. That being said, there are some fundamental principles of Fourth Amendment jurisprudence upon which one can rely, at least at present, although given the political climate in the wake of the events of 9/11, these rules are subject to change. (The recent challenge in *Dickerson v. United*

States, 530 U.S. 428, 120 S. Ct. 2326, 147 L. Ed. 2d 405 (2000), to the giving of Miranda warnings necessary for the admission of statements—the bedrock of Fifth Amendment rights-offers a prime example of the uncertainty of even extremely well-established criminal due process rights.)

Case law arising out of the Fourth Amendment's single sentence weaves a crazy quilt of search and seizure jurisprudence. The four borders of that quilt triggering Fourth Amendment protections upon which the practitioner can ordinarily rely are: warrants, search and seizure, probable cause and government action. The fringe around the quilt is standing and the exclusionary rule. The following is a brief overview of the four borders and the fringe. Specific litigation strategies on these issues and the Warrant Requirement itself and its exceptions are discussed in detail in the subsequent chapters to assist the practicing attorney in understanding Fourth Amendment issues.

General Fourth Amendment Principles

Warrant Requirement

Ordinarily, a search or seizure is not lawful unless preceded by a warrant issued by a neutral and detached magistrate, except in very specific and well-delineated exceptions. The Warrant Requirement of the Fourth Amendment, also known as the Warrant Clause, requires warrants to be issued upon probable cause. The Warrant Clause of the Fourth Amendment does not require warrants to be issued in all searches and seizures. Courts have held that searches and seizures are unreasonable unless executed pursuant to a warrant or well-established exception. *See Johnson v. United States*, 333 U.S. 10, 14, 68 S. Ct. 367, 369, 92 L. Ed. 436, 440 (1948). There are numerous well-established exceptions including exigent circumstances, consent, plain view, etc.

For a more detailed overview of warrants, *see Chapter Six: Warrants.*

Searches and Seizures

The Fourth Amendment clearly protects against unreasonable searches and seizures. To trigger this protection, there must be an actual search or seizure. (NB: the Fourth Amendment does not apply to the search and seizure of non-resident aliens in foreign countries. *See United States v. Verdugo-Urquidez*, 494 U.S. 259, 110 S. Ct. 1056, 108 L. Ed. 222 (1990).) The terms "search" and "seizure," however have taken on meanings beyond the obvious.

A search is legally defined as an invasion of an individual's legitimate expectation of privacy. *See Katz v. United States*, 389 U.S. 347, 88 S. Ct. 507, 19 L. Ed. 2d 576 (1967). This requires that an individual have a subjective expectation of privacy and that the expectation be an objectively reasonable one, meaning one that society is prepared to accept as reasonable. If contraband is left in plain view, abandoned in an alley, or voluntarily given to a police officer, there is no reasonable expectation of privacy and hence no Fourth Amendment search.

As with most legal terms, the definition of search is complex and often confusing. For example, when Sniffy the dog comes up to a piece of luggage and gives it the once over with his nose, an ordinary citizen would likely view that as a type of search. The courts, however, have determined that it is not a search through a balancing test of the need for the information against the degree of intrusion. *See United States v. Place*, 462 U.S. 696, 703, 103 S. Ct. 2637, 2642, 77 L. Ed. 2d 110, 118 (1983). Paradoxically, a police officer's small shift of a stereo in order to record stereo numbers even when the officer is legitimately on the premises can constitute a search. *See Arizona v. Hicks*, 480 U.S. 321, 107 S. Ct. 1149, 94 L. Ed. 2d 347 (1987).

There are two different types of seizures: seizures of people and seizures of property. "[T]he Fourth Amendment protects people, not places." *Katz*, 389 U.S. at 351, 88 S. Ct. at 511, 19 L. Ed. 2d at 582. The seizure of a person is determined by an objective standard and a totality of the circumstances analysis that asks the question whether the person stopped by government officials reasonably believes he or she is "free to leave." *See Michigan v. Chesternut*, 486, U.S. 567, 108 S. Ct. 1975, 100 L. Ed. 2d

565 (1988). This might happen with or without formal arrest. Seizure of property occurs when a government official meaningfully interferes with a person's possessory interest in that property. *See United States v. Jacobsen*, 466 U.S. 109, 104 S. Ct. 1652, 80 L. Ed. 2d 85 (1984). In plain English, the police take the bag, impound the car, and voucher the purse.

For a more detailed overview of Search and Seizure Law, *see Chapter Two: Search and Seizure Law Overview.*

Probable Cause

Probable cause is a level of suspicion necessary to obtain a warrant or effect an arrest and is generally required in order for the search or seizure to be reasonable. (If there is probable cause to believe a person committed a felony, an arrest does not require a warrant; if a misdemeanor or other non-felony is committed in the presence of an officer, a warrant is not required). To obtain a warrant, probable cause requires a finding of a "fair probability" that contraband or evidence will be found in a particular place as to a warrant. For an arrest, probable cause requires that an offense has been committed or that the offense is being committed. *See Illinois v. Gates*, 462 U.S. 213, 103 S. Ct. 2317, 76 L. Ed. 2d 527 (1983); *Beck v. Ohio*, 379 U.S. 89, 85 S. Ct. 223, 13 L. Ed. 2d 142 (1964). Probable cause is determined by a totality of the circumstances analysis, and is reviewed de novo by the appellate court, giving deference to the historical facts as found by the reviewing judge and the local law enforcement officers, and great deference to warrant determinations. *See Ornelas v. United States*, 517 U.S. 690, 116 S. Ct. 1657, 134 L. Ed. 2d 911 (1996). Where less than a full seizure is made, such as a stop and frisk or a protective sweep, the requisite level of suspicion may be less than that required for probable cause—mere reasonable suspicion to believe that criminal activity may be afoot can warrant the intrusion. *See Terry v. Ohio*, 392 U.S. 1, 30, 88 S. Ct. 1868, 1884, 20 L. Ed. 2d 889, 911 (1968).

For a more detailed overview of probable cause, *see Chapter Three: Probable Cause.*

Government Action

Government action is required to trigger the mandates of the Fourth Amendment. If an ordinary citizen breaks into a home and takes contraband that is later turned over to the authorities, there is no governmental action and therefore no requirement for a warrant or probable cause. The interesting question for the criminal attorney is what constitutes governmental action. For example, if an otherwise private citizen, such as an airport employee, is acting as an agent of the federal government, his or her actions could be considered government action, and, thus, trigger Fourth Amendment protections. *See*, e.g., *United States v. Doe*, 61 F.3d 107 (1st Cir. 1995) (nongovernmental airport personnel's administrative search triggered Fourth Amendment protections since the FAA prescribes extensive administrative directives to airport personnel).

For a more detailed overview of government action, *see Chapter Four: Government Action.*

Standing

Standing is the right to make a Fourth Amendment claim. Fourth Amendment rights are personal and cannot be litigated vicariously. In other words, a defendant cannot seek to preclude the use of evidence against him that was obtained from a location where he had no expectation of privacy, as the right is legally known. Thus, to make a Fourth Amendment claim, the movant must be the aggrieved party; her own rights must have been violated. For example, if Drug Enforcement Administration (DEA) agents unlawfully break into a home and seize two kilograms of cocaine, this might trigger Fourth Amendment issues. But unless the drugs were in a place or container in which the defendant had a reasonable expectation of privacy, the defendant ordinarily has no standing to challenge the admissibility of the evidence. *See Rawlings v. Kentucky*, 448 U.S. 98, 104-05, 100 S. Ct. 2556, 2561, 65 L. Ed. 2d 633, 641-42 (1980). In other words, if it was not the defendant's home or she was not a legitimate overnight guest, she would lack standing to challenge the unlawful search and the introduction of the evidence at her trial.

For a more detailed overview of standing, see *Chapter Five: Issues of Standing.*

The Exclusionary Rule

The concept of standing is closely tied to the exclusionary rule that surrounds and often dictates Fourth Amendment jurisprudence. The sanction for violating the Fourth Amendment is the exclusion of the evidence from use at trial. *See Weeks v. United States*, 232 U.S. 383, 34 S. Ct. 341, 58 L. Ed. 652 (1914). The evidence subject to exclusion includes any direct evidence and also evidence obtained through the exploitation of the illegal conduct, known as the "fruit of the poisonous tree." *See id.* The exclusionary rule was judicially created to deter and serve as a practical solution to police misconduct. Because the rule does not derive from the actual text of the Fourth Amendment, it arguably lacks constitutional legitimacy. Nevertheless, the rule was extended to the states through the Fourteenth Amendment. *See Mapp v. Ohio*, 367 U.S. 643, 81 S. Ct. 1684, 6 L. Ed. 2d 1081 (1961).

For a more detailed overview of the Exclusionary Rule, *see Chapter Seven: The Exclusionary Rule.*

Exceptions to the Warrant Requirement

Increasingly, the judiciary has taken a more positive view of law enforcement, and has provided loopholes to circumvent the exclusionary rule's arguably harsh mandates. Instead of focusing on the need to deter police misconduct through judicial review of probable cause, the view of the courts more often has been the need to enforce the laws and not handcuff the police in their efforts to do so. The many exceptions to the Warrant Requirement (more than 20 at last count, see listing below) are an obvious example.

Given the fact that a warrant is constitutionally prescribed and can be obtained relatively easily over the telephone and now even by facsimile machine, it is surprising that more warrants are not obtained. Although the Supreme Court has provided what it calls an "incentive" to use warrants by providing "great deference" to judicial decisions, *See Ornelas* 517 U.S. at 698-9, 116 S. Ct. at 1663, 134 L. Ed. 2d at 920, surprisingly very few searches proceed by warrant and there is a definite police culture where the rumored phrase in the ranks is that only rookies get warrants. (Failure to get a warrant may also be due to reluctance on the part of prosecutors to subject their law enforcement officers to yet another document under oath detailing case information when there are so many exceptions to the Warrant Requirement to validate the search.)

As the courts have grappled with the exclusionary effect of a violation of Fourth Amendment requirements, specifically the preclusion of evidence at trial, a myriad of exceptions to the Warrant Requirement have developed.

List of Exceptions to the Warrant Requirement

The following is a list of many exceptions to the Warrant Requirement. Included within the list are bases for avoiding the application of the exclusionary rule sanction all together. The most well-established and delineated exceptions are discussed in detail in subsequent chapters.

Abandonment

Administrative Searches

Airport Searches

Attenuation

Automobile

Boat Boarding

Border Searches

Consent

Container Searches

Exigent Circumstances

Foreign Searches

Good Faith

Government Offices

Hot Pursuit

Incident to Arrest

Independent Source

Inevitable Discovery

Inventory Search

Investigatory Stops

Mobile Home Exception

Open Fields

Plain Feel

Plain Hear

Plain Smell

Plain View

Prison Searches

Private Searches

Probation Searches

Public View

Regulated Industries

School Searches

Special Needs

Welfare Searches

Recognizing Fourth Amendment Issues

It is never too early in a case for a practitioner to begin assessing Fourth Amendment ramifications. Indeed, every significant fact should be held up against the filter of the Fourth Amendment for relevance and application to these issues. When attorneys first get a case, they should ask themselves a number of Fourth Amendment related questions. These questions provide a useful framework at the outset of a case when a criminal practitioner is assessing the possibility of Fourth Amendment issues in litigation.

Although the list of questions provided below is not exhaustive, it is a good starting point to get a general sense of what Fourth Amendment issues might arise. Many of the answers to these questions will not be known initially, and, particularly at the federal level, some of these questions will not be answered until much later in the case.

It is important, however, that the lawyer appreciate the issues in thinking about potential Fourth Amendment motions and in formulating hearing and trial strategies. The questions themselves assist a lawyer in evaluating which facts are unknown and must be discovered to consider Fourth Amendment issues adequately. For the experienced practitioner, many of these questions have been assimilated into the lawyer's typical case analysis so that he or she might not even realize the specific Fourth Amendment aspect actually being assessed, but simply jots "lack of consent" on the yellow note pad.

Useful Fourth Amendment Case Questions

First, how did the arresting officer know to arrest this person?

What was the source of that information?

Was that source reliable?

Was that information sufficient?

Was a warrant required?

Was a warrant obtained?

How was the warrant obtained?

Was the warrant supported by probable cause under oath?

If no warrant was obtained, is there a possible exception to the Warrant Requirement?

Second, how was the person stopped or arrested?

Where was the person stopped or arrested?

What did the officers do when they stopped or arrested the person?

Would a person at that time reasonably believe he was free to leave?

What did the officers know at the time the person was stopped or arrested?

Did the information known by the officers amount to probable cause to arrest?

Did the information known by the officers amount to reasonable suspicion?

Did the officers have a right to be where they were when they arrested the person?

Did an arrest at that particular place require a warrant?

Was a warrant obtained?

How was the warrant obtained?

Was the warrant supported by probable cause under oath?

If no warrant was obtained, is there a possible exception to the Warrant Requirement?

Third, was evidence seized?

How did the officers get the evidence?

When was the evidence seized relative to the arrest?

Where was the evidence seized?

Did the person have a reasonable expectation of privacy in the area searched?

Did the person have a reasonable expectation of privacy in the thing seized?

Did seizure of the evidence require a warrant?

Was a warrant obtained?

Was the warrant supported by probable cause under oath?

If no warrant was obtained, is there a possible exception to the Warrant Requirement?

Courageous Lawyering under the Fourth Amendment

The Fourth Amendment, as stated, does not require a warrant for every search or seizure; only that when a warrant is issued it must be supported by probable cause and it must be particularized. Rather than categorically requiring a warrant for searches and seizures, the amendment merely requires that a search or seizure be reasonable. Initially, the courts interpreted the Fourth Amendment to require a warrant supported by probable cause, unless there existed a well-established exception such as exigent circumstances, in order for the search to be reasonable. However, more recently, Fourth Amendment jurisprudence has increasingly focused on the balancing of an intrusion against the needs of law enforcement to determine whether the government action is reasonable; the courts less often demand a warrant to justify a Fourth Amendment intrusion.

Defense lawyers litigating Fourth Amendment issues will likely become discouraged by the absence of cases requiring warrants or suppressing evidence, and the corresponding explosion of cases allowing for so many exceptions to the Warrant Requirement on account of the eagerness of judges to uphold searches under those exceptions—seemingly at any cost—to keep the evidence in the case. Creative advocacy for those whose rights are most affected and whose liberty is at stake is an essential part of the defense function. The defense role is an important one and should not be shunted and marginalized just because of post-9/11 national security concerns, with those in power increasingly willing to accept nearly any means necessary to reach the ends, regardless of the impact on fundamental rights and previously established constitutional principles.

Litigating under the Fourth Amendment requires a certain amount of courage and persistence on the part of defense counsel to take on issues that are likely to be decided against the defense and in favor of the prosecution and law enforcement. Yet, so many of the Supreme Court's decisions in this area have been split decisions, often determined by a vote of 5 to 4. By the time a case comes before the Supreme Court, there is frequently a split in the circuits and reversals by higher courts of lower court findings. Thus, there are judges and jurisdictions that have upheld the defense arguments, even if the Supreme Court ultimately has rejected most of those defense arguments. This should give defense attorneys some confidence in continuing to make their arguments and distinguishing their individual case facts. After all, today's 4 to 5 vote might just be tomorrow's 5 to 4 vote in the defense's favor.

Some Useful Cases

Johnson v. United States, 333 U.S. 10, 68 S. Ct. at 367, 92 L. Ed. at 436 (1948).

Katz v. United States, 389 U.S. 347, 88 S. Ct. 507, 19 L. Ed. 2d 576 (1967).

Michigan v. Chesternut, 486, U.S. 567, 108 S. Ct. 1975, 100 L. Ed. 2d 565 (1988).

United States v. Jacobsen, 466 U.S. 109, 104 S. Ct. 1652, 80 L. Ed. 2d 85 (1984).

Illinois v. Gates, 462 U.S. 213, 103 S. Ct. 2317, 76 L. Ed. 2d 527 (1983).

Beck v. Ohio, 379 U.S. 89, 85 S. Ct. 223, 13 L. Ed. 2d 142 (1964).

Ornelas v. United States, 517 U.S. 690, 116 S. Ct. 1657, 134 L. Ed. 2d 911 (1996).

Terry v. Ohio, 392 U.S. 1, 88 S. Ct. 1868, 20 L. Ed. 2d 889 (1968).

Weeks v. United States, 232 U.S. 383, 34 S. Ct. 341, 58 L. Ed. 652 (1914).

CHAPTER TWO
SEARCH AND SEIZURE LAW OVERVIEW

Search or seizure of a person or property is generally determined to be unreasonable unless pursuant to a warrant supported by a finding of probable cause by a "neutral and detached magistrate." *Johnson v. United States*, 333 U.S. 10, 14, 68 S. Ct. 367, 369, 92 L. Ed. 436, 440 (1948). The starting point for every case involving a search or a seizure is the presumption that a warrant is required and it is the prosecution's burden to demonstrate that absent a warrant, the search and seizure were within a recognized exception. That being said, there are many exceptions to the "Warrant Requirement" including investigatory detentions, the automobile exception, and exigent circumstance situations, as listed in Chapter One.

Even before conducting a client interview, meeting with a case agent, investigating a scene, or negotiating with opposing counsel, counsel must review the facts of the case within the context of current search and seizure law. If a search or seizure in the case was arguably unlawful, a very different disposition might be reached in negotiations, and it certainly will influence the course and strategy of any investigations and interviews.

There are countless tomes written on Fourth Amendment law, but no lawyer should rely on treatises alone. There is no substitute for good old roll-up-your-sleeves case law research, particularly in the applicable jurisdiction. Many of the issues are fact specific and require application of the law to the facts by using and distinguishing supporting and contrary cases. Textbooks typically rely on excerpted Supreme Court cases, which are helpful for general principles of Fourth Amendment law, but lower-level court decisions provide the factual applications critical to the lawyer's analysis in motions and litigation.

Due to the factual nature of Fourth Amendment inquiries, however, a lawyer is unlikely to find a case that fits the individual facts on all fours. Rather, the lawyer's argument will likely develop by analyzing and analogizing from the case law within each jurisdiction under the umbrella holdings of the highest state court for state cases, the controlling circuit for federal cases, and, of course, the Supreme Court. From the following basic analysis of the seminal Supreme Court cases, a lawyer can then particularize and update the research for the individual case within the applicable jurisdiction at the local level.

Attorneys also should be aware that passage of the USA PATRIOT Act ("Uniting and Strengthening America by Providing Appropriate Tools Required to Intercept and Obstruct Terrorism") has broadened governmental powers to invade and intercept information. As detailed in *Chapter Sixteen: Wiretaps and Electronic Surveillance*, the most dramatic effect has been on the ability to gather and track communications including expansion of pen registers and roving surveillance. The Act has also authorized so-called "sneak and peak" warrants (allowing execution of warrants with delayed notification where essentially no tangible evidence or electronic communications evidence is seized) and allows the Attorney General to collect DNA samples from prisoners convicted of any federal crime of violence or terrorism. It has also provided the government with increased access to confidential information including library records. Attorneys must consider the impact of the Act with respect to any expectation of privacy and use the most recent statute and case law as the law continues to change, seemingly daily, in the aftermath of 9/11.

The Law of Seizure Generally

Seizure of a person is generally determined by an objective standard of whether the person stopped by government officials reasonably believes he or she is not "free to leave." *Michigan v. Chesternut,* 486 U.S. 567, 573, 108 S. Ct. 1975, 1979, 100 L. Ed. 2d 565, 572 (1988). The "free to leave" standard, however, has been deemed a necessary but not a sufficient condition for seizure. *See California v. Hodari D.*, 499 U.S. 621, 628, 111 S. Ct. 1547, 1551 , 113 L. Ed. 2d 690, 698 (1991). The Supreme Court has resisted bright lines and has adopted a contextual approach and consequently the test is not to look to one particular factor for this determination. The ultimate test for seizure involves an assessment of the "totality of the circumstances" by taking into account all the circumstances surrounding the incident. *See Chesternut*, 486 U.S. at 572-73, 108 S. Ct. at 1979, 100 L. Ed. 2d at 571.

Seizure of property occurs when there is government intrusion that meaningfully interferes with a person's possessory interest in the property. *See United States v. Jacobson*, 466 U.S. 109, 113, 104 S. Ct. 1652, 1656, 80 L. Ed. 2d 85, 94 (1984). Seizure of property is governed by the same principles as seizure of a person and the reasonableness of a seizure will depend primarily on how tailored the intrusion is to the needs of law enforcement. *See United States v. Place*, 462 U.S. 696, 703, 103 S. Ct. 2637, 2642, 77 L. Ed. 2d 110, 118 (1983). An example of a property seizure case may involve airline luggage and an intrusion that meaningfully interferes with the person's possession. Whether the interference is meaningful requires an examination of the circumstances of the detention of the bag (is the guy about to miss his plane) and the length of detention (a few minutes to let a dog sniff the luggage versus holding it for four hours to find the dog to do the search).

The subjective belief of the police officer is not determinative of a seizure. "Subjective intentions play no role in ordinary, probable-cause Fourth Amendment analysis," and, indeed, a stop can be pretextual by the officer and still not trigger Fourth Amendment protections. *Whren v. United States*, 517 U.S. 806, 813, 116 S. Ct. 1769, 1774, 135 L. Ed. 2d 89, 98 (1996). In other words, even if the police officer clearly did not intend to let the person go it might not be considered a seizure. If, however, the subjective intent of the officer not to let that person leave were communicated to the suspect, such as the officer telling the individual "I am not going to let you go," or "you need to stay here with me," it would obviously become a relevant and even dispositive factor in some cases. However, if there were a show of authority such that a reasonable person would believe she was not free to leave but if that person actually did leave, then there would be no seizure for Fourth Amendment purposes. *See Hodari D.*, 499 U.S. at 628, 111 S. Ct. at 1552, 113 L. Ed. 2d. at 699.

Moreover, the show of authority must be willful on the part of the government actors and not an unknowing act, such as a parked police car that slips its brake and pins in a vehicle driven by a wanted felon. *See Brower v. County of Inyo*, 489 U.S. 593, 596, 109 S. Ct. 1378, 1381, 103 L. Ed. 2d 628, 635 (1989). When the restriction of movement is the result of circumstances not created by the arresting officer, such as the fact that the suspect is on a bus, the standard is more precisely "whether a reasonable person would feel free to decline the officers' requests or otherwise terminate the encounter." *Florida v. Bostick*, 501 U.S. 429, 436, 111 S. Ct. 2382, 2387, 115 L. Ed. 2d 389, 400 (1991).

Whether a person reasonably feels free to leave does not require the officer to inform that person that he or she is free to leave, though doing so or failing to do so is a factor considered in the totality of the circumstances analysis. *See Ohio v. Robinette*, 519 U.S. 33, 39-40, 117 S. Ct. 417, 421, 136 L. Ed. 2d 347, 355 (1996). Other factors frequently considered important in determining whether a reasonable person would feel free to leave (although not individually required or dispositive) include whether the police activated sirens or flashers, commanded the person to halt, displayed weapons, operated their cars in a manner intended to block the person, or controlled the person's direction or movements. *See Chesternut*, 486 U.S. at 575, 108 S. Ct. at 1980, 100 L. Ed. 2d at 573. Additional examples of particularly relevant conduct include "the threatening presence of several officers, the display of a weapon by an officer, some physical touching of the person of the citizen, or the use of language or tone of voice indicating that compliance with the officer's request might be compelled." *United States v. Mendenhall*, 446 U.S. 544, 554, 100 S. Ct. 1870, 1877, 64 L. Ed. 2d 497, 509 (1980). As discussed in more detail in *Chapter Eight: Litigating Investigatory Detentions*, courts tend to focus more on the actions of the officers in creating a seizure than on circumstances that were not created by the officers unless the officers took advantage of those circumstances.

Consensual, Investigatory, and *Terry* Stops

An officer may approach someone on the street or a public place and ask questions such as inquiring as to that person's identity, requesting identification or asking for consent to search the person's property, without Fourth Amendment consequences. *See Bostick*,

501 U.S. at 434-35, 111 S. Ct. at 2386, 115 L. Ed. 2d at 398. "While most citizens will respond to a police request, the fact that people do so, and do so without being told they are free not to respond, hardly eliminates the consensual nature of the response." *I.N.S. v. Delgado*, 466 U.S. 210, 216, 104 S. Ct. 1758, 1762, 80 L. Ed. 2d 247, 255 (1984). In short, it is not a seizure if the person is free to "disregard the police and go about his business." *Hodari D.*, 499 U.S. at 628, 111 S. Ct. at 1552, 113 L. Ed. 2d. at 698. But if the officer, through a show of authority or use of physical force, restrains that person's liberty, that person has been seized for Fourth Amendment purposes. *See Terry v. Ohio*, 392 U.S. 1, 19 n.16, 88 S. Ct. 1868, 1879 n.16, 20 L. Ed. 2d 889, 905 n.16 (1968).

Prior to the Supreme Court's landmark holding in *Terry*, 392 U.S. at 30, 88 S. Ct. at 1884-85, 20 L. Ed. at 911, any restraint resulting in a seizure required probable cause. *Terry* carved out a limited exception to this probable cause requirement: the police only need *articulable suspicion* that a person has committed or is about to commit a crime to support a temporary seizure. This temporary seizure is limited to the extent necessary to investigate the reasonable suspicion and for a stop and frisk for weapons to assure the officers' safety when the police have reason to believe that the suspect is armed and dangerous. *See United States v. Brignoni-Ponce*, 422 U.S. 873, 880, 95 S. Ct. 2574, 2580, 45 L. Ed. 2d 607, 616 (1975). For more detail on investigatory detentions, see *Chapter Eight: Investigatory Detentions*.

Making Sense of Fourth Amendment Seizure Versus Fifth Amendment Custody

There is some confusion in the case law with respect to the difference, if any, as to what constitutes a Fourth Amendment "seizure" and what constitutes "custody" for Fifth Amendment purposes triggering the requirement of Miranda warnings. The Supreme Court itself has acknowledged that defining custody for Miranda purposes is a "slippery one." *Oregon v. Elstad*, 470 U.S. 298, 309, 105 S. Ct. 1285, 1293, 84 L. Ed. 2d 222, 232 (1985). There is no direct equation of the two standards, although some opinions have appeared to use them interchangeably. The key difference for Fourth Amendment purposes is that if a suspect reasonably does not feel free to leave, the government's intrusion amounts to a seizure and yet the suspect may not be in custody for Miranda purposes.

At the end of the day, the practitioner should be aware that ordinary *Terry* stops do not require the giving of Miranda warnings even though the person is "seized" for Fourth Amendment purposes. In addition, exclusion of evidence obtained as a "fruit" of the poisonous tree for Fourth Amendment violations, technically does not apply to Fifth Amendment Miranda violations meaning that information obtained in violation of Miranda and used to obtain other evidence will not be suppressed on that basis. *See Missouri v. Seibert*, 124 S.Ct 2601, 2616-17 (2004). (O'Connor, J. dissent, agreeing with the plurality in part). That said, an analysis similar to the Fourth Amendment "fruits" type analysis may be used to determine whether the statements were free from compulsion and any taint attenuated. *Id.* For an excellent road map through this confusing state of the law, see Circuit Judge Jon O. Newman's opinion in *Cruz v. Miller*, 255 F.3d 77 (2d Cir. 2001), discussing the differing standards at the Supreme Court level, as well as various circuit court discrepancies.

The Law of Searches Generally

For the lay person a search is not a particularly difficult concept. When four-year-olds play hide and seek, they "search" for hidden children. But in order to constitute a search under the Fourth Amendment there must be a reasonable expectation of privacy. Using this analogy, under the Fourth Amendment there is no search if the four-year-old (assumed to be spykids working for the government in this analogy) attempts to hide by crouching down in the middle of an open hay field. Although the other kids may have to search or hunt for him, the kid in the open hay field has no reasonable expectation of privacy in his location. Conversely, the four-year-old who stuffs himself inside an old tractor tire in the back shed after closing the door behind him has a reasonable expectation of privacy and the hunt for this kid constitutes a search. The kid in the middle of the field might have subjectively expected some privacy, i.e., not to be found, but society (including other four-year-olds) would not recognize that expectation as reasonable.

In sum, a search, for Fourth Amendment purposes, is an intrusion into an area where there has been exhibited a subjective expectation of privacy which society recognizes as reasonable. *See Katz v. United States*, 389 U.S. 347, 361, 88 S. Ct. 507, 516, 19 L. Ed. 2d 576, 588 (1967) (Harlan, J., concurring). By definition, then, there is no Fourth Amendment search unless a two-pronged test is met: 1) the individual manifested a subjective expectation of privacy; and 2) that expectation is one society is willing to accept as reasonable. *See California v. Ciarolo*. 476 U.S. 207, 211, 106 S. Ct. 1809, 1811, 90 L. Ed. 2d 210, 215 (1986). Thus, physical or other government intrusion is not a search unless there is a reasonable expectation of privacy.

Whether a search is really a search for Fourth Amendment purposes also depends on a balancing of the intrusion against the legitimacy and need of the police action. *See United States v. Place*, 462 U.S. 696, 703, 103 S. Ct. 2637, 2642, 77 L. Ed. 2d 110, 118 (1983). The lynchpin of this analysis is "reasonableness," but the Supreme Court has not maintained a consistent or explicable pattern of reasonableness. Some illustrative examples follow. Use of a pen register at the telephone company to monitor phone calls made within a home is not considered a search. *See Smith v. Maryland*, 442 U.S. 735, 99 S. Ct. 2577, 61 L. Ed. 2d 220 (1979). Aerial surveillance by a helicopter 400 feet above a home for the purpose of looking into a greenhouse in the yard is not a search (the boy in the hay field comes to mind). See *Florida v. Riley*, 488 U.S. 445, 109 S. Ct. 693, 102 L. Ed. 2d 835 (1989). Intrusion into a public telephone booth, no matter how minimal, is a search. *See Katz v. United States*, 389 U.S. 347, 88 S. Ct. 507, 19 L. Ed. 2d 576 (1967). Intrusion into a prison cell is not a search. *See Hudson v. Palmer*, 468 U.S. 517, 104 S. Ct. 3194, 82 L. Ed. 2d 393 (1984). Visual observation alone is no search at all ("I see you"). *See Dow Chemical v. United States*, 476 U.S. 227, 106 S. Ct. 1819, 90 L. Ed. 2d 226 (1986). A narcotics dog sniffing luggage is not considered a search. *See United States v. Place*, 462 U.S. at 707, 103 S. Ct. at 2644-45, 77 L. Ed. 2d at 121. A police officer's small shift of a stereo that was otherwise in plain view to record serial numbers constitutes a search. *See Arizona v. Hicks*, 480 U.S. 321, 107 S. Ct. 1149, 94 L. Ed. 2d 347 (1987).

Under ordinary circumstances, searches require warrants approved by a neutral and detached magistrate. *See Johnson*, 333 U.S. at 14, 68 S. Ct. at 369, 92 L. Ed. at 440. The courts, however, have developed a number of exceptions to the "Warrant Requirement," such as the automobile exception, exigent circumstances, investigatory detentions, and inventory searches, through the balancing of public policy concerns against the degree of intrusion. Again, the focus tends to be more on what is reasonable and less on the constitutional requirement for a warrant.

Using a similar reasoning, since warrantless searches are presumptively unreasonable, the courts have focused significantly on whether something is in fact a "search" and might not necessarily reach the issue of whether the intrusive action was reasonable. In other words, the courts have defined away many of the problems, usually to avoid the exclusionary rule. If law enforcement action is not defined under the law as a search within the Fourth Amendment, even though an ordinary person might consider it a search in the customary use of the word, then such action does not trigger the amendment's protections.

The Home Is Still the Castle

The highest privacy protections are reserved for the home, which is still regarded as the proverbial castle. These are the search areas where a defense attorney is likely to have the most success, particularly where the officers lacked a warrant. "With few exceptions, the question whether a warrantless search of a home is reasonable and hence constitutional must be answered no." *Kyllo v. United States*, 533 U.S. 27, 31, 121 S. Ct. 2038, 2042, 150 L. Ed. 2d 94, 100 (2001). The defense should remind the judge that "[t]he overriding function of the Fourth Amendment is to protect personal privacy and dignity against unwarranted intrusion by the State." *Schmerber*, 384 U.S. at 767. As Justice Scalia explained in *Kyllo*:

"In the home, our cases show, all details are intimate details, because the entire area is held safe from prying government eyes. Thus, in Karo, the only thing detected was a can of ether in the home; and in Arizona v. Hicks, the only thing detected by a physical search that went beyond what officers, lawfully present, could observe in "plain view" was the registration number of a phonograph turntable. These were intimate details because they were details of the home... ."

533 U.S. at 37-38, 121 S. Ct. at 2045, 150 L. Ed. 2d at 104.

Absent exigent circumstance or consent, the police need an arrest warrant to enter a person's home in order to execute the arrest. *See Payton v. New York*, 445 U.S. 573, 100 S. Ct. 1371, 63 L. Ed. 2d 639 (1980). But if the subject of an arrest warrant is in the home of a third party, the police need a search warrant to enter the third-party home. *See Steagald v. United States*, 451 U.S. 204, 101 S. Ct. 1642, 68 L. Ed. 2d 38 (1981). That being said, no warrant is required to observe information in plain view of outsiders including police officers. "The Fourth Amendment protection of the home has never been extended to require law enforcement officers to shield their eyes when passing by a home on public thoroughfares." *See Ciarolo*, 476 U.S. at 213, 106 S. Ct. at 1812, 90 L. Ed. 2d at 216.

Is the Body a Temple?

Intrusions into the body involve human dignity and privacy of the highest order. In the absence of exigent circumstances or other well-delineated exceptions to the Warrant Requirement, searches within the body, like the home, require a warrant. If there are emergency considerations, such as the loss of evidence during the time it would take to get a warrant to extract blood, the intrusion must be reasonable. That is, the manner and method by which the extraction is made, *e.g.*, a small amount of blood taken by licensed medical personnel with a syringe, must be reasonable. The Supreme Court has upheld the warrantless taking of a blood sample to test for alcohol where there was probable cause to believe the person was intoxicated and the search was a valid search incident to arrest. *See Schmerber v. California*, 384 U.S.

757, 86 S. Ct. 1826, 16 L. Ed. 2d 908 (1966). The Patriot Act allows for the taking of DNA samples of prisoners convicted of federal terrorism felonies.

Routine, warrantless searches of persons entering the country are considered reasonable and may be conducted by law enforcement officers without any suspicion whatsoever. *See United States v. Montoya de Hernandez*, 473 U.S. 531, 537-39, 105 S. Ct. 3304, 3309-3310, 87 L. Ed. 2d 381, 389-91 (1985) ("[N]ot only is the expectation of privacy less at the border than in the interior, the Fourth Amendment balance between the interests of the Government and the privacy right of the individual is also struck much more favorably to the Government at the border."). Although some categories of searches, i.e., body cavity, strip, pat down and involuntary x-ray searches, are so intrusive as to be clearly non-routine, the Supreme Court has not yet ruled on the requisite level of suspicion for any of these searches when performed during the course of a border search. A number of circuits have upheld strip searches where the officer has reasonable or "real" suspicion that the person is carrying drugs on the body. *See, e.g., United States v. Vance*, 62 F.3d 1152, 1156 (9th Cir. 1995); *United States v. Okeyan*, 786 F.2d 832, 837 (8th Cir. 1986).

Technology and Searches

With continual advancements in technologies that allow for inside observations of dwellings and other containers without physically entering those structures, Fourth Amendment protections have been challenged. The advent of aerial observations technologies means that areas of the home which were previously private are now in plain view from the skies. The courts have upheld these plain view searches because people no longer have a reasonable expectation that their property will not be exposed to those in airplanes. *See Ciarolo*, 476 U.S. at 213, 106 S. Ct. at 1812, 90 L. Ed. 2d at 216. However, there are limitations on the extent to which observations obtained outside the home are constitutionally permissible. Justice Scalia, writing for the majority, recently traced the advent of enhanced observation technology in Kyllo, in which the Court found that thermal-imaging technology used to monitor the amount of heat emanating from a home required a warrant. 533 U.S. at 40, 121 S. Ct. at 2046, 150 L. Ed. 2d at 106. A key factor in this analysis deals with how widespread and publicly available the technology is; whereas airplane travel is common and routine, thermal imaging technology is not routine or in general public use. *See id.*

The bottom line, at least with respect to the use of technology to observe a home, is that "[w]here, as here, the Government uses a device that is not in general public use, to explore details of the home that would previously have been unknowable without physical intrusion, the surveillance is a 'search' and is presumptively unreasonable without a warrant." *Id.* This is true even when the information obtained might seem minor or innocuous.

Some Useful Cases

Johnson v. United States, 333 U.S. 10, 68 S. Ct. 367, 92 L. Ed. 436 (1948) (ruling that search or seizure of a person or property is generally unreasonable unless performed pursuant to a warrant supported by a finding of probable cause by a neutral and detached magistrate).

Katz v. United States, 389 U.S. 347, 88 S. Ct. 507, 19 L. Ed. 2d 576 (1967) (defining search as the invasion of an individual's legitimate expectation of privacy).

Terry v. Ohio, 392 U.S. 1, 88 S. Ct. 1868, 20 L. Ed. 2d 889 (1968) (holding that law enforcement officers only need reasonable suspicion that a person has committed or is about to commit a crime to support a temporary seizure of that individual).

United States v. Place, 462 U.S. 696, 103 S. Ct. 2637, 77 L. Ed. 2d 110 (1983) (providing that, for Fourth Amendment purposes, a search depends on a balancing of the quality and nature of the intrusion against the legitimacy and need of the police action).

Horton v. California, 496 U.S. 128, 110 S. Ct. 2301, 110 L. Ed. 2d 112 (1990) (affirming that a search compromises the individual interest in privacy, while a seizure deprives the individual of dominion over his or her person or property).

Kyllo v. United States, 533 U.S. 27, 121 S. Ct. 2038, 150 L. Ed. 2d 94 (2001) (ruling that the warrantless search of a home is generally unreasonable and unconstitutional, and that the use of thermal-imaging technology to monitor the amount of heat emanating from a home requires a warrant).

CHAPTER THREE
PROBABLE CAUSE

Probable Cause in General

The commonly proffered definition of probable cause is the general concept that it exists when the known facts and circumstances are sufficient to allow a man of reasonable prudence to believe that contraband or evidence of a crime will be found; or in the belief that a crime has been committed and a particular individual committed it. *See Brinegar v. United States*, 338 U.S. 160, 203 S. Ct. 1302, 93 L.3d 1879 (1949). This standard purportedly "protects citizens from rash and unreasonable interferences with privacy and from unfounded charges of crime while giving fair leeway for enforcing the law in the community's protection." *Id.* In other words: "[r]equiring more would unduly hamper law enforcement. To allow less would be to leave law-abiding citizens at the mercy of the officers' whim or caprice." *Id.* But the general definition begs the question: what facts and circumstances render a determination sufficient?

It has been acknowledged by the Supreme Court that the standards for probable cause are not "readily, or even usefully, reduced to a neat set of legal rules." *Ornelas v United States*, 517 U.S. 690, 698-9, 116 S. Ct. 1657, 1662-3, 134 L. Ed. 2d 911, 920 (1996) (citing *Illinois v. Gates*, 462 U.S. 213, 231,103 S. Ct. 2317, 2328, 76 L. Ed. 2d 527, 544 (1983)). They are "fluid concepts" that take their "substantive content" from the particular contexts in which the standards are addressed with each case decided on its own facts and circumstances. *Id.* Probable cause involves "factual and practical considerations of everyday life on what reasonable and prudent men, not legal technicians, act." *Gates*, 462 U.S. at 231, 103 S. Ct. at 2328, 76 L. Ed. 2d at 544. However, when examining probable cause, courts are advised to determine the historical facts, and then view those historical facts from the standpoint of an objectively reasonable police officer. *See*

Ornelas, 517 U.S. at 696, 116 S. Ct. at 1662, 134 L. Ed. 2d at 919 (emphasis added).

The evidence necessary for probable cause is generally less than the evidence necessary to "justify condemnation." Moreover, the amount of proof appropriate in ordinary judicial proceedings is inapplicable to probable cause determinations, meaning that the standard is not proof beyond a reasonable doubt or preponderance of the evidence; these "finely tuned" standards have no place in a probable cause decision according to the Supreme Court. *See Gates*, 462 U.S. at 231, 103 S. Ct. at 2328, 76 L. Ed. 2d at 544 (cited in *Maryland v. Pringle*, 124 S. Ct. 795, 800, 157 L. Ed. 2d 769, 775 (2003)).

Trial courts evaluate probable cause under a totality of the circumstances analysis. Appellate courts will review probable cause determinations under a de novo standard, unless the officers obtained a warrant. *See Ornelas* 517 U.S. at 699, 116 S. Ct. at 1663, 134 L. Ed. 2d at 920. In cases where there is a warrant the reviewing courts will give great deference to the issuing judge in order to provide an incentive for the use of warrants. *Id.*

Probable Cause to Arrest

Every arrest must be based upon probable cause whether made with or without a warrant. Probable cause to arrest essentially boils down to two prongs: 1) reasonable belief of guilt; and 2) belief of guilt particularized to a specific person. *Ybarra v. Illinois,* 444 U.S. 85, 91, 100 S. Ct. 338, 342, 62 L. Ed. 2d 238, 245 (1979). The determination of probable cause must be made at the time the arrest is made and not from information obtained after the arrest such as evidence discovered during any search incident to the arrest. In other words, the officer cannot simply have a hunch that the young kid on the street in a bad neighborhood has drugs, search him, find drugs and then arrest him. Something less than probable cause, however, would be sufficient for an investigatory stop or *Terry* stop, as detailed in *Chapter Eight: Investigatory Detentions*.

The officer's subjective reason for arresting someone is ordinarily not relevant. It is only relevant whether objectively there was probable cause to arrest. Otherwise, as the First Circuit observed, "[i]f subjective good faith alone were the test, the protections of the Fourth Amendment would evaporate and the people would be secure in their persons, houses, papers and effects, only in the discretion of the police." *Rivera v. Murphy*, 979 F.2d 259, 263 (1st Cir. 1992). However, given the deference to police officer determinations in reality, despite the de novo review on appeal described above, Fourth Amendment protections rely increasingly on the discretion of the police and such protections have tended to erode with each new Fourth Amendment decision upholding warrantless arrests.

Probable cause to arrest must be particularized to the individual. Although in an era of increasing use of conspiracy charges, courts still will pause when the probable cause smacks of guilt by association. The nature of the case, however, will affect the success of this argument by the defense. For example, if the case involves allegations of organized crime or "mob" activity, very little is required for probable cause purposes because the crime itself is intimately tied to association. For example, a "walk talk" where suspected organized crime members individuals meet and walk around in conversation, presumably to avoid being overheard or detected, could be enough to support probable cause in an organized crime case. Narcotics is another type of case where association itself can provide probable cause if the person is present where criminal activity is openly conducted over a period of time. *See, e.g., Ker v. California*, 374 U.S. 23, 37, 83 S. Ct. 1623, 1631, 10 L. Ed. 2d 726, 740 (1963) (plurality opinion) (finding probable cause to arrest the wife where her husband used home for narcotics operations and marijuana was in prominent place in a room which had been occupied by the wife).

There are some limits to what might seem like probable cause by association. In *United States v. Di Re*, 332 U.S. 581, 68 S. Ct. 222, 92 L. Ed. 210 (1948), the Supreme Court found there was no probable cause to arrest the passenger in a vehicle driven by a suspect involved in a counterfeit ration-coupon case without probable cause to believe the passenger was also involved in the scheme. A very recent Supreme Court decision from a unanimous Court made clear, however, that $763 in a glove compartment along with drugs in a backseat armrest and no satisfactory explanation for the drugs or money was sufficient to arrest all three individuals in a vehicle including the passenger in the front seat. *Pringle*, 124 S. Ct. 795, 157 L. Ed. 769 (2003). The fact that the individuals were in a vehicle may give rise to an inference that all of them "have the same interest in concealing the fruits or the evidence of their wrongdoing," unlike customers in a tavern. *See Wyoming v. Houghton*, 526 U.S. 295, 304-5, 119 S. Ct. 1297, 1302, 143 L. Ed. 2d 408, 417 (1999). As with most Fourth Amendment arguments, it is much harder to argue lack of particularized probable cause in car cases. *See also*, *Chapter Fourteen: The Automobile Exception.*

Counsel must tease through the probable cause supporting the arrest of each individual so as to ensure that the particularized belief of criminal activity is properly applied to that individual defendant. Defense counsel should emphasize that our society still abhors guilt by association, and, despite recent erosions of the Fourth Amendment protections in the current political climate, the dragnet of rounding up the usual suspects or "sweeping" a street hoping to catch a criminal is still a violation of Fourth Amendment principles against unreasonable search and seizure. These probable cause challenges may be made at the initial appearance or in motions to suppress evidence. *See Chapter Eighteen: Fourth Amendment Issues at the Initial Appearance* and *Chapter Twenty Three: Motion Practice Under the Fourth Amendment.*

Probable Cause to Search

Searches conducted without a warrant are presumed to be illegal. *See Katz*, 389 U.S. at 347, 88 S. Ct. at 507, 19 L. Ed. 2d at 576. The Supreme Court has reiterated that, despite the reasonableness analysis often determining the propriety of a search conducted without a warrant, there is still a "strong preference" for warrants to search. *See Ornelas*, 517 U.S. at 699, 116 S. Ct. at 1663, 134 L. Ed. 2d at 920 (giving great deference to searches conducted pursuant to a warrant as opposed to de novo review for warrantless searches as a means of maintaining some incentive to proceed by warrant).

Probable cause to search essentially involves a two-pronged analysis: 1) a reasonable belief that a crime has been committed; and 2) a reasonable belief that evidence of the crime will be found in the place to be searched. As with probable cause to arrest, the probable cause to search must be individualized to a specific area or person. This second prong is often a fruitful area of litigation for defense lawyers in multiple defendant cases where officers typically detail one umbrella probable cause for all defendants.

The concept of an individualized basis for a search was well illustrated in *Ybarra, supra*, where the Supreme Court determined that a warrant allowing for the search of a tavern and bartender for narcotics did not permit a search of a customer present in the tavern. In other words, "search by association" is not permitted. The *Ybarra* Court's explanation is a helpful quote for the defense in litigating searches on the grounds that the authorities have gone beyond the individualized probable cause:

> [A] person's mere propinquity to others independently suspected of criminal activity does not, without more, give rise to probable cause to search that person. Where the standard is probable cause, a search or seizure of a person must be supported by probable cause particularized with respect to that person. This requirement cannot be undercut or avoided by simply pointing to the fact that coincidentally there exists probable cause to search or seize another or to search the premises where the person may happen to be.

Id. at 801 (citations and internal quotations omitted). (For those reaching for their dictionaries, "propinquity" means nearness or proximity, as you no doubt suspected.) For additional challenges to probable cause *see also, Chapter Six: Warrants, Attacking Warrants—Probable Cause.*

Anonymous Tips and Confidential Informants

The basis for probable cause can come from a confidential informant, or from an anonymous tip and may even be based entirely on hearsay. In contrast to an anonymous tip or confidential informant, a crime victim's motive and access to information is

31

ordinarily reasonably relied on by officers for probable cause for the alleged crime. Similarly, information from a private citizen, where reliability can be determined based on the nature of the information and the opportunity to see or hear coupled with verification by police investigation, is usually sufficient.

Most litigation in this area will arise when probable cause depends exclusively or primarily on anonymous tips or confidential informants. In those situations, the defense has a lot to work with in challenging the basis of probable cause. The challenge will revolve around the reliability of the information and the level of corroboration, if any, of the information. There is also an overlay of whether the officer's reliance on the information was reasonable given the circumstances known to the officer at the time and the officer's experience.

As to informants, it used to be that informant information was subject to a strict two-pronged analysis under the so-called Aguilar-Spinelli test requiring that the informant's basis of knowledge be specified and the informant's truthfulness could be shown by the fact that he had provided reliable information in the past or the information is inherently reliable. This test was rejected by the Supreme Court in favor of a totality of the circumstances analysis used today. *See Gates*, 462 U.S. at 213, 103 S. Ct. at 2317, 76 L. Ed. 2d at 527. Although the strict two-pronged analysis was abandoned, the underlying precepts contained in the test are still highly relevant in assessing the totality of the circumstances and both counsels should be aware of this during any challenges to the reliability of informant information.

An informant's information will almost always survive scrutiny if the informant has provided reliable information in the past. Defense counsel should still challenge the basis of the information and how the informant came to obtain this information as well as the relationship between the informant and the defendant. The defense should also challenge how reliable the information was and seek to discover the underlying facts and documents in the cases where the informant is alleged to be reliable. Defense counsel should insist that the prosecution or agent detail the facts and call witnesses relied upon to support such a conclusion to enable the neutral and detached magistrate to make an independent inquiry into the reliability of the informant.

The identities of informants are often closely guarded from the defense so the opportunity to learn the name of the informants and even interview the informant early in the case is a bonus to the defense. This opportunity could arise in the context of challenging the use of the informant's information contained in a warrant application when used as the basis for probable cause. Most judges, however, will allow the prosecution to proffer the information about the informant and not require the personal presence of the informant or even the informant's name.

Anonymous tips are the bottom of the food chain when it comes to reliability of information. Most troublesome for judges is the fact that the tipster, by not identifying himself, is not subjected to any penalties if the information turns out to be false. Tips by someone who identifies himself and has no apparent motive to frame, harass or falsify the information will be inherently more trustworthy than a tip by someone who refuses to identify himself and/or fails to provide the necessary information to determine his relationship to the alleged suspect or the motive for providing the information. There is little if any reason for the defense not to challenge probable cause that is based on an anonymous tip or informant, if only to require the prosecution to set forth information on why the person is reliable or otherwise trustworthy, allowing the defense to discover additional case facts.

If the tipster is willing to come down to the station and make the complaint in person, as compared with an anonymous telephone call, this gesture would enhance the informant's reliability and reasonableness of the reliance on the information. Importantly, coming to the station in person also would subject the person to repercussions if the information was false.

Frequently the issue in anonymous tip cases is grappling with the use of such a tip in the context of articulable suspicion and limited seizure in a *Terry* stop. As a result, the defense can argue that when the use of the information is offered to establish probable cause, a higher standard than reasonable or articulable suspicion, the scrutiny should be even greater and the level of reliability and corroboration higher.

Both counsel should make every effort to interview any tipster (no doubt impossible in most anonymous tip cases) to ascertain a possible invidious motive for providing information. For example, in *United States v. Walker*, 7 F.3d 26 (2d. Cir 1993) Amtrak officers received an anonymous tip about a "very large and fat" black man who was allegedly transporting guns on the train. Although the district court upheld the man's seizure under a totality of circumstances analysis because of the corroboration of the facts by officer surveillance, the court was troubled by the possibility that someone was actually harassing an overweight person by calling the police on him. Even so, if the officers reasonably relied on the information in good faith and the information would have been sufficient if true as told, courts will uphold the search or seizure.

Corroboration of tips can include prediction of past, present and future events, such as describing what the person is wearing and where the person will go. The point being that if the suspect can describe what transpired, what is transpiring and what will transpire in particular, the caller must have access to the suspect in some significant manner. Visual surveillance of a suspect who has come to the attention of an officer through an anonymous tip confirming the information given in the tip can provide a basis for articulable suspicion and even probable cause depending on the level of corroboration. Tips where the person refuses to identify himself but still reveals the basis of his information can increase the reliability of the information.

Anonymous tips must have some corroboration and be determined to be reliable both for the identity of the person and the alleged offense before they can be used even for the lesser intrusion of an investigatory stop. *See Florida v. J.L.*, 529 U.S. 266, 120 S. Ct. 1375, 146 L. Ed. 2d 254 (2000). Defense counsel must dissect each basis for corroboration and the nexus between that corroboration and the suspicious behavior relied on for probable cause as well as for the specific individual.

For example, the fact that the caller might have described the suspect as being in his teens wearing a t-shirt would not necessarily mean the person has some inside information since one would be hard pressed to find a teen these days who did not wear a t-shirt. However, if the caller described the person as wearing a black Nirvana T-shirt with a camouflage backpack who will take a train from Penn Station to Philadelphia on the 2:45, and thereafter the person is seen as described taking that train, this would provide a higher level corroboration. Still, the defense could argue that the caller could have been a person behind him a ticket line who simply wanted to harass him because the one claimed the other had cut in front of him. The informant would be able to describe what he was wearing and where he was going without any inside information into what was contained in the backpack. In other words, the reliability of the identification of the person might have been established but not as to the offense itself.

Innocent Behavior

A common defense argument for information relied on by officers in assessing probable cause is that the activities observed are consistent with innocence. The Supreme Court has noted, nonetheless, that "innocent behavior will frequently provide the basis for a showing of probable cause." *Gates*, 462 U.S. at 243-4, 103 S. Ct. at 2335, 76 L. Ed. 2d at 551-2, n.13. The Court went on to instruct that in "making a determination of probable cause the relevant inquiry is not whether particular conduct is 'innocent or guilty,' but the degree of suspicion that attaches to particular types of non criminal acts." *Id.* The defense should maintain when appropriate that there are no suspicious activities, each factor demonstrates innocence, and even when viewed in totality, the combination of factors demonstrates innocence. The underlying policy argument of the defense's position that should be made clear to the judge is that these requirements are not to put obstacles in the path of law enforcement without reason, but to safeguard against the invasion of the liberty and dignity of individuals without proper justification.

The Supreme Court has also rejected what amounts to a sort of dissection of probable cause by taking each factor relied on and determining whether it individually meets a probable cause standard. In the Court's most recent search and seizure case, a unanimous court rejected the analysis of the Court of Appeals of Maryland's dismissal of the fact that there was $763 seized from the glove compartment as a factor in the probable cause determination on the grounds that without more, money is innocuous. The Court admonished that isolation of the money was "mistaken," and that the lower court should have included that factor in a totality of the circumstances analysis. *Pringle*, 124 S. Ct. at 800, 157 L. Ed. 2d at 776, n. 2.

Whether otherwise innocent behavior amounts to probable cause is determined in hindsight which is problematic for the defense. It is crucial, therefore, that the alleged probable cause be put in context. Buying tickets with cash in an airport in Las Vegas would not seem suspicious. Looking around nervously in a bus station in New York would not seem suspicious (perhaps not looking around nervously would seem more suspicious). Carrying only a briefcase from Philadelphia to Boston would not be suspicious.

The Supreme Court applies such contextualization to find probable cause, but the defense can turn it around in the right case, to challenge such a finding by arguing the opposite context:

> For example, what may not amount to reasonable suspicion at a motel located alongside a transcontinental highway at the height of the summer tourist season may rise to that level in December in Milwaukee. That city is unlikely to have been an overnight stop selected at the last minute by a traveler coming from California to points east. The 85-mile width of Lake Michigan blocks any further eastward progress. And while the city's salubrious summer climate and seasonal attractions bring many tourists at that time of year, the same is not true in December. Milwaukee's average daily high temperature in that month is 31 degrees and its average daily low is 17 degrees; the percentage of possible sunshine is only 38 percent. It is a reasonable inference that a Californian stopping in Milwaukee in December is either there to transact business or to visit family or friends. The background facts, though rarely

the subject of explicit findings, inform the judge's assessment of the historical facts.

Ornelas, 517 U.S. at 699, 116 S. Ct. at 1663, 134 L. Ed. 2d at 921.

The argument defense counsel should impress on the court is that any innocent person could be subject to the indignities of a search and seizure as a result of factors that fail to show criminality even when combined. The defense should also make sure to read carefully cases offered by the prosecution for upholding arrests based on anonymous information because often they will involve determinations of reasonable suspicion rather than the higher standard of probable cause.

Racial and Drug Courier Profiling

Race alone will not provide the reasonable suspicion necessary for a *Terry* stop let alone probable cause. Indeed, stops made on the basis of race will be found constitutionally impermissible. *See United States v Brignoni-Ponce*, 422 U.S 873, 885-6, 95 S. Ct. 2574, 2582-3, 45 L. Ed. 2d 607, 619 (1975). That being said, courts have permitted race as one of the factors in a determination of reasonable suspicion or probable cause. *See, e.g., United States v. Fouche*, 776 F.2d 1393, 1042-403 (9th Cir. 1985) "although race or color alone is not a sufficient basis for making an investigatory stop...racial appearance may be considered as a factor contributing to a founded suspicion of criminal conduct."

Consider the use of ethnicity in the profile the officers in *United States v. $31,990 in United States Currency*, 982 F.2d 851, 856 (2d Cir. 1993) proffered to justify an arrest: "whenever two Dominicans are driving a cab on the New York State Thruway between Schenectady and New York City, any money found in the trunk ... must be connected with the illegal sale of drugs." The Second Circuit rejected this profile as unrealistic because it described a large category of presumably innocent travelers who would be subject to virtually random search. This justification clearly shows the use of ethnicity in profiles and provides a chilling example of the "war on drugs" mentality of many law enforcement officers at the expense of individual privacy and dignity.

More often employed by officers (at least overtly) is the straight up use of drug courier profiles rather than explicitly race. These profiles are characteristics, otherwise innocent, *e.g.*, flying from a drug city like Miami, buying a ticket in cash, traveling alone, not checking luggage, etc., but are alleged to be consistent with drug courier profiles to form a basis for an investigatory stop.

Drug courier profiling as sufficient to support reasonable suspicion was upheld by the Supreme Court in *United States v. Sokolow*, 490 U.S. 1,109 S. Ct. 1581, 104 L. Ed.2d 1 (1989). Justice Marshall's dissent is a blistering critique of the drug courier profile particularly its "chameleon-like way of adapting to any particular set of observations." *Id.* at 13-14, 109 S. Ct. at 1589, 104 L. Ed. 2d at 14-15. In short, it can encompass nearly any fact to the point where it becomes meaningless, but is still relied on heavily by arresting officers.

The defense should make clear that although the courts may have allowed racial profiling as sufficient for reasonable suspicion to further investigate, racial profiling without more is not sufficient for the higher standard of probable cause. *See, e.g., United States v. $31,990 in United States Currency*, 982 F.2d 851, 856 (2d Cir. 1993) (prohibiting the use of drug courier profile to establish probable cause). Courts often refer to drug courier profiles as starting points for investigation; defense counsel must make sure that the court understands that such a profile alone cannot be an ending point for probable cause.

Some Useful Cases

Brinegar v. United States, 338 U.S. 160, 203 S. Ct. 1302, 93 L.3d 1879 (1949).

Ornelas v. United States, 517 U.S. 690, 116 S. Ct. 1657, 134 L. Ed. 2d 911 (1996).

Ybarra v. $31,990 in United States Currency, 982 F.2d 851, 856 (2d Cir. 1993) (prohibiting the use of drug courier profile to establish probable cause). Courts often refer to drug courier profiles as starting points for investigation; defense counsel must make sure that the court understands that such a profile alone must not be an ending point for probable cause.

Ybarra v. Illinois, 444 U.S. 85, 100 S. Ct. 338, 62 L. Ed. 2d 238 (1979).

Maryland v. Pringle, 124 S. Ct. 795, 157 L. Ed. 769 (2003).

Illinois v. Gates, 462 U.S. 213, 103 S. Ct. 2317, 76 L. Ed. 2d 527 (1983).

United States v. Sokolow, 490 U.S. 1,109 S. Ct. 1581, 104 L. Ed.2d 1 (1989).

CHAPTER FOUR
GOVERNMENT ACTION

Government Action in General

The Fourth Amendment prohibition against unreasonable searches and seizures is limited to searches and seizures by government agencies and does not apply to private citizens. The Supreme Court has recounted how the Amendment's "origin and history clearly show that it was intended as a restraint upon the activities of sovereign authority and was not intended to be a limitation upon other than governmental agencies...." *Burdeau v. McDowell*, 256 U.S. 465, 475, 41 S. Ct. 574, 576, 65 L. Ed. 1048, 1051 (1921).

The facts of Burdeau, more reminiscent of some law school exam question rather than reality, involve a true scenario where corporations were in litigation and detectives hired by one of the corporation went into the other corporation's offices and blew up safes and forced open desks to recover materials. Some of the documents were subsequently turned over to the Justice Department, who used them in a grand jury presentation. Although the Court in *Burdeau* conceded that the evidence was obtained illegally, it determined that because no official of the federal government had anything to do with the wrongful seizure of the property or any knowledge about it until months after it had been taken, the federal agents would not be precluded from using the documents on Fourth Amendment grounds.

Conceptually it makes sense to limit the exclusion of the evidence to improper behavior by the government since the primary purpose of the exclusionary rule is deterrence of unconstitutional conduct by government officials and officers. If the officer has no role in the illegality, the need for deterrence is absent. One could at least suggest to the court, however, that for judicial or governmental integrity reasons, the information should not be used because it sullies the government's hands and gives an appearance of impropriety and even accessory after the fact. Although courts have consistently upheld the use of such information, it is a point that could boost an argument with additional factors showing government action. Justice Brandeis joined by Justice Holmes in dissent in Burdeau provides an eloquent condemnation of the government's use of illegal information to bolster the defense position:

> That the court would restore the papers to plaintiff if they were still in the thief's possession is not questioned. That it has power to control the disposition of these stolen papers, although they have passed into the possession of the law officer, is also not questioned. But it is said that no provision of the Constitution requires their surrender and that the papers could have been subpoenaed. This might be true. Still I cannot believe that action of a public official is necessarily lawful, because it does not violate constitutional prohibitions and because the same result might have been attained by other and proper means. At the foundation of our civil liberty lies the principle which denies to government officials an exceptional position before the law and which subjects them to the same rules of conduct that are commands to the citizen. And in the development of our liberty insistence upon procedural regularity has been large factor. Respect for law will not be advanced by resort, in its enforcement, to means which shock the common man's sense of decency and fair play.

Id. at 477, 41 S. Ct. at 576-7, 65 L. Ed. at 1051. Certainly this argument could be included by defense counsel if the issue is not clear as to the extent of the government's participation as well as to encourage judges to give a broad reading of what is meant by government action.

What Constitutes Government Action

It might seem obvious what is or is not government action but there exists extensive litigation on the issue. As Justice Scalia observed, "[we have] said many times, that actions of private entities can sometimes be regarded as government action for constitutional purposes. It is fair to say that our cases deciding when private action might be deemed that of the state have not been a model of consistency." *LeBron v. National Railroad Passenger Corporation*, 513 U.S. 374, 115 S. Ct. 961,130 L. Ed. 2d 902 (citations and internal quotations omitted). For example, search of a student by a school official in a public school constitutes government action. *See New Jersey v. T.L.O.*, 469 U.S. 325, 336, 105 S. Ct. 733, 740, 83 L. Ed. 2d 720, 731 (1985).

More recently the Supreme Court addressed the issue in the context of a civil case involving allegations of First Amendment violations against Amtrak. The Supreme Court found that even though Congress specifically provided by statute that Amtrak was not a government agency, it was not up to Congress to make that determination. The Court concluded that Amtrak was, indeed, an agency or instrumentality of the United States for purposes of individual constitutional rights. Certainly searches and seizures by Amtrak police officers involved in narcotics or firearm interdiction invoke Fourth Amendment review by courts. *See, e.g., United States v. Walker*, 7 F.3d 26 (2d.Cir 1993).

The threshold question the parties need to ask themselves is whether the action was by an obvious government actor: police officer, prosecutor, FBI agent, etc. If not, can the argument be made that the nonofficial entity should be regarded as government action for constitutional purposes? For example, does the entity receive public funding or is it heavily regulated by the government like a school system or public railway? For what purposes was the entity created and was it done so by official sanction or support? Does the government hold stock in the entity or have voting power or control over the entity? Etc.

Private Party as Government Agent

Although evidence obtained by private citizens is admissible even if the private party violated a reasonable expectation of privacy or obtained the information unlawfully, if the government commissioned or caused the private party to do the searching it is government action triggering Fourth Amendment protections. In that situation, the private party is actually an instrument or agent of the government and would fall within the protections of the Fourth Amendment.

In determining whether a private party is an agent or instrument, some circuits, such as the Ninth Circuit, have adopted a two-pronged inquiry: 1) whether the government knew or acquiesced in the intrusive conduct; and 2) whether the private party performing the search did so intending to assist law enforcement or to further private goals. *See, e.g., United States v. Reed*, 15 F.3d 928, 931 (9th Cir. 1994).

Determinations of whether a party is a government agency are fact specific and can involve actions before any search takes place, as well as actions after a search takes place. For example, what might start out as an entirely private search by private actors, could be converted into a government search if the private actors are enlisted by the government. For example, in *United States v. Knoll*, 16 F.3d 1313 (2d Cir. 1994), documents from an attorney's officer were obtained through burglary entirely by private entities. Subsequent to the burglary, however, documents were turned over to the federal prosecutor. This prosecutor requested that the private entity get more detailed information and suggested and condoned a further search through the stolen documents.

The court in *Knoll* remanded the case for a determination by the lower court as to whether the documents requested by the prosecutor would have required additional searching by the private entity, which would have constituted an additional search by a government agent without a warrant in violation of the Fourth Amendment. From the defense perspective, this is a good case to bring to a court's attention because it shows how greedy some prosecutors can be with respect to obtaining evidence, seemingly indifferent to the fact that the information was obtained through the commission of a crime.

Partial Government Involvement

If it is mostly a private search but a government agent is involved in the illegal search, it is usually considered a government action for purposes of the Fourth Amendment. In a case decided before the Fourth Amendment was incorporated and applicable to the states, the state officers had been involved in an illegal search of a hotel room. During the search a federal secret service agent was called in who reviewed the evidence and made suggestions as to which evidence would be useful in a federal prosecution. In finding federal government action, the Supreme Court observed that:

> It surely can make no difference whether a state officer turns up the evidence and hands it over to a federal agent for his critical inspection with the view to its use in a federal prosecution, or the federal agent himself takes the articles out of a bag. It would trivialize law to base legal significance on such a differentiation....To differentiate between participation from the beginning of an illegal search and joining it before it had run its course, would be to draw too fine a line in the application of the prohibition of the Fourth Amendment....It is immaterial whether a federal agent originated the idea or joined in it while the search was in progress. So long as he was completely accomplished, he must be deemed to have participated in it. Where there is participation on the part of federal officers it is not necessary to consider what would be the result if the search had been conducted entirely by State officers. Evidence secured through such federal participation is inadmissible for the same considerations as those which made Weeks v. United States...governing principle in federal prosecutions.

Lustig v. United States, 338 U.S. 74, 78-9, 69 S. Ct. 1372, 1374, 93 L. Ed. 1819, 1823 (1949) (citations omitted).

In a more recent Supreme Court case, however, the Court refined the extent of official participation where the search starts out as a private matter. In *United States v. Jacobsen*, 466 U.S. 109, 104 S. Ct. 1652, 80 L.Ed 2d 85 (1984) a package was opened by a private entity (in that case Federal Express employees) where a sealed tube was cut open revealing a bag of white powder. The federal agents were called in and they took a small sample of the powder for testing. The Supreme Court found that the federal officers were not in violation of the Fourth Amendment.

Although the Court in *Jacobsen* upheld the search, it did not do so on the basis that there was no government action. Instead, in typical Supreme Court fashion, it affirmed the initial taking of the package out of the tube on the grounds that the federal agents' actions could not be defined as a search. Specifically, the Court determined that the government actors had not exceeded the search previously conducted by the private entities; therefore the government's conduct was not violative of any legitimate expectation of privacy, ergo, by definition, did not constitute a search. As to the additional testing, which clearly exceeded what had been done by the private entities, the Court rationalized that although it was clearly an interference with possessory interests (destroying a small amount of substance to do the test) to constitute a seizure, such a seizure was determined to be reasonable given the balancing of Fourth Amendment rights versus important law enforcement interests, particularly in light of the so-called "de minimus" intrusion.

The important factors courts will typically focus on in determining whether the government officer's participation warrants a finding of a "government search" include whether the government agents requested that the container be opened, whether the government officers were present when it was opened and/or whether the agents participated in searching the package. The government agents' actions must be viewed from the moment of the intrusion: "[t]he fact that [private agents] independently opened the package and made an examination that might have been impermissible for a government agent cannot render otherwise reasonable official conduct unreasonable. The reasonableness of an official invasion of the citizen's privacy must be appraised on the basis of the facts as they existed at the time that invasion occurred." *Jacobsen*, 466 at 114-15, 104 S. Ct. at 1657, 80 L.Ed. 2d at 94-95.

Although courts have increasingly found government actors acting reasonably when involved with private entity searches, it is still crucial to analyze thoroughly the actions of every participant. Each side must break down the various searches to determine who was involved and in what manner at what stage in the search. It might be that part of the search is truly private without

Fourth Amendment protections; whereas, subsequent searches could easily involve government actors once the police or federal authorities are notified. Counsel should never assume that an actor is truly a private entity without full investigation and research. Nor should counsel ever assume that because a private entity initiated the search it could not become a search by government authorities triggering protections under the Fourth Amendment at some time after the initial private intrusion.

Some Useful Cases

Burdeau v. McDowell, 256 U.S. 465, 41 S. Ct. 574, 65 L. Ed. 1048 (1921).

United States v. Walker, 7 F.3d 26 (2d.Cir 1993).

United States v. Reed, 15 F.3d 928 (9th Cir. 1994).

United States v. Jacobsen, 466 U.S. 109, 104 S. Ct. 1652, 80 L. Ed 2d. 85 (1984).

CHAPTER FIVE
ISSUES OF STANDING

Standing to Make a Fourth Amendment Claim Generally

The government has the burden to prove that the evidence admitted at trial was obtained lawfully. The defense, however, has the burden of putting the legality of the search or seizure in issue at the outset. To meet this burden of "going forward," the defendant must assert that his own Fourth Amendment rights were violated. The right to assert this claim is known as standing.

To make out standing in a Fourth Amendment issue, the defendant must aver that he or his property was unlawfully seized, or that there was an unlawful search and he had a reasonable expectation of privacy in the area searched. Fourth Amendment rights are personal and cannot be litigated vicariously. For example, unless the items taken were in a place or container in which the defendant himself had a reasonable expectation of privacy, the defendant ordinarily has no standing to challenge the admissibility of the evidence offered against him at trial. *See Rawlings v. Kentucky*, 448 U.S. 98, 104-05, 100 S. Ct. 2556, 2561, 65 L. Ed. 2d 633, 641-42 (1980). Similarly, co-conspirators, though involved in a joint enterprise of smuggling narcotics, do not have an automatic reasonable expectation of privacy in a car where drugs are found. Each conspirator must have an individual expectation of privacy in the area searched or the thing seized to make a Fourth Amendment claim. The conspiracy contributes nothing to the privacy analysis. *See United States v. Padilla*, 508 U.S. 77, 113 S. Ct. 1936, 123 L. Ed. 2d 635 (1993).

Asserting Standing in Personal Seizure Cases

To assert standing for an unlawful personal seizure, the defendant must claim that he was seized and that the officers lacked reasonable suspicion or probable cause necessary to conduct the

49

degree of seizure that took place. In claiming personal seizure, the defendant ordinarily must assert a subjective belief that he did not feel free to leave, and also allege facts showing that a reasonable person in the defendant's position would not have felt free to leave. Courts will determine standing based on the totality of the circumstances. *See Rakas v. Illinois*, 439 U.S. 128, 152, 99 S. Ct. 421, 435, 58 L. Ed. 2d 387, 406 (1978) (Powell, J., concurring).

Important factors in determining whether a reasonable person would not feel free to leave—though not individually required or dispositive—include whether the police activated sirens or flashers, commanded the person to halt, displayed weapons, operated their cars in order to block the person, or controlled the person's direction or movements. *See Michigan v. Chesternut*, 486 U.S. 567, 575, 108 S. Ct. 1975, 1980, 100 L. Ed. 2d 565, 573 (1988). Additional factors, particularly relevant when the police walk up to a person on the street, include "the threatening presence of several officers, the display of a weapon by an officer, some physical touching of the person of the citizen, or the use of language or tone of voice indicating that compliance with the officer's request might be compelled." *United States v. Mendenhall*, 446 U.S. 544, 554, 100 S. Ct. 1870, 1877, 64 L. Ed. 2d 497, 509 (1980). These factors are the ones a lawyer should be focused on in client interviews to determine whether there was an unlawful seizure. *See also Chapter Seventeen: Client/Agent Interviews.*

Whether a person reasonably feels free to leave does not require the officer to inform that person that he or she is free to leave, though doing so or failing to do so is a factor in the totality of the circumstances analysis. *See Ohio v. Robinette*, 519 U.S. 33, 39-40, 117 S. Ct. 417, 421, 136 L. Ed. 2d 347, 355 (1996). If the officer does tell the suspect that he is free to leave, that will go a long way toward convincing the judge that the person did feel free to leave. Prosecutors should stress that fact if present in a particular case. On the other hand, if the officer did not tell the suspect he was free to leave, the defense needs to concentrate on how a person who is surrounded by uniformed officers asking him questions would not believe that he could just walk away, particularly if the cops approached the defendant with sirens, in uniforms, and never told the defendant he was free to go about his business.

Defense lawyers should paint a scene for the judge of the defendant's position in the moving papers as well as at any hearing. For example, three fully uniformed and armed officers approached the defendant in three separate marked police cars with their sirens flashing. All three walked up to the defendant at the same time. One of the uniformed officers had a flashlight that he shone in the defendant's face. One of the uniformed officers went behind the defendant and the other officer went to the side and put his hand on the butt of his holstered gun. The officers were less than one foot away from the defendant. The third officer with the flashlight did a quick pat down of the defendant and asked him why he was in the park at 4:00 in the morning. There were no other people around. The area is a parking lot out on a pier. The subway is five blocks away and not visible from where the defendant was standing. There is one exit from the parking lot and all three police vehicles were positioned between the defendant and that exit.

Asserting Standing in Search Cases

The issue of standing with respect to a search is really an affirmation that a Fourth Amendment violation occurred, because the standing threshold is the same as that required to show a search: the officers unlawfully invaded an area where the defendant had a reasonable expectation of privacy. By circular definition, if there is no reasonable expectation of privacy, there is no search of Fourth Amendment consequence.

A separate analysis of "standing" is no longer the inquiry for search and seizure of property, though many courts still refer to the right to bring the claim as a standing issue. *See Rakas*, 439 U.S. at 140, 99 S. Ct. at 428, 58 L. Ed. 2d at 399. That being said, most judges recognize and require a threshold showing of standing even if the Supreme Court has conflated a search by definition with the standing requirement. Judges are less concerned with the academic distinction and more concerned with whether the defendant has met his burden of going forward. Most judges expect to see a standing section in the defendant's motion. *See also Chapter Twenty Three: Motion Practice Under the Fourth Amendment.*

Because the remedy for a violation of the Fourth Amendment is exclusion of the evidence in order to deter improper police behavior, conceptually it would make sense to have any defendant against whom the evidence were being used make a Fourth Amendment claim even if that defendant did not personally have a reasonable expectation of privacy, provided some Fourth Amendment right were at issue. This type of standing would be similar to the broad standing allowing a defendant charged with an overly broad or unduly vague offense to bring a First Amendment claim, even when that particular defendant's offense is not speech related, as a means of preventing the chilling of First Amendment protected speech. Such a broad standing for the Fourth Amendment was specifically rejected in *Alderman v. United States*, 394 U.S. 165, 174, 89 S. Ct. 961, 966-67, 22 L. Ed. 2d 176, 187 (1969).

For lawyers just starting to litigate these issues, it undoubtedly seems counterintuitive that a defendant charged with possession of certain contraband would not have automatic standing to contest the search or seizure of the property particularly if he is alleged to have owned it. Indeed, for two decades, from 1960 to 1980, there was automatic standing to contest the taking of items when the defendant owned the evidence, was charged with possession of the contraband, or was legitimately on the premises at the time of the search. Automatic standing is no longer the standard.

In *Rakas v. Illinois*, the Supreme Court significantly redefined who could make a Fourth Amendment claim, allowing it only when the defendant has a reasonable expectation of privacy in the thing searched or the property seized. 439 U.S. at 148, 99 S. Ct. at 433, 58 L. Ed. 2d at 404. A few years later the Court specifically overruled earlier precedent which held that a defendant has automatic standing to contest the taking of the items due to a possessory interest in the property, if he is being charged with its possession, or by virtue of being legitimately on the premises at the time of the search or seizure. *See United States. v. Salvucci,* 448 U.S. 83, 100 S. Ct. 2547, 65 L. Ed. 2d 619 (1980), overruling *Jones v. United States*, 362 U.S. 257, 80 S. Ct. 725, 4 L. Ed. 2d 697 (1960); *see also Rakas*, 439 U.S. at 142, 99 S. Ct. at 429, 58 L. Ed. 2d at 400. The Supreme Court's current position is that standing is not an issue of property interests focusing on trespass, but rather one of privacy interests. *See, e.g., Rakas,* 439 U.S. at 149, 99 S. Ct. at 433, 58 L. Ed. 2d at 405 n.17 (arcane notions of property law should not determine standing to make a Fourth Amendment claim). Today the standard is whether the defendant has an expectation of privacy in the thing searched or the items seized, and whether that expectation is one society is prepared to accept as reasonable.

Property Interests and Standing

Although the courts have focused on the privacy aspect rather than the property aspect in Fourth Amendment analysis, making clear in *Katz,* 389 U.S. at 351, 88 S. Ct. at 511, 19 L. Ed. 2d at 582, that the "Fourth Amendment protects people not places," ownership of the property searched or seized certainly still weighs in on whether the person had a reasonable expectation of privacy. Conversely, if the person has no ownership in the property, he is unlikely to have a reasonable expectation of privacy in the property. Ownership of contraband alone, however, is ordinarily not enough to meet Fourth Amendment standards if there is no reasonable expectation of privacy by virtue of such things as the contraband's location or packaging.

The defendant in *Rawlings v. Kentucky,* for example, owned the drugs found in his companion's purse—he had, in fact, put them there—but the Court held that he did not have a reasonable expectation of privacy in his companion's bag. *See* 448 U.S. at 105-06, 100 S. Ct. at 2561-62, 65 L. Ed. 2d at 642. Slightly different facts, however, might have made a difference with respect to standing in that case. Given Rawlings' ownership of the property, had he testified that he believed that the purse would be free from intrusion, or had there been a lock on the bag or a more formalized agreement to keep his property safe, the Court may have found that Rawlings had a reasonable expectation of privacy in the handbag.

Rawlings teaches us that in setting out the right to make a Fourth Amendment claim in this kind of situation, the defense needs to do more than base that claim solely on ownership of the contraband. Generally speaking, unlawful possession of contraband *per se* is not something society is prepared to accept as a reasonable expectation of privacy. Nevertheless, society is prepared to accept that someone who has property in her own home, in a package wrapped to avoid someone else finding out what is inside, or kept in her own bag or purse, ordinarily has a reasonable expectation of privacy. It is the expectation that is the focus of reasonableness, not the property itself, though ownership obviously is tied to how reasonable the expectation is. That being said, the fact that the property might be contraband does not in itself preclude the possessor from having a reasonable expectation that such property will remain private from governmental intrusion and unreasonable searches and seizures. *See, e.g., United States v. Jeffers,* 342 U.S. 48, 52-54, 72 S. Ct. 93, 96, 96 L. Ed. 59, 65 (1951) (while there are no property rights in contraband, it is still considered property for purposes of the Fourth Amendment).

Although the fact that the property is contraband does not itself preclude a finding of reasonable expectation of privacy, defense counsel should avoid any righteous indignation about property interests in making Fourth Amendment claims. Judges are more likely to be persuaded by the reasonableness of the privacy concern itself, no doubt sharing on some level society's skepticism that ownership of contraband should ever be reasonable. Defense counsel needs to separate the illegality of the ownership from the protected privacy interests as much as possible. An argument to the judge might be: suppose, Your Honor, that the brick of cocaine was in fact a cake of fungal medicine to treat an embarrassing disease. Would society be prepared to accept as reasonable the defendant's expectation of privacy in the manner in which he possessed and stowed the article? In short, the Fourth Amendment "extends to offenders as well as to the law abiding." *United States v. Lefkowitz,* 285 U.S. 452, 464, 52 S. Ct. 420, 423, 76 L. Ed. 877, 882 (1932).

Standing in Automobile Searches

The owner of a vehicle has standing to object to a search of that vehicle for Fourth Amendment purposes. A passenger in the vehicle may or may not have a right to object to a search of the vehicle. If the search includes bags or containers owned by the passenger, she is likely to have a reasonable expectation of privacy in the contents of those bags or containers. However, merely riding in a car where contraband is found does not amount to a legitimate expectation of privacy by the passenger. The two men stopped in *Rakas v. Illinois* did not own the car and did not claim ownership of the rifles under the seat. As a result, they had no standing to challenge the admissibility of the evidence against them as violating the Fourth Amendment. *See Rakas*, 439 U.S. at 148-49, 99 S. Ct. at 433, 58 L. Ed. 2d at 404. Again, the focus will be on the reasonableness of the defendant's expectation. If the defendant does not own the car but was given the keys by the owner, kept other personal belongings in the car, etc., there might be an expectation of privacy society would be prepared to accept as reasonable even though the defendant does not own the car or had not been driving at the time.

Overnight Guests and Standing

The defendant clearly has a reasonable expectation of privacy in his own home. The harder cases are when the defendant is staying at a third party's home, the container with the contraband is owned by the defendant but being kept by a third party or a third party owns the container. If the defendant is a bona fide overnight guest, ordinarily he will have a reasonable expectation of privacy in the home where he is visiting. *See Minnesota v. Olsen*, 495 U.S. 91, 98-99, 110 S. Ct. 1684, 1689, 109 L. Ed. 2d 85, 94-95 (1990). However, if the defendant is on the premises as an invitee for the purpose of conducting a business, such as the packaging of cocaine, there is a lessened expectation of privacy. Depending on the extent of the relationship between the owner of the premises and the defendant, and how long the defendant is on the premises, the defendant might not be considered a guest for purposes of standing. *See Minnesota v. Carter*, 525 U.S. 83, 91, 119 S. Ct. 469, 474, 142 L. Ed. 2d 373, 381 (1998) (use of home for commercial purposes—where defendants were allowed to use the home to package cocaine, where no previous relationship existed between lessee of the apartment and defendants, and where defendants were only on the premises for a few hours—did not give defendants a reasonable expectation of privacy in the apartment).

Factors the courts look to (but are not individually dispositive) in deciding whether a person is indeed a guest for Fourth Amendment purposes include: the extent of the relationship between the owner or lessor of the premises and the defendant; how long they had known each other; whether the defendant had a key; the extent of the permission to stay, and whether it included excluding or inviting others; whether the defendant kept personal property on the premises; how long he stayed there; and whether he contributed to the rent or expenses. In considering these factors, courts are looking to see if the relationship between the guest and the owner of the premises is like that of a guest who is invited into a home to stay the night and may therefore claim the protection of the Fourth Amendment. These are the factors defense lawyers must focus on in questioning clients as to their interests in the house, the containers, and the property itself. How much does the defendant's interest in third-party property resemble ownership interests such that society would be prepared to accept as reasonable the defendant's expectation of privacy? *See also, Chapter Seventeen: Fourth Amendment Issues and Client/Agent Interviews.*

Hotel Rooms

Like the defendant in his own home, the defendant in a properly rented hotel or motel room also has a legitimate expectation of privacy in the room during the rental period. *See, e.g., United States v. Morales,* 737 F.2d 761 (8th Cir. 1984). The Ninth Circuit has even found that a camper on a public campground has a legitimate expectation of privacy in her pitched tent. *See United States v. Gooch,* 6 F.3d 673 (9th Cir. 1993). But if the defendant, by her own volition, opens the door to her hotel room, she no longer has a reasonable expectation of privacy in the room—even if the police use subterfuge. *See, e.g., United States v. Gori,* 230 F.3d 44, 52 (2d Cir. 2000) (citing *United States v. Vaneaton,* 49 F.3d 1423 (9th Cir. 1995), and *United States v. Carrion,* 809 F.2d 1120 (5th Cir. 1987)).

Affidavit Concerns

In order to meet the burden of going forward on a Fourth Amendment claim, the defendant will need to affirm the basis for the claim in a sworn affidavit or declaration under penalty of perjury. An affirmation in a seizure case must include facts that the defendant did not feel free to leave, as well as relevant factors in his personal knowledge supporting a finding that a reasonable person in his position would not have felt free to leave.

The defendant will usually need to set out some basis for why the officers lacked reasonable suspicion if it was a *Terry* stop, or probable cause if it was an arrest or effectively an arrest. If the facts necessary to meet the defendant's burden of going forward are set out in a sworn statement by the officers, *e.g.*, a complaint detailing why the particular individual was arrested or an affidavit for a search warrant, then the defense lawyer may assert those facts based on the sworn court documents in the lawyer's own affidavit or declaration. By using a lawyer affidavit or declaration, the attorney need not include such facts in the defendant's declaration. (In many cases the defendant will not know all the information the officers had at the time of the arrest and whether those factors amounted to probable cause or articulable suspicion.)

In search cases, the defendant must assert that he had a reasonable expectation of privacy in the area searched or the thing seized. These facts also must be set out in an affidavit or declaration sworn to by the defendant under the penalty of perjury. When the defendant is the person with personal knowledge as to the facts necessary to assert standing to raise the issue, such as who owns the suitcase, then the defendant personally will have to allege those facts under oath. The lawyer ordinarily cannot assert the facts based on conversations with the defendant—personal knowledge is needed to put a fact in issue properly and to avoid a claim of frivolousness. *See, e.g., United States v. Gillette*, 383 F.2d 843, 848 (2d. Cir. 1967) (someone with personal knowledge must assume the risk of a perjury prosecution if the affidavit is false or misleading, otherwise the court is justified in denying the motion or a hearing on the motion).

Although the defendant must swear to facts within his personal knowledge in order to meet the burden of going forward on the claim, not all facts known need be alleged. Typically, the prosecutor will proffer facts in opposition to the defendant's motion but usually will not submit a sworn affidavit by the arresting officer. Depending on the jurisdiction and custom of the court, defense counsel may be able to argue that in order to counter sworn facts asserting a claim, the prosecution must submit sworn testimony from the officer based on personal knowledge. *See also, Chapter Twenty Three: Motion Practice Under the Fourth Amendment.*

There are important strategic considerations when the defendant or agent must swear to facts to support or counter a motion to suppress. Indeed, both sides should be cautious in unnecessarily committing an agent or client to a detailed account that can later be used to impeach the affiant should she take the stand and misstate a detail. The defendant is severely disadvantaged when an officer's version differs, even if the defense version is truthful because sworn statements by the defendant contradicted by law enforcement officers are often used to support obstruction of justice and perjury charges or enhancements at sentencing. Moreover, in the absence of objective evidence undermining the officer's version, most judges are likely to credit the officer's testimony as against the defendant's.

Defense counsel in particular needs to appreciate that the affidavit serves a narrow purpose: to meet the burden of going forward. It is not testimony. If there are factual disputes as to what transpired in the case, the judge will hold a hearing to resolve those disputed facts. At the hearing, the facts set out in the affidavits or declarations ordinarily are not used by the judge to decide the issue, although there are times when the judge will proceed on sworn affidavit. Only the facts that come out at the hearing under oath and subject to cross examination form the basis for the judge's decision unless the facts are agreed to by the parties. As a result, the defense and the prosecution need only assert in affidavits those facts necessary to meet the burden of going forward or to contest the other side's position. Counsel should craft any declaration carefully to ensure that it includes only the minimal information needed to support or oppose the motion. In short, less is more.

Asserting Standing and Fifth Amendment Privileges

The more connection the defendant has to the dwelling that is searched, the more likely he will be able to make out a Fourth Amendment claim. Then again, the more he makes out a connection between himself and the place that was searched (or the contraband that was seized), the more he ties himself to the crime. The obvious problem is that in asserting standing, the defendant frequently has to admit to being on the premises, owning the container, owning the contraband, etc. This conflicts with the defendant's Fifth Amendment rights against self-incrimination.

Although it is technically not "compelled" testimony, asserting rights and interests in property and places to meet standing requirements pits one constitutional right against another—the right to enforce Fourth Amendment protections versus preserving Fifth Amendment privileges. The Supreme Court has effected a compromise that allows the defendant to make the incriminating assertions necessary to establish her right to bring a Fourth Amendment claim: the defendant may make such affirmations, but the prosecution is not allowed to use that information in its case-in-chief to establish guilt. *See Simmons v. United States*, 390 U.S. 377, 394, 88 S. Ct. 967, 976, 19 L. Ed. 2d 1247, 1259 (1968). Defense counsel should be wary, however, because the prosecution could use the information to impeach the defendant were he to take the stand at trial and contradict what was contained in the affidavit. The prosecution could also use the information in its investigation once it is revealed in a court document.

Defense counsel must ensure that information contained in the defendant's affidavit is not used inappropriately at trial in contravention of *Simmons*. This requires that the defense make a timely objection in order to avoid waiver of the issue. The Supreme Court is quite specific: "We therefore hold that when a defendant testifies in support of a motion to suppress evidence on Fourth Amendment grounds, his testimony may not thereafter be admitted against him at trial on the issue of guilt unless he makes no objection." *Id.* (emphasis added).

Some Useful Cases

Simmons v. United States, 390 U.S. 377, 88 S. Ct. 967, 19 L. Ed. 2d 1247 (1968) (when a defendant testifies that his own Fourth Amendment rights were violated by the challenged search or seizure, his testimony may not later be used to establish guilt in the prosecution's case-in-chief).

Rakas v. Illinois, 439 U.S. 128, 99 S. Ct. 421, 58 L. Ed. 2d 387 (1978) (proper Fourth Amendment focus is whether the defendant has a legitimate expectation of privacy in the searched premises, and whether the defendant has fulfilled the burden of establishing it; automobile passengers could not assert Fourth Amendment protection against the seizure of incriminating evidence from a vehicle where they owned neither the vehicle nor the evidence seized).

Minnesota v. Olsen, 495 U.S. 91, 110 S. Ct. 1684, 109 L. Ed. 2d 85 (1990) (guest who had permission to stay overnight in another's home, even though he did not have a key or exclusive use of the dwelling, had a reasonable expectation of privacy in the home and therefore standing to challenge a warrantless arrest inside the home).

Minnesota v. Carter, 525 U.S. 83, 119 S. Ct. 469, 142 L. Ed. 2d 373 (1998) (guests who were using the apartment of a third party to package cocaine, who had no pre-existing relationship with the third party, and who had been on the premises for only a few hours did not have standing to challenge a warrantless search of the apartment).

CHAPTER SIX
WARRANTS

Warrants Generally

Ordinarily a search or seizure is not lawful unless preceded by a warrant issued by a neutral and detached magistrate except in specific and well-delineated exceptions. *See Chapter Seven: The Exclusionary Rule and Chapter One: List of Exceptions to the Warrant Requirement.* The Warrant Requirement of the Fourth Amendment, also known as the Warrant Clause, requires warrants to be issued upon probable cause. Although the Fourth Amendment does not require warrants to be obtained for all searches and seizures, it is well established that searches and seizures are unreasonable unless executed pursuant to a warrant or recognized exception.

Probable cause is a relatively low standard merely requiring a determination that there is a substantial basis for finding fair probability that contraband or other evidence of a crime will be found in the place to be searched, or that an offense has been committed or is being committed to support an arrest. It is based on the totality of the circumstances presented to the judge at the time of the request. *See Illinois v. Gates*, 462 U.S. 213, 103 S. Ct. 2317, 76 L. Ed. 2d 527 (1983). *See also, Chapter Three: Probable Cause.*

A "neutral and detached" magistrate or other judicial officer must make the finding of probable cause for a warrant. *See United States v. United States District Court Eastern District of Michigan*, 407 U.S. 297, 92 S. Ct. 2125, 32 L. Ed. 2d 752 (1972). The Attorney General, for example, cannot be the one deciding whether there is probable cause since the Attorney General is the chief federal prosecutor. *See Coolidge v. New Hampshire*, 403 U.S. 443, 91 S. Ct. 2022, 29 L. Ed. 2d 564 (1971).

As the Supreme Court explained:

> The point of the Fourth Amendment, which often is not grasped by zealous officers, is not that it denies law enforcement the support of the usual inferences which reasonable men draw from evidence. Its protection consists in requiring that those inferences be drawn by a neutral and detached magistrate instead of being judged by the officer engaged in the often competitive enterprise of ferreting out crime.

Johnson v. United States 333 U.S. 10, 68 S. Ct. 367, 92 L. Ed. 436 (1948) (footnotes omitted).

In addition to the requirement of probable cause to support a warrant, the Fourth Amendment demands that the warrant be particularized by naming the "place to be searched, and the persons or things to be seized." The particularity requirement is a strict one. In a recent decision, the Supreme Court found that the failure of the officer to describe the person or things to be seized was not reasonable for Fourth Amendment purposes, even though the items were described in the search warrant application. *Groh v. Ramirez*, 124 S. Ct. 1284, 157 L. Ed. 2d 1068 (2004).

Issuance of Warrants in Federal Court

FRCrP 41 governs search and seizure of property and people. It is important for both prosecutors and defense attorneys practicing in federal court to know the detailed requirements of the rule, which might differ from the requirements in their state jurisdictions, although many states have similar requirements based on the federal rules.

A federal judge or state judge must issue a warrant under FRCrP 41. Probable cause for a warrant may be presented in person, by affidavit, over the phone and even by facsimile provided it is given under oath. *See* FRCrP 41(c)(2) for the specific procedures for the use of various types of testimony in federal court. The rule specifically allows for the use of hearsay to establish probable cause although the court may require the affiant to appear in person. FRCrP 41(c)(1). (Although the use of computer generated transmissions to submit affidavits to support a warrant were considered in 1993, the idea was ultimately rejected because it was believed to lack the authenticity of the handwriting that can be observed on a facsimile transmission. *See* FRCrP 41, Committee Notes 1993 Amendments.)

The warrant must identify the property or person to be seized and it must name or describe the person or place to be searched. A warrant may be issued under Rule 41 for:

(1) property that constitutes evidence of the commission of a criminal offense; or

(2) contraband, the fruits of crime, or things otherwise criminally possessed; or

(3) property designed or intended for use or which is or has been used as the means of committing a criminal offense; or

(4) person for whose arrest there is probable cause, or who is unlawfully restrained.

FRCrP 41.

Any search by warrant granted under FRCrP 41 must take place within a specified time period not to exceed 10 days and ordinarily must be executed during the day time meaning 6:00 a.m. to 10:00 p.m. unless the court finds reasonable cause to allow it to be executed at night. *Id.* Search warrants related to narcotics offenses, however, can be served at any time if a judge is satisfied that there is probable cause to believe drugs will be found then. *See* 21 USC § 879. FRCrP 41 allows for anticipatory warrants for executions outside the district of the original request when the property or person is expected to move from the original district such as luggage on an airplane. FRCrP 41(a).

FRCrP 4 provides for issuance of an arrest warrant or summons upon a complaint or affidavit where there is probable cause to believe that an offense has been committed and the defendant committed the offense. To obtain the warrant the officer or prosecutor would come before the magistrate judge and swear to an affidavit, which is usually prepared by a prosecutor. In some cases there might be an oral application that would be recorded.

If the prosecutor has successfully sought a grand jury indict-ment she can obtain an arrest warrant under FRCrP 9, and no further evidence of probable cause is required for issuance of a warrant or a summons. This is because the grand jury's determi-nation of probable cause is sufficient provided the grand jury is properly constituted under FRCrP 6. If the prosecution proceeds by information under FRCrP 9 (allowable in misdemeanors and lesser offenses), the warrant must be supported by an affidavit demonstrating probable cause. A prosecutor's information alone, which simply tracks the elements of the offense, without an af-fidavit establishing probable cause, is insufficient. *Gerstein v. Pugh*, 420 U.S. 103, 95 S. Ct. 854, 43 L. Ed. 2d 54 (1975). *See also Practice Commentaries Federal Rules of Criminal Procedure* Natali, Parsons, Statsinger & Wolfe, Commentary to Fed. R. Crim. P. 4, 9, and 41 (2002-2003).

Anticipatory Warrants

Judges may issue search warrants in anticipation that a person or certain specified evidence will be in a particular location even though the person or evidence is not at the location at the time the warrant is requested. These types of warrants are known as "Anticipatory Warrants." Because a warrant may issue only when probable cause exists at the time the warrant is issued, there have been many challenges to the constitutionality of anticipatory war-rants *per se* by the defense. All of the circuits that have consid-ered the issue have rejected a *per se* ban on anticipatory warrants. Counsel should know the status of such warrants in their particu-lar jurisdiction. Largely courts have viewed anticipatory warrants under the same rubric as any warrant: if the warrant is supported by sufficient probable cause to believe that the anticipated events will occur the warrant will survive scrutiny. That being said, the defense should carefully analyze, as with any warrant, whether there is a sufficient nexus between the expected contraband and the place to be searched.

Anticipatory warrants are usually issued with the requirement that a particular triggering event occur such as the delivery of drugs or the arrival of a suspect. If the anticipated events do not occur, the warrant is not considered "ripe" or "mature" for execution. Premature execution of a warrant will provide grounds for a defense challenge.

The defense can attack anticipatory warrants as they would any warrant with particular emphasis on the possibility of the staleness of the information and the nexus between the location and the evidence. The defense should scrutinize why the officer believed the event would occur, how the information was obtained and the reliability of any sources. *See Chapter Three: Probable Cause.* Prosecutors can counter that an anticipatory warrant is an effective and constitutional means of protecting Fourth Amendment rights perhaps even more than an ordinary warrant, because if the triggering events do not occur the privacy of the home or area will not be invaded at all.

Finally, the availability of anticipatory warrants can assist the defense in challenging warrantless arrests or searches where the officers claim exigent circumstances. If the officers had sufficient time to obtain an anticipatory warrant, then a claim of exigent circumstances could be invalidated. *See, e.g., United States v. Santa*, 236 F.3d 662, 671-76 (11th Cir. 2000) (analyzing the constitutionality of anticipatory warrants and finding that federal agents who had arranged a controlled drug delivery in advance could have obtained an anticipatory warrant, thus, the warrantless arrest inside the defendant's home violated the Fourth Amendment). In cases where the defendant is arrested in his home without a warrant, the defense could be in a position to argue that the officers' failure to obtain an anticipatory warrant resulted in police created exigencies that do not justify a warrantless entry or arrest. *See also Chapter Thirteen: Exigent Circumstances.*

Attacking Warrants

Probable Cause. Warrant affidavits are entitled to a presumption of validity, although that does not mean that they can never be challenged, just that the defense starts with the "laboring oar" in terms of overcoming the presumption. In some cases the defense might have an argument that the warrant was not supported by probable cause despite the issuance by the proverbial neutral and detached magistrate judge. Judges see a lot of warrant applications. Many judges have a rubber stamp and might not have scrutinized the basis for probable cause very carefully.

Defense counsel should obtain a copy of the affidavit and any supporting documents to determine whether the affidavit contains more than a mere assertion that a statute has been violated, though not every element of the offense needs to be supported. Importantly, the basis for probable cause cannot be simply a conclusory statement that the affiant believes there is probable cause to obtain a warrant, *e.g.*, "I observed the defendant committing mail fraud," or "the defendant was arrested after a determination that there was probable cause to believe she had sold narcotics."

A finding of probable cause on a warrant application is the role of the neutral and detached magistrate assessing the facts underlying that belief. The court is actually not supposed to be a "rubber stamp" for the law enforcement officer. If such conclusory statements are the basis for probable cause, the defense should challenge their sufficiency, ideally at the initial appearance. *See also, Chapter Three: Probable Cause* and *Chapter Nineteen: Fourth Amendment Issues at the Initial Appearance.*

Probable cause, however, is a relatively low standard requiring only that it persuade a person of reasonable caution that a crime is being committed or the evidence of a crime will be found at a particular location. Probable cause can be found in an accumulation of affidavits and can be based entirely on hearsay. Courts look to the totality of the circumstances and a reviewing court must give "great deference" to a probable cause determination made by a magistrate judge in issuing a warrant. Warrantless searches and seizures, on the other hand, are reviewed de novo. The higher deference afforded to searches and seizures pursuant to warrants is maintained in order to promote the use of warrants by police officers. *See Ornelas v. United States*, 517 U.S. 690, 698-9, 116 S. Ct. 1657, 1662-3, 134 L. Ed. 2d 911, 920-1 (1996).

If information contained in a warrant was obtained unlawfully, that information may not be relied on to support probable cause. If the lawfully obtained information would still support probable cause absent the tainted information, the warrant and the accompanying search are still valid. When a search or seizure would be justified without a warrant, insufficiency of a search warrant becomes immaterial. These issues would be litigated in pretrial motions.

Confidential Informants. If the information relied on comes from an informant, the basis for the reliability of that information should be set out in the affidavit. Challenging the sufficiency of the affidavit at a minimum could provide valuable discovery to the defense as to the source and content of the prosecutor's information. Prosecutors should avoid such challenges by including the basis for information detailing why the informant is reliable to the extent possible without compromising the case investigation. If the information cannot be revealed without seriously compromising the safety of an individual or the case investigation, the prosecution should seek ex parte to have the affidavit filed under seal. For a more in-depth discussion on challenging probable cause based on confidential informants and anonymous tips, *see Chapter Three: Probable Cause.*

Stale Information. Information that is old or outdated, is usually a more fruitful challenge than attacking a magistrate judge's determination of probable cause. Defense counsel should obtain a copy of the affidavit or other documents supporting the issuance of the warrant and review it for the date of the information upon which the officer relied. That dated information should be compared with the date when the warrant was issued. Anticipatory warrants are especially vulnerable to this sort of challenge. *See Anticipatory Warrants* above.

Critical factors in assessing the staleness of the information are the age of those facts and the nature of the conduct alleged. Defense counsel could be in a position to argue that the information is old and should not have been relied upon for an arrest. The delay will be contextual. In some cases a few weeks or even a few days could be too long depending on the nature of the information; whereas, in other cases a time lapse of several months would be required to find that the information was stale. If the conduct is considered ongoing or a continuing course of conduct, the amount of time between the last dated act and the application is less significant. *See, e.g., United States v. Martino,* 664 F.2d

860, 866-7 (2d Cir. 1981) (warrant authorizing wiretap had not become stale even though the latest event described had occurred 22 days before the issuance of the warrant).

Good Faith Exception. In *United States v. Leon,* 468 U.S. 897, 104 S. Ct. 3405, 82 L. Ed. 2d 677 (1984) the Supreme Court provided an enormously important safety net for the prosecution in that if the executing officer relies on a defective warrant in good faith the evidence will not be suppressed. The rationale behind the "good faith" exception is related to the purpose of the exclusionary rule: to deter police misconduct. If the issuing judicial officer or a court clerk is the person who made a mistake on the warrant and the police officer reasonably relies on the warrant, there is no police misconduct. In such cases, excluding evidence would not further the underlying policies of deterrence and the preference for the admission of the evidence is paramount.

The critical question in litigating *Leon* issues is whether the police officers relied on the warrant in good faith. Most of the time courts will find they did. In rare cases, the warrant might be so facially defective that no reasonable officer could rely on the probable cause in good faith. In *Groh*, for example, the Supreme Court not only found that the warrant lacked the necessary particularization, but that there was no good faith reliance on the warrant because it was so facially deficient that the officer could not reasonably presume it was valid. *Groh*, 124 S. Ct. at 1289, 157 L. Ed. 2d at 1077-8.

Defense counsel should obtain a copy of the warrant and review it for defects. If the defects were such that no reasonable officer could have considered the warrant valid, an argument for exclusion may be made notwithstanding Leon. Realistically, such arguments are very difficult to win. Defense counsel will be attacking the issuing judge's determination to issue a warrant and the officer's judgment in relying on that judicially approved document. Neither argument is likely to prevail, unless there are total omissions or absences of information as in Groh. Though the task is difficult it is not impossible and it might highlight to the court the overzealousness of the officers in support of other arguments in the case. Finally, if the information submitted to the court was false or misleading, the good faith exception is inapplicable. *See*

Lo-Ji Sales Inc. v. New York, 442 U.S. 319, 99 S. Ct. 2319, 60 L. Ed. 2d 920 (1979).

Lack of Particularization. A potentially viable challenge to a search executed pursuant to a warrant is that the warrant was not particularized as required by the Fourth Amendment or the search exceeded the scope of the warrant, i.e., the places to be searched and the things to be seized. The concern is what is known as a "general warrant" allowing for essentially a fishing expedition in a person's home. The Supreme Court recently revisited the issue of particularization in *Groh*, where the Court emphasized that "we are not dealing with formalities....Because the right of man to retreat into his own home and there be free from unreasonable governmental intrusion stands at the very core of the Fourth Amendment." *Groh* 124 S. Ct at 1290, 157 L. Ed. 2d at 1079 (internal quotations and citations omitted). Moreover, the particularization argument has constitutional legitimacy since the Fourth Amendment specifically requires particularization.

An overly broad warrant may be "cured" by reference to the supporting affidavit in many jurisdictions if it ensures that the officers knew for what they were specifically looking, though the terms of the warrant itself might be impermissibly broad. *See, e.g, U.S. v. Bianco*, 998 F.2d 1112, 1115-17 (2d Cir. 1993) (court upheld validity of search where the warrant impermissibly contained no particular description of items and made no mention of any criminal statute or criminal conduct, because the supporting affidavit was sufficiently particular). However, if the warrant failed to reference the supporting affidavit, it will not cure an unparticularized warrant. *See Groh* 124 S.Ct at 1290, 157 L. Ed. 2d at 1079. Courts will also consider whether the officers did the best they could with the information they had at the time of the application of the warrant. In short, a warrant will be read in a reasonable manner and counsel can craft arguments in that same vein.

Prosecutors often use the catch-all phrase "evidence of crime at this time unknown" on the warrant as long as it adequately limits the discretion of the executing officers and defines the particular offenses. Attaching the affidavit to the warrant and specifically incorporating the affidavit in the warrant can often assist in particularizing the search. The good news for prosecutors is that the courts understand that the warrants and affidavits must be viewed realistically and with common sense to avoid a "technicality." Moreover, if the officers relied on an overly broad affidavit in good faith, the search will usually be upheld under *Leon*.

Exceeding the Scope of the Warrant

Defense counsel must be on the look out for searches that extend beyond the scope of the warrant. The Supreme Court's description of the scope of a lawful search in *United States v. Ross*, 456 U.S. 798, 102 S. Ct. 2157, 72 L. Ed. 2d 572 (1982), is instructive:

> [The scope of a lawful search is] defined by the object of the search and the places in which there is probable cause to believe that it may be found. Just as probable cause to believe that a stolen lawnmower may be found in a garage will not support a warrant to search an upstairs bedroom, probable cause to believe that undocumented aliens are being transported in a van will not justify a warrantless search of a suitcase.

Id.

Defense counsel should obtain a copy of the return of the warrant detailing the evidence gathered to compare it against the scope of the warrant. It might be that lawfully owned ammunition was seized during the search of an office for suspected wire fraud although the warrant did not specify a search for firearms or ammunition. If the executing officers "flagrantly disregard" the terms of the warrant a court could suppress all of the evidence recovered, even that which was properly described. *See, e.g., United States v. Medlin*, 842 F.2d 1194, 1199-1200 (10th Cir. 1988) (court suppressed all evidence including firearms where ATF agents recovered 667 items in flagrant disregard of the scope of warrant issued solely for firearms). In most cases, however, the court is likely to suppress only that evidence taken outside the scope. Moreover, obvious contraband in plain view where the police are legitimately on the premises may be seized even if the contraband is not listed in the warrant. *See Chapter Twelve: Plain View.*

Prosecutors and law enforcement officers might avoid many of these challenges by making sure that the warrant covers possible contraband including any fruits, instruments or evidence of a crime such as money, firearms, etc. In setting out the terms of the warrant, the prosecutor must balance the need for particularization to avoid a "general search" against the possibility that the warrant will be too particularized to allow officers to take potential evidence. In cases which involve mostly documents, such as mail fraud cases, the judge will usually allow a class of items to be seized such as business records if the prosecution can establish that such records are expected to be "permeated with fraud."

Material Omissions and False Information. If the warrant is facially invalid or contains deliberate omissions the defense might be able to get the fruits of the search excluded. Where the affidavit contains false statements, the defense should request a Franks hearing pursuant to *Franks v. Delaware*, 438 U.S. 154, 98 S. Ct. 2674, 57 L. Ed. 2d 667 (1978) and ultimately a request for invalidation of the warrant.

To obtain a *Franks* hearing, the defense needs to make a "substantial preliminary showing" that the affidavit contained false information and that the false information was submitted deliberately or from a reckless disregard of the truth. *Id.* at 155-56, 98 S. Ct. at 2676, 57 L. Ed. 2d at 672. If only part of the information is tainted but the remainder is sufficient to establish probable cause, the search usually will be considered valid and no Franks hearing even need be held.

First Amendment Considerations and Pornography Cases. When documents are the target of the warrant, First Amendment rights are often implicated and the description of those documents must be met with "scrupulous exactitude." *See Stanford v. Texas*, 397 U.S. 476, 85 S. Ct. 506, 13 L. Ed. 2d 431 (1965). Alleged obscene materials present their own difficulties in this regard and counsel for both sides in these cases should become aware of the more exacting requirements. That being said, courts have allowed for very broad warrants for computer files in child pornography cases, often allowing the officers to take the entire computer, in part because the computer itself is considered an instrumentality of the crime.

Execution Errors. The method of execution of a warrant is governed by the Fourth Amendment and must be reasonable. *See Pennsylvania v. Mimms*, 434 U.S. 106, 98 S. Ct. 330, 54 L. Ed. 2d 331 (1977). The police actions in executing the warrant need to be related to the objectives of the "authorized intrusion." Bringing a "media tag along," for example, is not related to the objectives of the "authorized intrusion." *See Wilson v. Layne*, 526 U.S. 603, 119 S. Ct. 1692, 143 L. Ed. 2d 818 (1999).

Excessive or unnecessary destruction of property in the course of a search might also violate the Fourth Amendment, even when the entry is otherwise lawful. *See United States v. Ramirez*, 523 U.S. 65, 118 S. Ct. 992, 140 L. Ed. 2d 191 (1998). That being said, federal law provides that an officer may "break open any outer door or window of a house, or any part of a house, or anything therein, to execute a search warrant, if, after notice of his authority and purpose, he is refused admittance or when necessary to liberate himself or a person aiding him in the execution of the warrant." 18 USC § 3109. Counsel should determine the type of force used and whether the entry resulted in destruction of property to assess whether there might be an argument that the entry was not reasonable under the circumstances.

Knock and Announce Requirement. Federal officers (and state officers executing warrants resulting in federal charges) are required to follow the statutory "knock and announce" provisions in 18 USC § 3109 unless there are exigent circumstances involving the officers' safety or destruction of evidence justifying a "no knock" entry. Failure to give notice of purpose and authority before forced entry where there are no exigent circumstances might be violative of the Fourth Amendment.

There is no "rigid rule" requiring announcement in all instances, and the Supreme Court has left it to lower courts to determine the circumstances under which an unannounced entry is reasonable under the Fourth Amendment. *See Wilson v. Arkansas*, 514 U.S. 927, 115 S. Ct. 1914, 131 L. Ed. 2d 976 (1995). In general, the Fourth Amendment does not require officers to "knock and announce" when they have a "reasonable suspicion that knocking and announcing their presence, under the particular circumstances, would be dangerous or futile, or that it would inhibit the effective investigation of the crime by, for example, allowing the destruction of evidence." *See Richardson v. Wisconsin*, 520 U.S. 385, 394 S. Ct. 1416, 1422, 137 L. Ed. 2d 615, 117 (1997). Moreover, the officer may use forcible entry even if he is not refused admittance, if exigent circumstances "ripen." *United States v. Banks*, 124 S. Ct 521, 157 L. Ed. 2d 343 (2003). The reasonableness of when to force entry will also depend on the type of case. "Police seeking a stolen piano may be able to spend more time to make sure they really need the battering ram." *Id.*

Exigent circumstances often arise in narcotics cases, although the Supreme Court has rejected a *per se* rule of exigency in drug cases, requiring officers to have at least a reasonable suspicion that knocking and announcing their entry would be "dangerous, futile, or destructive to the purposes of the investigation." *See Id.* Defense counsel should insist that the prosecution submit individualized factual support for exigent circumstances in the particular case, and urge the court to reject a blanket, "it was a drug case of course it was dangerous" rationale. As the Ninth Circuit advised, "While it is true that 'exigent circumstances' can justify immediate entry, incantation of that phrase does not dissolve the shield that our law provides." *United States v. Becker* 23 F.3d 1537, 1540 (9th Cir. 1994) (police violated Fourth Amendment in methamphetamine case by announcing their presence and simultaneously breaking down front door of defendant's house where no exigent circumstances when enforcing warrant where suspects were still in bed). Defense counsel must listen carefully for generalized statements about drug cases and demand that the basis be more specific or that defense's motion be granted. At a minimum, this particularization could provide crucial pretrial discovery.

Both counsels should investigate the method of execution of a warrant to determine whether there was a violation of the knock and announcement requirement. The first determination is whether the officers were required to knock and announce. If exigent circumstances were present, notably the destruction of evidence, the actual facts that gave rise to the claimed exigency should be delineated; *e.g.*, the type of case, the possibility of weapons, history of violence of the offenders, possible destruction of evidence such as flushing water sounds and opening of windows. If a knock and announcement was required, the parties should assess whether the actual announcement and the length of time between the announcement and the actual entry was reasonable. *See also Chapter Thirteen: Exigent Circumstances.*

No court has held a bright line rule regarding the amount of time necessary between the announcement and the entry. The courts look to whether the amount of time was reasonable under the circumstances. As the Sixth Circuit explained, given the knock and announcement principle's fact-sensitive nature, it "cannot be distilled into a constitutional stop-watch where a fraction of a second assumes controlling significance." *United States v. Spikes*, 158 F.3d 913, 926 (1998) (emphasis in original).

The Patriot Act now specifically allows judges to issue "sneak and peak" warrants which do not require a knock and announce or even notice of the execution of the warrant. Instead, entire notification of the warrant may be delayed until after the police enter and search provided the court finds "reasonable cause to believe that providing immediate notification of the execution of the warrant may have an adverse result" such as endangering life or physical safety of an individual; destruction or tampering with evidence; initimidation of potential witnesses or seriously jeopardizing an investigation or delaying a trial. *See* 18 USC §§ 3103a, 2705(b). In addition, the warrant must prohibit the seizure of any tangible property or communications unless a court finds such seizure to be a reasonable necessity. The warrant also must provide notice of the execution within a reasonable period which may be extended upon a showing of good cause. 18 USC § 3103a(b). The purpose is to allow the officers to go into the house, make observations and then come back and use what they have seen to obtain full search warrants without giving notice to the occupants or owners. Probable cause is still required to issue the warrant.

Remedies. The general remedy for a Fourth Amendment violation is exclusion of the evidence from trial. *See Weeks v. United States,* 232 U.S. 383, 398, 34 S. Ct. 341, 346, 58 L. Ed. 652, 658 (1914). Failure to follow the requirements of obtaining a warrant under FRCrP 41 could lead to suppression of the evidence under the exclusionary rule, although FRCrP 41 no longer contains a specific exclusionary provision having been deleted in the 1989 amendments.

The usual remedy for violation of the knock and announce provision is exclusion of the evidence. *See, e.g., Becker* 23 F.3d at 1541-42 (finding that the officers violated the knock and announcement requirement and failed to show sufficient exigent circumstances, the court remanded the case for a new trial, ordering that the evidence seized during the first search as well as evidence obtained in reliance upon the fruits of that search, including the evidence obtained during the second search, shall be excluded). Although the Supreme Court has not specifically held that the exclusionary rule is the remedy for violation of knock and announce provisions, it allowed for that remedy back in 1958 when officers broke into a home without prior notice and made an unlawful arrest. *See United States v. Miller,* 357 U.S. 301, 313-14, 78 S. Ct. 1190, 1198, 2 L. Ed. 2d 1332, 1341 (1958). Still, there appears to be some division in the circuits whether the remedy of exclusion of the evidence is applied in knock and announce violations. *See, e.g., United v. Espinoza,* 256 F.3d 718 (7th Cir. 2001) (holding that a violation of the knock and announce rule did not compel exclusion where the privacy and property interests of the defendant whom the rule was meant to protect were not impacted by the violation of the rule). *See also, Chapter Seven: The Exclusionary Rule and Chapter One: List of Exceptions to the Warrant Requirement.*

Defense counsel should be prepared not only to argue a Fourth Amendment violation, but also that the remedy should be exclusion of the evidence in order to deter errant police behavior and as a proportionate remedy to the harm incurred. The defendant also might have civil causes of action against the police officers through a *Bivens* claim allowing for damages from Fourth Amendment violations, *see Bivens v. Six Unnamed Agents of the*

Federal Bureau of Narcotics, 403 U.S. 388, 91 S. Ct. 1999, 29 L. Ed. 2d 619 (1971), or a possible civil rights claim under 42 USC § 1983.

Some Useful Cases

United States v. United States District Court Eastern District of Michigan, 407 U.S. 297, 92 S. Ct. 2125, 32 L. Ed. 2d 752 (1972).

Gerstein v. Pugh, 420 U.S. 103, 95 S. Ct. 854, 43 L. Ed. 2d 54 (1975).

United States v. Leon, 468 U.S. 897, 104 S. Ct. 3405, 82 L. Ed. 2d 677 (1984).

United States v. Ross, 456 U.S. 798, 102 S. Ct. 2157, 72 L. Ed. 2d 572 (1982).

Franks v. Delaware, 438 U.S. 154, 98 S. Ct. 2674, 57 L. Ed. 2d 667 (1978).

See Pennsylvania v. Mimms, 434 U.S. 106, 98 S. Ct. 330, 54 L. Ed. 2d 331 (1977).

Wilson v. Arkansas, 514 U.S. 927, 115 S. Ct. 1914, 131 L. Ed. 2d 976 (1995).

United States v. Becker 23 F.3d 1537, 1540 (9th Cir. 1994)

Bivens v. Six Unnamed Agents of the Federal Bureau of Narcotics, 403 U.S. 388, 91 S. Ct. 1999, 29 L. Ed. 2d 619 (1971).

CHAPTER SEVEN
THE EXCLUSIONARY RULE

Exclusionary Rule in General

The sanction for violating the Fourth Amendment is the exclusion of the evidence from use by the prosecution at trial, *see Weeks v. United States*, 232 U.S. 383, 34 S. Ct. 341, 58 L. Ed. 652 (1914). The Exclusionary Rule was judicially created to deter police misconduct and is one of the most controversial aspects of criminal law.

The courts have frequently sought to distinguish fact situations and precedent to avoid the application of the Exclusionary Rule in order to circumvent the situation of a criminal going free because the police blundered. The Exclusionary Rule also explains why courts have often abandoned the requirement of a warrant as the *sine qua non* of a reasonable search and adopted a standard that assesses the actions of the officers under a reasonableness standard independent of the Warrant Requirement. As Justice Scalia observed in his concurrence in *California v. Acevedo*, there was an "explosion" of Fourth Amendment litigation after the Exclusionary Rule was adopted in 1914, and the Supreme Court's jurisprudence has "lurched back and forth between imposing a categorical warrant requirement and looking to reasonableness alone." 500 U.S. 565, 582, 111 S. Ct. 1982, 1992, 114 L. Ed. 2d 619, 635 (1991) (Scalia, J., concurring).

Exclusion of Evidence

The basic purpose of the Exclusionary Rule is to deter police misconduct; it is not to provide a "remedy" to the defendant for violation of his Fourth Amendment rights (*See United States v. Leon*, 468 U.S. 897, 906, 104 S. Ct. 3405, 3412, 82 L. Ed. 2d 677, 687 (1984)), although the defendant and other victims of Fourth Amendment violations may have civil remedies including claims under 28 USC § 1983. Application of the Exclusionary

Rule is dependent upon whether its objective of deterrence is furthered through the exclusion. It is important to remember that even though this remedy is trial related, a Fourth Amendment violation is "fully accomplished" at the time the unreasonable act is committed. *See United States v. Calandra*, 414 U.S. 338, 354, 94 S. Ct. 613, 623, 38 L. Ed. 2d 561, 575 (1974). In other words, the Fourth Amendment prohibits "unreasonable searches and seizures" regardless of whether the evidence is ultimately used at trial.

In practice, the effect of a violation does not come to the attention of criminal courts and until defense counsel files a motion to suppress the evidence seized in violation of the amendment. Not every defendant will have "standing" to make the claim. *See Chapter Five: Issues of Standing.*

The fact that these issues arise because the officers actually found incriminating evidence that the defense is moving to suppress increases judicial dislike of the Exclusionary Rule since such evidence often confirms the defendant's guilt. The result is that the burden the defense realistically carries in challenging the admissibility of evidence is great even though it is the prosecution's burden to show that the evidence was obtained lawfully. In short, it is difficult to win a motion to suppress especially in federal court.

Fruit of the Poisonous Tree

The evidence subject to exclusion includes direct evidence and evidence obtained through the exploitation of the illegal conduct known as the "fruit of the poisonous tree." *Wong Sun v. United States*, 371 U.S. 471, 487-88, 83 S. Ct. 407, 417, 9 L. Ed. 2d 441, 455 (1963). The taint of this poisonous tree is quite far reaching under the Fourth Amendment and includes: "tangible, physical material actually seized in an illegal search, items observed or words overhead in the course of the unlawful activity, or confessions or statements of the accused obtained during an illegal detention." *See United States v. Crews*, 445 U.S. 463, 470, 100 S. Ct. 1244, 1249, 63 L. Ed. 2d 537, 555 (1980).

There is some limit to what constitutes "fruit" from the poisonous tree. For example, in Crews, the Supreme Court determined that a defendant's person cannot be the "fruit" of an illegal arrest. *Id.* The defendant in that case had argued that he was entitled to immunity from prosecution and suppression of an in-court identification as a result of his illegal arrest.

Even so, defense counsel should think creatively in determining what constitutes tainted evidence once it is determined that there has been an illegal search or seizure. It is helpful to make a chronological chart of what happened before and after the illegal event: when was the evidence obtained, when was consent obtained, when were statements taken, etc.?The argument being that even if there was consent or waiver of rights, they may have been tainted by the illegal search and seizure. *See also Attenuation* below.

Attenuation

If there is a Fourth Amendment violation, the prosecution has the task of trying to show that the evidence which was recovered was not a fruit of the poisonous tree because any taint was dissipated by subsequent events or actions by the officers or the defendant. This dissipation or purging of the taint is known as "attenuation" and the prosecution must prove attenuation. See *Brown v. Illinois,* 422 U.S. 590, 603, 95 S. Ct. 2254, 2261, 45 L. Ed. 2d 416, 427 (1975).

The key to attenuation is the strength of the nexus between the Fourth Amendment violation and the discovery or procurement of the evidence the prosecution seeks to introduce at trial. It is when the nexus has "become so attenuated as to dissipate the taint" that the evidence can be used by the prosecution despite the Fourth Amendment violation. *See Nardone v. United States,* 308 U.S. 338, 341, 60 S. Ct. 266, 268, 84 L. Ed. 307, 312 (1939). The Supreme Court's code word is "exploitation"; i.e., did the police officers exploit the primary taint or was the taint sufficiently disconnected to purge the evidence of the taint. *See Wong Sun,* 371 U.S. at 487-88, 83 S. Ct. at 417, 9 L. Ed. 2d at 455.

There are three factors at which the courts look in assessing whether the evidence constitutes fruit of the poisonous tree: 1) the purpose and "flagrancy" of the misconduct; 2) the time lapse between the misconduct and the procurement of the evidence; and 3) any intervening circumstances. *See Brown*, 422 U.S. at 603-04, 95 S. Ct. at 2261-62, 45 L. Ed. 2d at 427.

It is often difficult for the defense to convince a judge that the police officer's actions were flagrant and it may require something as drastic as a confession or admission of wrongdoing on the part of the officer. For example, in *United States v. Caro*, 248 F.3d 1240, 47-48 (10th Cir. 2001), the Tenth Circuit found the police misconduct flagrant because officer asked to search the car in the "hope that something might turn up." Prosecutors will focus heavily on the lack of flagrancy as it ties in with their position that the Exclusionary Rule should not be used against officers who may have been mistaken but were not acting in bad faith. Where there is no bad faith by the officers, the rationale is there is little if any deterrent value to the use of the Exclusionary Rule.

Time elapsed is an important factor. If there was an illegal search and directly after that the officers sat down and took the defendants' statements in the same place searched, a court is not likely to find attenuation. As a general rule, contemporaneous actions are not going to be purged of any taint. The defense should focus on brevity between the violation and the procurement of evidence. In *Taylor v. Alabama*, 457 U.S. 687, 691, 102 S. Ct. 2664, 2667, 73 L. Ed. 2d 314, 320 (1982) the Supreme Court found that a confession was not admissible when only six hours had elapsed between the illegal arrest and the defendant's confession, and during that time the defendant had been fingerprinted and subject to a lineup. Each circuit will have different standards with time frames varying from hours to days.

Intervening circumstances resulting in attenuation include police leaving the scene; abandonment of the evidence by the defendant; *Miranda* warnings given after an illegal arrest (although this alone not always enough to purge the taint without some other intervening circumstances or elapsed time, *see e.g., Brown*, 422 U.S. at 601-02, 95 S. Ct. at 2261, 45 L. Ed. 2d at 426). Again, the issues are very fact specific and judges look at a totality of the circumstances to determine whether there has been sufficient attenuation.

When statements are the fruit of an illegal arrest, judges will look to at a number of factors including among others whether warnings were given, whether the defendant was given an opportunity to contact a lawyer, whether the defendant signed a waiver of rights form, whether the defendant initiated the discussions with the officers. The defense needs to emphasize to the judge that the illegal arrest itself compelled any cooperation or waiver by the defendant stemmed from a poisonous search.

When physical evidence is found, the defense will want to show that even though there may be intervening circumstances such as the police officers leaving and coming back and asking for consent to search, that reasonably the defendant would not deny consent given the fact that the officers were already in the house without a warrant. If nothing transpired during the period the police left, *e.g.* the defendant did not contact a lawyer, or a spouse did not arrive on the scene, etc., the defense can argue that the factors are the equivalent of a contemporaneous action given the mindset of the defendant.

Good Faith

Although the need for a warrant supported by probable cause is ordinarily required for most searches, if the police act in good faith upon a warrant that turns out to lack probable cause or is otherwise defective, the search will be upheld. *United States v. Leon*, 468 U.S. 897, 104 S. Ct. 3405, 82 L. Ed. 2d 677 (1984). The good faith exception makes it very difficult for defense counsel to challenge successfully a search warrant issued by a magistrate judge.

However, if the police have no reasonable basis for believing the warrant is valid the good faith exception does not apply. For example, where the officers have misled the magistrate as to the facts, the reliance is not in good faith. In addition, if the application is so lacking in indicia of probable cause or so facially deficient reliance upon the warrant is unreasonable and not in good faith.

Importantly, it is incumbent upon the police officers to review the warrant to ensure that the warrant "conforms to constitutional requirements." *Groh v. Ramirez*, 540 U.S. 551, 124 S. Ct. 1284, 1293, 157 L. Ed. 2d 1068, 1082 (2004). In *Groh*, the Supreme Court refused to apply the good faith exception under Leon, because the warrant failed to describe at all the persons or things to be seized. Although the application contained such information, the fact that the warrant itself did not list the persons or things to be seized was fatal.

Independent Source

If the evidence is discovered through a source independent of any Fourth Amendment violation then it is admissible even though there is police misconduct. *See Segura v. United States*, 468 U.S. 796, 813-14, 104 S. Ct. 3380, 3390, 82 L. Ed. 2d 599, 614 (1984). The Supreme Court has defined "independent source" from a law enforcement perspective. Defendants have argued that independent source should mean that evidence is obtained in the first instance through lawful means. *See, e.g., Murray v. United States*, 487 U.S. 533, 537-40, 108 S. Ct. 2529, 2533-34, 101 L. Ed. 2d 472, 480-82 (1988). The government has maintained that independent source includes evidence obtained as a result of an unlawful search but later obtained independently from activities untainted by the initial illegality, such as a warrant based on information independent of the unlawful actions of the officers. Id. The Supreme Court has agreed with the government's position with respect to the scope of independent source. *Id.*

The facts in *Segura* are instructive as to the Court's position. In *Segura*, the Supreme Court allowed evidence of drug trafficking obtained from an illegal search because the officers were in the process of obtaining a warrant for the search and thus operating in good faith. Officers had applied for the warrant based on information procured from police surveillance, but due to the late hour, were unable to obtain the warrant until the next day. Before obtaining the warrant, the officers arrested the defendants, secured the apartment and seized items in plain view in the apartment. Once the warrant was obtained (based on information that was known prior to any search or seizure) the officers completed the search. The Court found that police acted in good faith on the assumption that a warrant would be issued, and allowed all evidence seized prior to issuance of the warrant. These so-called "second look" warrants may only be obtained on facts known to the officers before the illegal search, based on an independent source such as a tip-off, or surveillance.

Inevitable Discovery

A similar exception to the Exclusionary Rule to that of independent source is the notion of inevitable discovery, which permits the introduction of tainted evidence if the prosecution can show that it would have been inevitably discovered by lawful means. The way the court has defined independent source covers most of the issues involved with inevitable discovery, and some judges have commented that there was little need for a separate inevitable source exception given the independent source doctrine.

The only way to understand fully why the inevitable discovery doctrine came about as something beyond independent source, is to review the facts of the seminal case setting forth the doctrine. *Nix v. Williams*, 467 U.S. 431, 104 S. Ct. 2501, 81 L. Ed. 2d 377 (1984) involved the search for the body of a young girl who had been abducted from a local YMCA and murdered. Rescue teams combed the surrounding area which involved miles of terrain. Williams had been seen at the YMCA putting a blanket covered bundle with skinny white legs sticking out of it. Williams eventually surrendered to authorities and was transported by officers in a police car. During the ride the police officers gave Williams what is known as the "Christian burial speech" about finding the girl's body so that she could have a proper Christian burial. Williams provided the location of the body in an area near where rescuers were searching. The officers knew that Williams was represented by counsel at the time they gave the speech which was found to have been done for the purposes of eliciting an incriminating response in violation of Williams' rights.

The Court determined that the evidence was not admissible under the independent source doctrine because the body was discovered by exploitation of the violation of Williams' rights.

Instead, the Court took on the task of justifying the finding of the body (obviously essential to the murder case) by contending that the searchers would have inevitably found the body in their search. To do so, the Court had to assess night temperatures, time of day, the trajectory of the search teams, etc., clearly a reach that recovery was inevitable as a matter of law.

It seems evident that the Court in *Nix* strained the concept of inevitable discovery to ensure that the criminal did not go free because the constable blundered due at least in part to the fact that the case involved the heinous murder of a child. Justice Stevens said as much in his concurrence:

> The facts are unusually tragic; it involves an unusually clear violation of constitutional rights; and it graphically illustrates the societal costs that may be incurred when police officers decide to dispense with the requirements of the law....the pressures on state executive and judicial officers charged with the administration of the criminal law are great, especially when the crime is murder and the victim a small child. But it is precisely the predictability of those pressures that makes imperative a resolute loyalty to the guarantees that the Constitution extends to us all.

Nix at 451 (quoting in part *Brewer v. Williams*, 430 U.S. 387, 406, 97 S. Ct. 1232, 1243, 51 L. Ed. 2d 424, 441 (citations and internal quotations omitted)).

There are certain facts in *Nix*, however, which are helpful to the defense in arguing against inevitable discovery. For example, in *Nix*, the process by which the discovery would have supposedly been inevitable was already in place at the time of the constitutional violation. Circuits are split on whether the police conduct has to have been started before the violation to constitute a proper exception. The defense should argue even in those jurisdictions not requiring the process to have started, that the failure of the officers to even start a legitimate process shows a lack of good faith and respect for the constitutional protections thus fulfilling the objective of deterrence underlying the Exclusionary Rule. In short, if the actions of the officers show a flaunting of Fourth Amendment requirements by not even bothering to do it legally, the amendment is undermined.

The notion of inevitable discovery has more appropriately been used in inventory searches where the police could search and voucher evidence from property anyway and would have discovered the evidence regardless of any previous violation. Although this argument could also be defended on the basis of independent source, inevitable discovery in this situation is more properly named. Assertion of the exception still requires that the prosecution establish by a preponderance of the evidence the prerequisites to an inventory search exception including that inventory search standards were in placed and followed. The defense must ensure that the prosecution is held to its burden. *See Chapter Fifteen: Inventory, Regulatory, and Border Searches.*

Uses of Tainted Evidence

Even though evidence was obtained in violation of Fourth Amendment rights, it may still be used at certain stages in a criminal proceeding and even during trial. For example, tainted evidence may be used to impeach the defendant's own testimony should she take the stand at trial. *Walder v. United States*, 347 U.S. 62, 74 S. Ct. 354, 98 L. Ed. 503 (1954). Tainted evidence may not be used, however, to impeach other witnesses. *See James v. Illinois*, 493 U.S. 307, 110 S. Ct. 648, 107 L. Ed. 2d 676 (1990).

Tainted evidence may be used at grand jury proceedings, *see United States v. Calandra*, 414 U.S. 338, 94 S. Ct. 613, 38 L. Ed. 2d 561 (1974) and basically any other proceeding outside the jury trial including sentencing (unless the defense can show the evidence was obtained specifically to enhance a sentencing guideline), *see, e.g., United States v. Tejada*, 956 F.2d 1256, 1263 (2d Cir. 1992); probation and parole hearings, *see Pennsylvania Bd. Of Probation and Parole v. Scott*, 524 U.S. 3571, 119 S. Ct. 1, 141 L. Ed. 2d 761 (1998); and deportation hearings *INS v. Lopez-Mendoza*, 468 U.S. 1032, 104 S. Ct. 3479, 82 L. Ed. 2d 778 (1984). Tainted evidence may not be used, however, in forfeiture cases. *See One 1958 Plymouth Sedan v. Pennsylvania*, 380 U.S. 693, 696, 85 S. Ct. 1246, 1248, 14 L. Ed. 2d 170, 172 (1965).

CHAPTER EIGHT
INVESTIGATORY DETENTIONS

Overview

The legal tension between protecting Fourth Amendment rights and still providing reasonable opportunities for officers to investigate crime is played out in full force in investigatory detentions. What can an officer do when he encounters a person? What level of suspicion must the officer have to detain someone? What level of suspicion must the officer have to place that person under arrest?

Far from the impersonal act of placing a parking ticket on a car windshield, police action that detains an individual person physically harkens up the tyranny of government that gave rise to many of our rights in the first place. Our society, and even the courts to some extent, still considers the personal integrity and security of an individual an important right. Although defense counsel represents a person accused of a crime, in arguing against an illegal seizure, the defense will be championing the protection of personal liberty. Defense attorneys should not lose sight of that fact in their arguments, despite the dwindling success rate of motions for suppression, particularly in the present political climate.

Consensual Encounters Generally

Like any ordinary citizen, an officer may approach someone on the street or in a public place and ask questions, such as inquiring as to that person's identity, and even requesting identification or asking for consent to search that person's property. It is called a *consensual encounter* and police may engage in such stops without warrants and without probable cause or even articulable suspicion, defined generally as some objective justification for suspecting criminal activity less than needed for probable cause.

The Supreme Court has made clear that "law enforcement officers do not violate the Fourth Amendment by merely approaching an individual on the street or in another public place, by asking him if he is willing to answer some questions, by putting questions to him if the person is willing to listen, or by offering in evidence in a criminal prosecution his voluntary answers to such questions." *Florida v. Royer*, 460 U.S. 491, 497, 103 S. Ct. 1319, 1324, 75 L. Ed. 2d 229, 236 (1983). Since the Fourth Amendment's protections involve the reasonableness of a seizure, by defining a consensual encounter as not constituting a seizure, the Fourth Amendment is not implicated.

However, if there is a "stop and identify" statute or ordinance which requires a person to provide a police officer with his name or face criminal sanctions, the police officer must have reasonable suspicion to enforce the statute. The Supreme Court recently upheld a Nevada statute making it a crime for failure to provide one's name to a police officer under the Fourth Amendment on the basis that the requirement is limited to a valid investigatory stop requiring reasonable suspicion. *See Hiibel v. Sixth Judicial District Court of Nevada*, 2004 WL 1373207 at 5 (June 21, 2004).

Free to Leave

The touchstone of a consensual encounter is whether a person objectively would have felt *free to leave*. If a person objectively felt free to leave he is not considered "seized" and the protections of the Fourth Amendment are not triggered. Lacking a detention or seizure, the police/individual encounter does not require articulable suspicion, probable cause, a warrant, or an established warrant exception. This means that officers may walk up to a person and ask questions based on hunches, profiles, racism, you name it. Unless there is more to the encounter, the person is not seized for Fourth Amendment purposes and there is nothing to litigate under this amendment despite the officer's subjective motives.

The notion that an individual would ever feel free to leave an encounter with police officers is a judicial construct. In reality how many people on the street truly believe they can walk away from a police officer's questions with impunity? But to hold otherwise would, pardon the expression, handcuff law enforcement and the courts have constructed this notion of "free to leave" focusing on the behavior of the officers in presenting such a show of authority as to distinguish the encounter from one with an ordinary citizen. Attorneys must likewise assess and litigate these issues under this judicial construct.

The standard of whether a person is "free to leave" an encounter with the police is an objective one. The courts consider the totality of the existing facts to determine whether a reasonable person in that position would have felt free to leave focusing on the police officer's actions. Even if the person subjectively felt he could not leave, if, objectively, a reasonable person in that position would have felt free to "disregard the police and go about his business" then he is not seized or detained under the Fourth Amendment. *See California v. Hodari D.*, 499 U.S. 621, 628, 111 S. Ct. 1547, 1552, 113 L. Ed. 2d. 690, 698 (1991).

Likewise, if the officer subjectively believed that the suspect was not free to leave and, in fact, would not have allowed that person to leave, the court could still find a consensual encounter unless there was manifested objective behavior on the part of the police officer signaling that the person was not free to go. That being said, there is still room for litigation even if the officer subjectively believed that it was a consensual encounter if the actions of the officer would have made a reasonable person not feel free to leave.

When a person reasonably believes he or she is no longer free to leave, at that point, the otherwise consensual encounter becomes a seizure triggering Fourth Amendment protections. This seizure at a minimum constitutes an investigatory detention, and might even be the equivalent of a formal arrest, depending on the extent of the show of authority.

When Does a Consensual Encounter Become an Investigatory Detention?

There are no bright line rules to determine when a particular consensual encounter becomes an investigatory detention. The Supreme Court in *United States v. Mendenhall*, 446 U.S. 544, 100 S. Ct. 1870, 64 L. Ed. 2d 497 (1980), grappled with the question of when a consensual stop becomes a seizure triggering Fourth Amendment protections. If counsel is confronting this issue, *Mendenhall* is a good starting point. In that case, the Court demonstrated the distinction by examining the facts in *Terry v. Ohio:*

> Officer McFadden approached the three men, identified himself as a police officer and asked for their names.... When the men "mumbled something" in response to his inquiries, Officer McFadden grabbed petitioner Terry, spun him around so that they were facing the other two, with Terry between McFadden and the others, and patted down the outside of his clothing.... Obviously the officer "seized" Terry and subjected him to a "search" when he took hold of him, spun him around, and patted down the outer surfaces of his clothing.

Mendenhall, 446 U.S. at 552-53, 100 S. Ct. at 1876, 64 L. Ed. 2d at 508. The focus of concern for the Court in *Mendenhall* was the actions of the police officers that transformed an otherwise consensual encounter into something more.

Defense counsel in particular will be tempted to focus on the state of mind of the client and the status of the client. For example, defense counsel might argue that because the client was a woman and alone on the street and the police officer was male that the encounter was necessarily one in which a reasonable person would not have felt free to leave. Though likely to be true, the courts are much less concerned with the defendant than they are with police action. The Court in *Mendenhall* made clear that:

> [A] person is "seized" only when, by means of physical force or a show of authority, his freedom of movement is restrained. Only when such restraint is imposed is there any foundation whatever for invoking constitutional safeguards. The purpose

of the Fourth Amendment is not to eliminate all contact between the police and the citizenry, but "to prevent arbitrary and oppressive interference by enforcement officials with the privacy and personal security of individuals."

446 U.S. at 553-554, 100 S. Ct. at 1877, 64 L. Ed. 2d at 509 (citing *United States v. Martinez-Fuerte*, 428 U.S. 543, 554, 96 S. Ct. 3074, 3081, 49 L. Ed. 2d 1116, 1126 (1976)).

Although the fact that the defendant is a woman and alone definitely belongs in the calculation, without some action on the part of the police officer, the status of the defendant will not be enough to find a seizure.

Investigatory Seizures

Perhaps the most fruitful area of litigation for the defense is when the officer claims that the officer-citizen encounter was consensual while the defendant argues that she reasonably did not feel free to leave. In such cases, the prosecution may have conceded that the officer lacked articulable suspicion or probable cause, key to any defense victory, but that such justifications were not required because the person was not seized for Fourth Amendment purposes. The defense will need to demonstrate how the encounter was not consensual in that a reasonable person in the defendant's position would not have felt free to leave and was actually responding to a show of authority.

Important factors in determining whether a reasonable person would not feel free to leave—though not individually required or dispositive—include whether the police activated sirens or flashers, commanded the person to halt, displayed weapons, operated their cars in order to block the person, or controlled the person's direction or movements. *See Michigan v. Chesternut*, 486 U.S. 567, 575, 108 S. Ct. 1975, 1980, 100 L. Ed. 2d 565, 573 (1988). Additional factors, particularly relevant when the police walk up to a person on the street, include "the threatening presence of several officers, the display of a weapon by an officer, some physical touching of the person of the citizen, or the use of language or tone of voice indicating that compliance with the officer's request might be compelled." *United States v. Mendenhall*, 446 U.S.

544, 554, 100 S. Ct. 1870, 1877, 64 L. Ed. 2d 497, 509 (1980). These are the same factors used when demonstrating standing in seizure cases. *See Chapter Five: Issues of Standing.*

The more successful arguments for the defense are typically those that do not challenge the officer's version of events or require the judge to find the officer lying or acting unlawfully. When the prosecution concedes a lack of reasonable suspicion relying instead on a claim that the encounter was consensual, the defense would not need to show that the officer lacked reasonable suspicion, which is a much harder hurdle to overcome before a judge. However, savvy prosecutors often maintain that it was a consensual encounter, but even if it arguably was not, alternatively the officer had reasonable suspicion. This double-barreled strategy is harder for the defense to overcome, particularly given the fact that reasonable suspicion is a lower standard than probable cause and likely to be found by a judge giving considerable deference to police officer actions.

Articulable, Individualized and Reasonable Suspicion

Prior to the Supreme Court's landmark holding in *Terry v. Ohio*, 392 U.S. at 30, 88 S. Ct. at 1884-85, 20 L. Ed. 2d at 911, the seminal "stop and frisk case," any restraint resulting in a seizure required probable cause even if it was simply an investigatory detention and not a full arrest. *Terry* set out an important exception to this probable cause requirement: the police only need articulable suspicion that a person has committed or is about to commit a crime to support a temporary seizure or brief investigatory stop. When officers have such suspicion they may temporarily seize someone, but they are limited to the extent necessary to investigate the reasonable suspicion. For example, an officer who reasonably suspects that someone has jumped a turnstile may stop and question that person, but the officer, without more, would not be justified in searching the person's backpack.

An investigatory detention can involve a stop and frisk or pat down for weapons to assure the officers' safety if the police have reason to believe that the suspect is armed and dangerous. *See*

United States v. Brignoni-Ponce, 422 U.S. 873, 880, 95 S. Ct. 2574, 2580, 45 L. Ed. 2d 607, 616 (1975). (N.B. The terms articulable suspicion, reasonable suspicion and individualized suspicion are used interchangeably in court opinions.)

Litigating Frisks and Pat Downs

A *Terry* stop, known colloquially as a "stop and frisk," allows police officers to do a routine pat down if the officers justifiably believe that the person is armed and dangerous. The average person influenced by television dramas and cop shows might assume that any stop by the police necessitates a pat down as standard police procedure. Some attorneys might make that assumption as well. It is wrong. When someone is being placed under arrest, a pat down is indeed standard police procedure and perfectly legal provided there is sufficient probable cause to justify the arrest in the first place.

Admittedly, in many cases where the officers have articulable suspicion that a crime has been committed or is about to be committed, there is also a justifiable belief that the person is armed and dangerous, particularly in narcotics cases or crimes of violence. But there are many crimes where such an assumption is not justified and the physical touching is an unwarranted intrusion in violation of a person's Fourth Amendment rights. Furthermore, such touching could turn what was otherwise an investigatory detention into a full arrest requiring probable cause. *See When Does a* Terry *Stop Turn Into an Arrest?* below.

Pre-arrest pat downs in documents cases, immigration offenses, fraud cases, and other typically non-violent offenses should raise a red flag to the criminal practitioner to determine whether the officers had a justifiable belief that the suspect was armed and dangerous. The defense attorney should determine from the client whether such a pat down occurred and at what point it occurred during the encounter with the officer. Likewise, the prosecutor should determine such information from the case agent. If the pat down was subsequent to an arrest supported by probable cause, there is no Fourth Amendment violation. If the pat down was before an arrest and before the officers had probable cause to arrest, there could be a viable defense motion if the officers lacked articulable suspicion as to the dangerousness of the suspect, even if the officers had articulable suspicion as to a particular crime, unless it was a violent crime.

If the evidence from the pat down formed the basis for probable cause for the subsequent arrest, counsel should determine the basis for the pat down separately from the fruits of the frisk. If the frisk was improper and the results of the frisk were used to establish probable cause to arrest, the evidence could be suppressed as fruits of that poisonous tree.

That being said, judges, who often watch the same television programs as everyone else, are unlikely to "punish" officers with exclusion of the evidence, particularly if a weapon or drugs were discovered during the pat down. The argument to suppress the fruits of a frisk might be more successful if the unjustified pat down revealed contraband or elicited statements rather than revealing a weapon. Judges generally give great deference to experienced officers, and the standard itself does not require certainty that a suspect is armed—it only requires that a reasonably prudent person would be warranted in believing he or others were in danger. *See Terry,* 392 U.S. at 27, 88 S. Ct. at 1883, 20 L. Ed. 2d at 909.

In litigating these issues, counsel should be mindful that the purpose of a pat down is officer safety and not to discover evidence. The facts and analysis in *Sibron v. New York,* 392 U.S. 40, 88 S. Ct. 1889, 20 L. Ed. 2d 917 (1968), decided the same day as *Terry,* are illuminating. In *Sibron,* a police officer had observed the defendant speaking to known drug dealers over the course of eight hours. The officer approached the defendant in a restaurant and told him to come outside. The defendant accompanied the officer outside where the police officer conducted a search of the defendant and found packets of heroin. The prosecution had conceded that there was no probable cause to arrest the defendant so the issue was whether the officer's search of the defendant was a proper frisk or an investigatory stop where the Court assumed for purposes of the argument that there was articulable suspicion to do the patdown:

The search for weapons approved in *Terry* consisted solely of a limited patting of the outer clothing of the suspect for concealed objects which might be used as instruments of assault. Only when he discovered such objects did the officer in *Terry* place his hands in the pockets of the men he searched. In this case, with no attempt at an initial limited exploration for arms, Patrolman Martin thrust his hand into Sibron's pocket and took from him envelopes of heroin. His testimony shows that he was looking for narcotics, and he found them. The search was not reasonably limited in scope to the accomplishment of the only goal which might conceivably have justified its inception—the protection of the officer by disarming a potentially dangerous man. Such a search violates the guarantee of the Fourth Amendment, which protects the sanctity of the person against unreasonable intrusions on the part of all government agents.

Sibron, 392 U.S. at 65, 88 S. Ct. at 1904, 20 L. Ed. 2d at 936.

If, during a pat down, officers discover apparent contraband or a weapon, they are justified in seizing the weapon or contraband. This is the so-called "plain feel" or "plain touch" doctrine. See *Minnesota v. Dickerson*, 508 U.S. 366, 370-71, 113 S. Ct. 2130, 2134, 124 L. Ed. 2d 334, 342-43 (1993). However, the officers are not justified in manipulating an object to determine whether it is indeed contraband, such as sliding and squeezing a lump to determine whether it is crack cocaine. Such behavior goes beyond the justification and limited purposes of the *Terry* stop. *See Dickerson*, 508 U.S. at 378, 113 S. Ct. at 2138-39, 124 L. Ed. 2d at 347-48. *See also, Chapter Eleven: Plain View.*

In cases where a pat down uncovers contraband, counsel should be sure to determine where the contraband was located on the person and whether it would have been plainly felt as contraband. This often requires physically examining the evidence. It is also useful to have the evidence available for demonstrations at the suppression hearing by either or both sides. *See Chapter Twenty Four: Fourth Amendment Hearings.*

Articulable Suspicion

The officers' suspicion to conduct an investigatory detention must be specific and articulable, that is, the officers must be able to detail the specific factors that lead them to suspect that the person had committed or was about to commit a crime. The officers' suspicion must be more than a "hunch" that criminal activity is afoot. *Terry*, 392 U.S. at 27, 88 S. Ct. at 1883, 20 L. Ed. 2d at 909. For example, the Supreme Court found that the Fourth Amendment was violated when police randomly chose vehicles to inspect drivers' licenses and registrations without "articulable and reasonable suspicion" that the drivers were unlicensed or unregistered. *Delaware v. Prouse*, 440 U.S. 648, 663, 99 S. Ct. 1391, 1401, 59 L. Ed. 2d 660, 673 (1979). The courts will evaluate reasonable or articulable suspicion from the "whole picture" as presented from a law enforcement perspective. *United States v. Cortez*, 449 U.S. 411, 417, 101 S. Ct. 690, 695, 66 L. Ed. 2d 621, 629 (1981).

One of the harder issues for the defense to prevail on is a claim that the officers lacked reasonable or articulable suspicion, and that they were simply acting on a hunch when they stopped or temporarily seized the defendant. One of the main difficulties in litigating a "hunch" issue is that a violation of the Fourth Amendment on the grounds that the officers lacked reasonable suspicion would not be litigated unless there was evidence from the unlawful seizure the government was intending to introduce into evidence at trial. In other words, a seizure violation is litigated only when there is evidence to be suppressed, essentially the sole criminal remedy for Fourth Amendment violations.

When physical evidence is in fact discovered during an investigatory detention, it is hard to convince a judge that the officers lacked reasonable suspicion in order to have the evidence suppressed. Even though judges are not allowed to justify the means by the ends, realistically the court is likely to decide that it must have been a pretty darn good hunch; so good it should be considered articulable suspicion because it turned out to be right. Moreover, given that reasonable suspicion is assessed within the whole picture from a law enforcement perspective and with the benefit of 20/20 hindsight, the judge is likely to side with the experienced law enforcer on the scene over any claims by the defense. Defense attorneys must separate this original intrusion from the results of any encounter (something judges often find difficult to do) when assessing and arguing investigatory detention issues.

When Does a Terry Stop Turn into an Arrest?

There is no bright-line rule to determine whether or when an investigatory *Terry* stop has turned into an arrest requiring probable cause—a higher degree of suspicion than reasonable suspicion. Essentially, the determination involves an assessment of the "character of the official intrusion and its justification." *Michigan v. Summers*, 452 U.S. 692, 701, 101 S. Ct. 2587, 2593, 69 L. Ed. 2d 340, 349 (1981). The heart of the inquiry is "whether the police are diligently pursuing a means of investigation which is likely to resolve the matter one way or another very soon...." *Id.* at n.14 (citing *3 W. LaFave, Search and Seizure* § 9.2, at 40 (1978)).

When the seizure has the "essential attributes" of a formal arrest, it must be supported by probable cause to be reasonable under the Fourth Amendment. The police may not conduct what amounts to a full search or full arrest of a person in the name of investigation. In *Dunaway v. New York*, 442 U.S. 200, 99 S. Ct. 2248, 60 L. Ed. 2d 824 (1979), the defendant was taken from his home to the police station without first being placed under formal arrest. At the station, he was interrogated for an hour as part of the officers' investigation of the case. The Court held that reasonable suspicion of criminal activity was insufficient to justify this custodial interrogation even though the interrogation was investigative in nature. The officer had to have probable cause to arrest.

The Court's analysis in *Florida v. Royer* is instructive as to the progression from consensual stop to *Terry* stop to de facto arrest:

What had begun as a consensual inquiry in a public place had escalated into an investigatory procedure in a police inter-rogation room, where the police, unsatisfied with previous explanations, sought to confirm their suspicions. The officers had Royer's ticket, they had his identification, and they had seized his luggage. Royer was never informed that he was free to board his plane if he so chose, and he reasonably believed that he was being detained. At least as of that moment, any consensual aspects of the encounter had evaporated, and we cannot fault the Florida Court of Appeal for concluding that *Terry v. Ohio* and the cases following it did not justify the restraint to which Royer was then subjected. As a practical matter, Royer was under arrest.

460 U.S. at 503, 103 S. Ct. at 1327, 75 L. Ed. 2d at 240.

The borderline cases—those most likely to be litigated—involve situations where there are a few factors ordinarily associated with arrest, but there are also other factors consistent with a *Terry* stop. These are the cases that must be analyzed and analogized to facts in existing case law. Often, whether police conduct is found to be a de facto arrest depends on the particular jurisdiction and even within a circuit there can be seemingly inconsistent determina-tions, providing something for both prosecution and defense. *See, e.g., United States v. Kirsh*, 54 F.3d 1062 (2d Cir. 1995) (find-ing no custody of a suspect taken out of her apartment during a search and questioned elsewhere in the building); c.f. *United States v. Moody*, 649 F.2d 124 (2d Cir. 1981) (finding custody where a suspect was taken to a private room at an airport for questioning).

Some Useful Cases

Terry v. Ohio, 392 U.S. 1, 88 S. Ct. 1868, 20 L. Ed. 2d 889 (1968) (holding that law enforcement officers only need articulable suspicion that a person has committed or is about to commit a crime to support a temporary seizure of that person).

United States v. Mendenhall, 446 U.S. 544, 100 S. Ct. 1870, 64 L. Ed. 2d 497 (1980) (ruling that a person is "seized" for constitutional purposes only when, by means of physical force or show of authority, law enforcement officers restrict his freedom of movement).

Florida v. Royer, 460 U.S. 491, 103 S. Ct. 1319, 75 L. Ed. 2d 229 (1983) (stating that law enforcement officers may approach an individual in a public place and conduct a consensual stop without violating the Fourth Amendment).

Florida v. Bostick, 501 U.S. 429, 111 S. Ct. 2382, 115 L. Ed. 2d 389 (1991) (maintaining that police may engage in consensual stops without warrants, probable cause, or even articulable suspicion).

CHAPTER NINE
CONSENT

General Principles of Consent

Consent is a very common exception to the Warrant Requirement. No warrant to search an area or enter a dwelling is required if the officers obtain proper consent to search. Officers do not even need probable cause to search if they obtain the necessary consent. Indeed, officers may simply walk up and ask for consent to search without any grounds justifying the request, provided the person is not detained or seized.

Unlike waiver of most other constitutional rights, such as the right to counsel or the right to trial, consent does not have to be knowingly and intelligently given. In other words, the person giving the consent does not have to be advised that he or she has a right not to give that consent or understand the right he or she is relinquishing. *See Schneckloth v. Bustamonte*, 412 U.S. 218, 241, 93 S. Ct. 2041, 2055, 36 L. Ed. 2d 854, 871 (1973).

The underlying rationale for the lack of a knowing requirement is another example of the balancing of the protection of constitutional rights against the need for unfettered law enforcement. This balancing act is done under the somewhat artificial delineation that because it is not a trial or pre-trial right before a judge in a structured environment, it is unrealistic to require a finding of "knowing and intelligent." In short, law enforcement convenience and effectiveness trumps; this is also the mind set of most judges, and lawyers must appreciate that mindset when litigating these issues.

The critical issues in consent cases are whether consent was actually given; whether the consent was given by someone who had the authority to give the consent, or at least the apparent authority to do so; whether the consent was given voluntarily or was simply acquiescence to authority; and whether the officers exceeded the scope of the consent. As with other challenges to the constitutional validity of a search, the prosecution bears the burden of proving by a preponderance of the evidence that the consent was voluntary under a totality of the circumstances analysis.

Lack of Consent

It is usually problematic when the defendant claims that the search was never given at all when the arresting officer maintains that the defendant consented to the search. Realistically, it is a rare case when the defendant will be believed over the officer unless there is strong, independent objective evidence supporting the defendant's version. Moreover, the defendant risks perjury charges, and the possibility of obstruction of justice enhancements at sentencing, if the judge finds that the defendant was lying or not credible in his claim that he did not give consent.

Before asserting such a claim, defense counsel should make an independent investigation into the credibility of the defendant's claim, particularly determining whether the defendant signed a form giving consent to search. It is not uncommon for a defendant, particularly one who does not speak English, to sign such a form believing that signing the form is necessary to get property back, only to discover that it was a consent to search form. If the form was signed, but done so involuntarily, that will add to the mix as to whether the defendant's consent was voluntary, particularly if the defense has some independent means of showing the involuntariness.

If ethically possible, the defense argument should be couched as one of misunderstanding or miscommunication, *e.g.*, the defendant did not believe he had given consent, even if the officer interpreted the defendant's responses as affirmatively or implicitly approving of the search. Defining the issue as a misunderstanding or miscommunication allows the judge to consider the defendant's version without necessarily requiring the judge to find the police officer a liar in order to suppress the evidence. Moreover, in many cases the defense will be that the consent was given involuntarily even if the police officers subjectively believed that the consent was freely given. Involuntariness is a legal standard applied to facts, rather than a straight credibility issue as to whether the officers or the defendant is lying. *See Voluntariness infra.*

In some cases the defense has no choice but to maintain that the officers are lying. If there are objective factors or the officers are inconsistent in their testimony, the defense might be able to convince a judge to suppress the evidence, particularly judges who have the courage to find officer testimony incredible. For example, a judge in the Southern District of New York found an officer's statement that he had received consent to search the defendant's bag incredible based on the evidence given by the officer himself. *See United States v. Brisbane,* 931 F.Supp 245 (S.D.N.Y. 1996).

In *Brisbane,* an Amtrak officer described how he had obtained consent to search two different bags owned by the defendant. When the officer asked to search the backpack, the defendant picked up the backpack and handed it to the officer saying in substance "go ahead." The officer unzipped the backpack and rifled through the contents. At the same time, the defendant was eating from a white paper bag that the officer claimed the defendant had also given consent to search. The officers testified that when the officer reached into the food bag and pulled out a hard "biscuit" of cocaine the defendant stood up and grabbed it back. The officer maintained that he never touched the food bag when he pulled out the "biscuit" despite claiming that he had consent to search the bag. Why didn't he rifle through it as he had done the backpack? The court found the officer's testimony "incredible" that he had been given consent to search the food bag by comparing how the defendant had reacted when the backpack was searched as compared to the white bag, and how the officer had handled the backpack compared to the white bag. *See id.*

Sometimes the judge will discredit the police testimony if the officer's version is inherently unbelievable. The same Southern District of New York judge as in the *Brisbane* case found another officer's testimony unbelievable, specifically where the officer claimed that the defendant raised his hands in some sort of "natural response," to the officer's request to frisk him rather than as an acquiescence to authority. *United States v. Floyd,* 1999 WL 673050 (SDNY 1999).

Judges might also find an officer's testimony unbelievable if it is inconsistent or contradicted by other witnesses, depending on the believability of the witness and their bias and social credibility, meaning whether they are upstanding and moral citizens unrelated to the defendant. Fellow crack dealers are unlikely to provide the objective evidence upon which a judge will rely to discredit a police officer's version. However, if the other witnesses are other police officers at the scene, there is a better chance of convincing a judge as to the incredibility of the arresting officer. That being said, minor inconsistencies will be tolerated, but if the inconsistencies relate to the main issue, a judge could find the officer incredible regardless whether there was consent. For example, a Maine judge found incredible the testimony of one officer that the defendant asked no questions but signed the consent to search form. Four other witnesses, including two other officers, contradicted the officer's testimony. *United States v. Muelter* 1993 WL 434081 (D.Me. 1993).

The standard on appeal for a judge's determination of credibility is clearly erroneous—a near impossible standard on any issue but particularly on credibility issues where the appellate judges ordinarily will not disturb any factual findings by the hearing judge who observed the witness on the stand. As a result, when the issue involves credibility it is almost never a successful appeal. Moreover, the Supreme Court has held that if "the district court's account of the evidence is plausible in light of the record viewed in its entirety, the court of appeals may not reverse it even though convinced that had it been sitting as the trier of fact, it would have weighed the evidence differently. Where there are two permissible views of the evidence, the factfinder's choice between them cannot be clearly erroneous." *Anderson v. City of Bessemer City,* N.C., 470 U.S. 564, 574, 105 S. Ct. 1504, 1512, 84 L. Ed. 2d 518, 528 (1985).

Third Party Consent and Apparent Authority

Someone other than the defendant can give consent to search property owned by the defendant or jointly owned by the defendant or containing the defendant's property provided the person maintains common authority or joint access over the thing or place to be searched. In order to give consent to search, the person either must have the authority to do so, or the apparent authority. The rationale for allowing third party consent is that the defendant assumes the risk that this other person will consent to a search given the joint ownership or common authority.

Apparent authority is determined from the perspective of the officer; does the person appear from the various circumstances to have the authority to give consent. Is the person a spouse, family member, roommate, co-worker, etc.? The reliance on apparent authority must be reasonable under the circumstances. The officer cannot simply grab someone in the neighboring apartment and ask whether it is okay to search the defendant's apartment where there is no indicia of common authority or joint ownership. Moreover, landlords and hotel clerks do not ordinarily have authority to consent to a search of a defendant's room or apartment, although the circumstances could provide the officers with a reasonable basis to conclude that the landlord has authority.

In assessing the validity of third party consent both parties must ascertain the actual relationship between the parties, how the relationship was presented to the officers, any joint occupancy or ownership of the search area, who owns or has access to the keys, etc. Defense counsel absolutely must interview the person who allegedly gave consent and be prepared to call that witness (bring a subpoena to the interview) should there be a conflict between the officers' version and what the individual says was his relationship with the defendant and any consent or acquiescence he might have given.

Voluntariness

The most common defense challenge to a consent search is that the consent, though given, was not given voluntarily. From the defense perspective this argument has the advantage of not directly attacking the credibility of the officer, though there might be inconsistencies as to what transpired that would show involuntariness.

Typically the argument is that the consent given was done in acquiescence to authority, see discussion below. But aside from the officer's actions, there are typical factors relied on in assessing whether the consent given was voluntary: 1) whether the person knew he had a right to refuse consent (though not required); 2) the person's age, education, intelligence; 3) whether the person spoke the same language as the officer; 4) whether the person giving the consent was under the influence of drugs or alcohol; 5) the person's familiarity and experience with law enforcement; 6) evidence of other cooperation with authorities; 7) the circumstances leading up to the consent including the length of detention and type of questioning; and 8) the presence or threat of coercion by the police officers. As with any totality of the circumstances analysis, no single factor is dispositive.

Advised By Officer Do Not Have to Give Consent. Although the person giving consent need not be advised that he can refuse to give consent, if the officers in fact advise the person and consent is given it goes a long way toward showing the voluntariness of that consent. When the police fail to advise the person that he has a right to refuse, some of the other factors become more crucial including the person's age, education and intelligence and familiarity with law enforcement. Not being advised of the right to refuse consent when an individual is unfamiliar with the American justice system can have some persuasive merit. If the person's only experience is his own country where there is no right of refusal or an expectation of physical punishment if no consent is given, the defense might be able to convince a judge that the consent was involuntary, provided the belief was a reasonable one and there is some corroboration that this is indeed the standard in the country.

Age, Intelligence, and Education. Someone who is very young could still have the capacity to give consent. Courts have upheld cases where a child as young as nine gave consent. *See, e.g., Lenz v. Wilburn*, 51 F.3d 1540, 1548-9 (11th Cir. 1995) (upholding a nine-year old girl's consent to guardian ad litem to search a trailer where the child resided). Although there is no categorical prohibition against a child giving consent, certainly a young person's "attendant vulnerability to coercion" is a factor in determining whether the consent was given voluntarily. *Id.*

Similarly, even if someone has a low I.Q. or is not well-educated, that does not preclude consent. The courts have determined that privacy is an "intuitive interest" and legal sophistication is not required. Nevertheless, where consent is given by a juvenile or a young child or a very old person who suffers from some dementia or other mental frailty, these are additional factors that can add to the totality of the circumstances in terms of the voluntariness or lack of voluntariness as to the consent.

Cooperation with Authorities. If the defendant was cooperative at the time and responded appropriately to any verbal or physical commands by the officer, judges will find that the consent was voluntary, even though the defendant might claim that he was simply acquiescing to authority (see discussion below). Factors the courts look to are whether the individual smiled, opened the door, gestured to come in, served tea or coffee, etc., consistent with welcoming the officers into the home.

Conceptually the concern as always in cases where the evidence could be suppressed, is the level of so-called culpability of the police officers. If they were given every indication that the person was consenting even though there was no specific, yes please come in, the courts are simply going to find consent.

Language Barriers. The fact that the defendant speaks a different language from the officer is helpful in terms of the defense arguing lack of consent. Because consent can be given without knowing that one has a right not to consent, however, a language barrier is not as dispositive as it might be where the issue is one of waiver of right to counsel or right to silence. It is still one layer added on top of any other factors in attempting to persuade the court that the consent was not voluntarily given.

To establish the language barrier requires eliciting from the officers or the defendant, should he be called to testify, the defendant's level of understanding of English, if any, and the language that was spoken by the officers. If the officers say they speak some Spanish, for example, it is important to draw out the level of Spanish. An interview of the officer(s) before the hearing is helpful but not always possible. Questions should be asked regarding what is the native language of the officer, where the officer learned the foreign language, how many years he studied, what type of program (basic or immersion), whether the officer is a certified interpreter (unlikely), etc. When these questions are being asked for the first time it is not uncommon for the officer to bolster his understanding of the foreign language. This should not deter defense counsel. The judge will rule against the defendant without some basis to challenge the voluntariness of the consent anyway, so defense counsel should challenge the officer's understanding, unless the officer has provided no basis for his ability to understand the language.

Unless the officer is a native speaker or trained interpreter it is unlikely that the officer has the capacity to provide a fair interpretation of legal concepts such as a consent to search form even if the officer speaks the language to some degree. If the officer claims to have been able to translate a consent to search form, for example, it might be useful to have the officer do so in court with the interpreter available to translate the officer's translation. For example, in a case in the Southern District of New York, the Federal Defender asked the officer to translate the consent to search form in Spanish with the court certified interpreter translating the officer's rendition. It turned out to be something to the effect that the defendant had a right to own property. True the officer might translate the form correctly, but it is likely the judge would have believed him anyway. However, the possibility that the officer has "overestimated" his language skills is often distinct and worth the risk, since the judge would otherwise rule against the defense without some objective evidence of mistranslation or communication.

As with any defendant who will be claiming a language barrier, it is important to speak to the defendant in front of the judge or jury through an interpreter or using the defendant's native language. Many non-English speaking defendants understand some basic things in English and it might be tempting to say sit down or stand up in English, for example. However, the impression this gives could be very damaging even though in reality the person would not be able to understand important legal concepts spoken in English. It will seem to the judge that the defendant is not (and you as the lawyer are not) being straight as to the defendant's level of English.

Effect of Drugs or Alcohol. It seems obvious that if someone is impaired by drugs or alcohol any consent would be involuntarily almost as a matter of course. Once again, however, the system balances the law enforcement need against the defendant's rights, almost in a retributive mind set. Even if the defendant is intoxicated, the implicit position of the legal system seems to be that the defendant brought such a state on himself and cannot hide behind that to impact the evidence against him. In short, a defendant who voluntarily impairs himself is usually not allowed to take advantage of that fact by having evidence suppressed.

It is true that a certain level of intoxication could render someone absolutely incapable of giving consent, in most cases it will be one factor for which the judge will give some, though typically minor, consideration. However, if the officer took advantage of the situation to obtain consent when the officer knew the defendant was inebriated or otherwise under the influence, a court is more likely to exclude the evidence to punish or deter the wrongdoing of the officer.

Familiarity with Law Enforcement. When a defendant has a prior record of any sort judges typically find that consent is voluntary in that they "know the ropes." Moreover, it is a way of punishing people judges no doubt presume are guilty (they did it before they will do it again mentality). If as the defense lawyer your client has any significant record, it will be difficult to make the argument that the defendant's consent was anything but voluntary unless there is obvious coercion. Still, it is important to get the facts of each prior arrest. If the prior convictions are for traffic type offenses, there might not have been formal arrest proceedings. If there was no search in the previous cases that could have some impact as well.

Coercion and Setting. It is essential in any consent case to elicit through interviews with the defendant, officers, etc., as well as independent investigation of the scene where the consent was given to get a full picture of how the consent was obtained. What were the officers wearing, holding, saying, etc., how many were there, where were they standing, what were they doing? When was the consent given? Was the person arrested, in handcuffs, been injured, etc. The courts focus on the officers' conduct primarily to determine whether it was indeed a coercive environment. Even if the individual subjectively felt coerced, if the environment did not appear objectively coercive to vitiate the voluntariness of consent, the judge will uphold the search. Because the analysis for coercion is still under a totality of the circumstances, any of the factors that undermine the notion of voluntary consent should be included in a claim that the consent was coerced.

Use of a Ruse. In some cases it is perfectly acceptable for the police to obtain consent to search through the use of a ruse or ploy. If the police come into a home or apartment pretending to be drug buyers and ask to look around or search and are given consent there is no constitutional violation even though the officers are not in fact drug dealers.

A ploy by officers might not pass constitutional muster, however, if the effect of the ruse is to convince a person that she has no choice but to invite the person in. If the officers pretended to have a dying person outside and needed to come in to use the phone to save someone's life and asked to look through the house for bandages, that would likely render the consent involuntary.

Effect of Prior Taint. In some cases consent can vitiate a prior illegal search, provided that there is attenuation between the violation and the consent. In other words, if the officers entered the premises unlawfully, but the consent was the product of free will and sufficiently removed from the illegality the search might still be lawful. The term used in that context is "dissipated."

Defense counsel should make sure to inquire as to all of the circumstances surrounding how consent was obtained. What happened before the defendant opened the door? How did the officers get on to the property or get into the house? Even if the defendant would have let them in anyway, if the officers violated the law to get into the house, it could affect the voluntariness of the consent that was subsequently obtained.

Acquiescence to Authority and Implied Consent

As the Supreme Court explained in *Florida v. Bostick*, 501 U.S. 429, 438, 111 S. Ct. 2382, 115 L. Ed. 2d 389 (1991), "[c]onsent that is the product of official intimidation or harassment is not consent at all. Citizens do not forfeit their constitutional rights when they are coerced to comply with a request that they would prefer to refuse." For example, a 66-year-old African American widow, who lived in a house located in a rural area at the end of an isolated mile-long dirt road, allowed four white law enforcement officials to search her home after they asserted they had a warrant to search the house. The Supreme Court held the alleged consent to be invalid, noting that "(w)hen a law enforcement officer claims authority to search a home under a warrant, he announces in effect that the occupant has no right to resist the search. The situation is instinct with coercion—albeit colorably lawful coercion. Where there is coercion there cannot be consent." *North Carolina v Bumper*, 391 U.S. 543, 550, 88 S. Ct. 1788, 1792, 20 L. Ed. 2d 797, 803 (1968).

Even though the officers cannot tell the occupant that they have a warrant if they do not, as in *Bumper*, an officer may advise that he will he go and get a warrant and search the house anyway provided he has probable cause. Furthermore, although a defendant is under arrest and handcuffed, the officers can still obtain consent to search unless there is additional coercion that would render the consent either involuntary or simply acquiescence to authority. (Obviously in some cases the police may be able to search areas near the defendant if the arrest was lawful without any consent as a search incident to arrest).

Although consent obtained while one is handcuffed and under arrest would seem to be inherently an acquiescence to authority, provided the circumstances would not so overcome free will, etc., the court will often uphold a search based on consent. In such cases the circumstances should be carefully scrutinized by the parties and the court in the analysis and argument. The defense should almost always make the argument that the consent was the result of acquiescence to authority and not freely given when the defendant has been arrested and/or was in handcuffs at the time. *See, e.g., United States v. Sanchez*, 635 F.2d 47, 61 (2d Cir. 1980) (finding consent invalid where defendant was handcuffed and driven to apartment and officers sought consent immediately before putting key in the door).

Scope of a Consent Search

The scope of the search can be general or limited, depending on what a reasonable person would understand the scope of the search to be given the object of the search. If the search is for a person there might be limitations on where the police could search, not in an ordinary dresser drawer for example. The standard is what a reasonable person would understand the scope of the search to be. Blanket consent for requests such as, "may we search the house," will basically have no limitations provided it is reasonable within the object of the search. If an officer advises they want to search the house for a fleeing burglar, it would be unreasonable for them to peel the wallpaper back. However, if the search is for drugs or contraband, there is little the police would be estopped from searching, including ripping up the carpet, floor boards, moving furniture, opening up drawers and boxes and taking down pictures.

Once consent is obtained the person giving consent can withdraw that consent or limit that consent. That being said, if what has already been found provides probable cause and exigency to continue with the search, consent might not be required. At a minimum, the officers could stop the search, secure the premises and seek a warrant over the phone. They are also permitted to tell the person that they would go ahead and seek the warrant in an effort to get consent, which is usually very effective.

Challenging Officer Testimony at a Suppression Hearing on Consent

Often the prosecution will only put one police officer on the stand at a suppression hearing to avoid inconsistencies between different officers, usually a very smart strategy on the part of the prosecution. Since hearsay is admissible at suppression hearings, the judges will usually credit the testimony of the single officer even though his knowledge of the issues was gleaned from discussions with other officers.

The defense should consider serving subpoenas on any other officers present at the scene or otherwise involved if there is reason to believe they would give different or helpful testimony particularly with respect to the notion of consent. Ideally, the defense will have interviewed the officers in advance to determine how helpful the other testimony would be or whether they would provide crucial corroboration of the main issue even if the officers are inconsistent on other details. Even if the officers serve only to corroborate the other officers, the opportunity to see these witnesses on the stand and to observe them in a suppression hearing where the prosecution is likely to prevail anyway could still be valuable.

Calling the other officers can irritate the judge if it appears to be simply a "fishing expedition" on the part of the defense to gain additional discovery. If the officer was unwilling to speak to the defense in advance, the argument to the judge is that this was the only means of determining the officers' knowledge of the case with respect to the relevant issues as to suppression. A judge, however, may preclude their testimony or quash the subpoena if the testimony would be "cumulative."

It is a rare case that the officers give the exact same version so there is little risk in calling the other officers provided the court will indulge the defense and the defense has not "won" through the first officer. In such situations where other officers are called, it is important that the defense ask that these witnesses not be present in the courtroom for the testimony of other witnesses and to have a defense witness or potential witness in the witness room to insure that the officers are not "refreshing" each others recollections or "coaching" each other as to what happened.

Defense counsel must not let the officers get away with a mere conclusion that the defendant "consented to the search." Such a conclusion is a legal determination that will be made by the judge not the interested officer. It is critical that the defense bring out all of the surrounding circumstances including exactly what the defendant did that indicated the so-called consent, *e.g.*, opening the door, nodding yes, not doing anything but standing at the door, in other words not saying no. It is also important to elicit the setting of the consent: how many officers were present, what they were wearing, what they were carrying, how they walked, talked and acted including tone of voice, where they were standing, etc.

Litigation Strategies When Consent Is Upheld

The fact that the defendant has consented to the search of an apartment or area where contraband is found, can provide a litigative boon to the defense on some level. If the defense theory is that the defendant did not know that there were drugs in the apartment, the fact that the defendant consented would tend to support that theory, as a person who knew the drugs were there would not have consented to the search. Although there are many cases where guilty defendants still consent to the search, the defense can make that argument to the jury.

Defense counsel should request from the court a jury instruction on "consciousness of innocence." The charge would be similar to a consciousness of guilt instruction with the opposite phrasing, *e.g.*, "You have heard testimony that the defendant consented to the search of the apartment. It is the defense theory that the defendant did not know there was contraband in the trunk at the base of the bed. You may but need not infer from the fact that the defendant consented to the search that the defendant did not know there was contraband in the trunk. On the other hand, there might be other reasons, as suggested by the prosecution, for why the defendant might have consented to the search."

Some Useful Cases

North Carolina v Bumper, 391 U.S. 543, 550, 88 S. Ct. 1788, 1792, 20 L. Ed. 2d 797, 803 (1968) key to understanding the notion of voluntariness where officers claim they have a warrant; consent is not voluntary where the officers say they have a warrant where there was no warrant justifying the search.

CHAPTER TEN
ABANDONMENT

Abandonment in General

"The Fourth Amendment protects people, not places." *Katz v. United States*, 389 U.S. 347, 351, 88 S. Ct. 507, 511, 19 L. Ed. 2d 576, 582 (1967). A person's property is ordinarily included in the Fourth Amendment's protection of an individual, provided the person manifests a reasonable expectation of privacy in the property. *See Chapter Five: Issues of Standing.* A reasonable expectation of privacy in an area may be modified by the behavior of the suspect: opening the door to the house and welcoming someone in, failing to pull down the blinds or conducting business out in an unfenced front yard, for example. Similarly, an individual can abandon or voluntarily relinquish a possessory interest by no longer having an expectation of privacy in an object. Such relinquishment is considered abandonment. Property can be abandoned by a number of means including throwing away or leaving the property behind, disclaiming ownership ("that's not my bag") or dropping the property and leaving, as in the so-called "dropsy" cases.

A warrantless seizure or search of abandoned property does not "offend" the Fourth Amendment. *See Abel v. United States,* 362 U.S. 217, 241, 80 S. Ct. 683, 698; 4 L. Ed. 2d 668, 687 (1960). By definition, if there is no reasonable expectation of privacy, there is no search either. By relinquishing any expectation of privacy or possessory interest in the object, the property is lawfully subject to search and to seizure without a warrant or any suspicion at all.

Challenging Abandonment Cases

The key factor in determining abandonment is the intent of the defendant as manifested by his actions. As with most Fourth Amendment issues, abandonment is intensely fact specific, perhaps even more so than other seizure and search issues because it depends almost entirely on the actions of the suspect as observed by police officers rather than police action itself. Defense counsel must also be cognizant that although the actions of the defendants are uppermost in the analysis, courts still look at the response of the police to those actions in assessing reasonableness.

Leaving Property. The quintessential abandoned property is the bag of garbage on the curb. Although not every bag of garbage outside the house is deemed abandoned, garbage in a bin put in a garage still has trappings of expectation of privacy, if the bag of garbage is out on the curb for collection or in an area available to the public there is no expectation of privacy, thus no Fourth Amendment violation for a warrantless search. In the words of the Supreme Court: "[i]t is common knowledge that plastic garbage bags left on or at the side of a public street are readily accessible to animals, children, scavengers, snoops and other members of the public." *California v. Greenwood*, 486 U.S. 35, 40-41, 108 S. Ct. 1625, 1628-29, 100 L. Ed. 2d 30, 36-37. Because the neighbor's dog, the homeless man with the shopping cart and anyone else, could rummage through that bag of garbage, there is no Fourth Amendment violation even if the ransacking is done by a police officer and the evidence recovered is introduced in a criminal case.

Property carried into public transportation or public areas is a frequent arena for abandonment cases, particularly in drug courier cases. Is putting the bag on top of the luggage rack in the train abandonment? Above the seat in a rack is the location where most people would put their luggage with a reasonable expectation that it will not be taken and rummaged through. The bag might be considered abandoned, however, if it were placed in the rack a number of seats away or in a different train car from where the suspect ultimately sits.

But if the bag were simply placed near the person or behind a person this is less likely to constitute abandonment. Defense counsel must truly determine the surrounding circumstances: where was the bag, where was the suspect, did the bag have a name tag; were there any other passengers around who could have claimed it; etc.

If transportation security officers recover a bag believed to be abandoned for security and safety reasons, the bag could also be searched for inventory under a standardized security procedure and would not constitute a Fourth Amendment violation even if the security personnel were determined to be government agents. *See Chapter Eight: Inventory, Regulatory, and Border Searches; see also Chapter Four: Government Action.*

In *Smith v. Ohio*, 494 U.S. 541, 543-44, 110 S. Ct. 1288, 1290, 108 L. Ed. 2d 464, 467-68 (1990), the Supreme Court found no abandonment when the suspect tossed his bag on the hood of a vehicle before confronting police officers. "As the state court properly recognized, a citizen who attempts to protect his private property from inspection, after throwing it on a car to respond to a police officer inquiry clearly has not abandoned that property." Id. In challenging these searches, both parties need to recreate the scene for the officer and consider whether a reasonable person in defendant's position would actually be abandoning the property.

Abandonment cases also come about in hotel situations. Ordinarily if the defendant leaves an item in a hotel wastepaper basket and checks out of the room the police can seize those items without Fourth Amendment repercussions provided the hotel management gives permission to enter. For example, in *United States v. Abel*, 362 U.S. 217, 80 S. Ct. 683, 4 L. Ed. 2d 668 (1960), the defendant had vacated his hotel room, at that point the hotel had exclusive right to its possession and the management gave consent for the police to search. The recovery of microfiche from a wastepaper basket without a warrant was considered lawful because "there can be nothing unlawful in the Government's appropriation of such abandoned property." *Id.* at 241. However, if the defendant leaves a locked briefcase in a hotel room which the defendant did not vacate for four hours past termination of the rental period, that would constitute a reasonable expectation of privacy, thus a search of the briefcase constituted a Fourth Amendment violation. *See United States v. Ramos*, 12 F.3d 1019, 1026 (11th Cir. 1994).

The key to this analysis is the reasonableness of the police action in response to the objective factors of the defendant's behavior. When the police are told by the hotel maid that the person had checked out of the room and the police go in and see a few items left in a trash can and no other indicia of occupancy, the officers could reasonably conclude that the room had been abandoned as well as the property in the trash can.

If however, they are told by the maid that the person checked out and they enter and find various pieces of luggage, personal items in the bathroom and clothes in the closet, their reliance mostly likely would not be found to be reasonable. If, in the first example, the person had not checked out of the room, under the good faith rationale of *Leon*, the court is likely to uphold the search as reasonable under an abandonment theory because the reliance on the representation was in good faith based on the totality of the circumstances, even though the defendant had not in actuality abandoned his expectation of privacy.

Disclaiming Ownership. Denying ownership or failing to admit to ownership of a bag can constitute abandonment given certain circumstances. In the above train scenario, if police pick up the bag and ask loudly and clearly if it belongs to anyone and there is no reply from the defendant, the bag ordinarily will be considered abandoned. In determining abandonment, the belief in abandonment must be objectively reasonable from a totality of the circumstances, including the police officers' own actions vis-à-vis a suspect's response or actions.

Disclaimer cases do provide a number of avenues for the defense to challenge the legality of the search. If the police waited until the suspect went into the bathroom or up to the café car in the train before asking if the bag belonged to anyone, it would not be considered a relinquishment of an expectation of privacy, particularly if the police suspected the bag belonged to the person who left. Similarly, if the police asked the question very softly or only once on a loud moving train or bus a non-response may not be a reasonable determination of abandonment, although an affirmative "that's not my bag," would constitute sufficient indicia of abandonment.

Moreover, even if there has been a disclaimer of ownership, if the disclaimer was made after an unlawful detention, the disclaimer ordinarily will be viewed as a fruit of the poisonous tree. Defense counsel must sort through the timing of the disclaimer and the reasonableness of the disclaimer to see whether it was tainted by previous illegality. *See Chapter Seven: The Exclusionary Rule.*

Dropping Property: Of all of the challenges to abandonment, the dropping of property by a suspect is probably the easiest justification to assert by officers. "Your Honor, when the suspect saw us in uniform he dropped the brown paper bag and ran. We recovered the abandoned property, opened it and found a kilogram of cocaine." In the typical case, who is to challenge the officer's version except the defendant who obviously has such a vested interest in the outcome as compared to the officer? Besides, the dropping of the incriminating evidence once the police are spied is helpful to the prosecution for an entirely separate reason beyond the search. Obviously, if believed, the dropping of the evidence gives the officers a way of opening the bag without having to obtain a warrant on the basis of abandonment. However, dropping the evidence at the sight of the police provides evidence of conscience of guilt to counter any claim by the suspect that he did not know what was in the bag, especially important if the bag contained a package wrapped in opaque material, *e.g.*, why drop what you say was a bologna sandwich when you saw the cops arrive. (Inference of guilt would not necessarily be available if the officers were not in uniform or did not announce themselves as police even if the suspect ran).

Because it is so easy to assert dropping of the evidence, particularly in jurisdictions where the testimony of the police officer ordinarily will be credited over a defendant in the absence of objective evidence to the contrary, it used to be the justification in thousands of drugs case. But there came a point in the 70s and 80s when "dropsy cases" as they are known, were so prevalent that the use of the justification became almost comical; could so many defendants be that stupid to leave the incriminating evidence literally at the feet of the cops? Judges would see the same almost too good to be true fact patterns over and over again to justify warrantless searches—often with the exact same language used in each complaint. The result was what can only be called a judicial backlash of skepticism. Eventually judges started discrediting these "dropsy" cases as being untrustworthy as a matter of law.

A New York Supreme Court's observation in *People v. Caesar,* 419 N.Y.S. 2d 319, 327-28 (1985) is representative: "We refuse to credit testimony [in this "dropsy" case] which has all appearance of having been patently tailored to nullify constitutional objections...Hence we reject the officer's testimony as a matter of law." *People v. Quinones,* 402 N.Y.S. 2d 196, 198 (1978) (citations and internal quotations omitted). A New York Supreme Court summed up the pinnacle of the use of the "dropsy" type mentality of police officers in rejecting the validity of a search not just on dropping the evidence, but every other conceivable exception to the Warrant Requirement:

> The People's evidence as a whole leaves no doubt in our minds that this is a classic, indeed textbook, example of evidence patently tailored to meet constitutional objections. In a case which conjures up practically every judicially recognized exception to the warrant requirement, consensual entry, "dropsy" evidence, plain view, spontaneous statements, not to mention the most alleged fortuitous set of facts imagineable [sic], open closets, open drawers, and exceptionably cooperative suspects, I cannot imagine any other way to treat the People's case than as anything but incredible as a matter of law.

People v. Caesar, 491 N.Y.S. 2d 319, 327-28 (1985).

Given the skepticism of these "dropsy" justifications by courts in such states as New York, prosecutors had either to introduce objective evidence of dropping apart from the officer's statement, or provide an independent basis for seizure of the article. For the defense, if the facts were too good to be true to uphold the search, chances are those facts were not true and judges were increasingly willing to agree. Even today, the defense can use the "dropsy" case mentality in alleged abandonment cases. As hard as it may be for many judges to disbelieve the testimony of police officers, particularly in federal jurisdictions, referring the judge to a sampling of these "dropsy" cases could provide some grounds for the courts at least to consider the possibility that the officers are not providing the full story on how they got the drugs.

Arguments requiring skepticism by police officers are likely to be more successful at the state level where the volume of cases is so high and the mentality of "testilying" by police officers is often given more credence. In such cases, if there was more then one officer involved, this may be the kind of case where the defense should interview everyone on the scene and be prepared to call other officers at the hearing to relate what really happened. *See, also, Chapter Twenty Four: Fourth Amendment Hearings.*

Some Useful Cases

Abel v. United States, 362 U.S. 217, 80 S. Ct. 683, 4 L. Ed. 2d 668 (1960).

CHAPTER ELEVEN
SEARCH INCIDENT TO ARREST

Search Incident to Arrest in General

If a suspect is properly under formal arrest the police may search him incident to the arrest without any additional suspicion or reason other than the probable cause for the arrest itself. *Rawlings v. Kentucky*, 448 U.S. 98, 100 S. Ct. 2556, 65 L. Ed. 2d 633 (1980). In order to search incident to arrest, the arrest itself must be a full custodial arrest, and a valid arrest made by an officer with authority to make the arrest.

Although the original rationale for such a search was to discover weapons and preserve evidence within the suspect's reach, the police do not need particularized suspicion that weapons or evidence will be found upon search. It is an automatic search right. Period. In addition, unlike a pat down or *Terry* frisk, a search incident to arrest allows the officer to do a comprehensive search for weapons and evidence. There is no requirement that he have particularized suspicion for the presence of either.

Even if the suspect is carrying a closed container like a briefcase, the officer may still search without consent provided it is done incident to arrest. That being said, once the police gain exclusive control over the container, a later search generally will not be permissible without a warrant.

Scope of the Search

The area of a search incident to arrest is limited to the suspect herself as well as to areas "within which [the suspect] might gain possession of a weapon or destructible evidence." *Chimel v. California*, 395 U.S. 752, 763, 89 S. Ct. 2034, 2040, 23 L. Ed. 2d 685, 694 (1969). This is the so-called "grabbable space." The courts interpret this area even more liberally when the defendant is arrested in a vehicle which adds to the exigency of the situation and broadens the scope of the search. (An area in reach of a third party present at the time of a valid arrest might be justified by the officers' fears of safety and destruction of evidence; accordingly the police may search that area as well under this exception.)

Courts have increasingly extended the reach of the average suspect. The area has become something of a fiction; a glass bubble of "okay" police behavior which has lost its roots of safety and evidence concerns. As long as the area was in the suspect's control at the time of the arrest, the fact that the suspect is no longer even in the room but handcuffed out in the patrol car, does not prevent the cops from going back and searching the area the suspect had been in at the time of the arrest. If the person reaches toward an area or lunges toward a container that might not otherwise be within his control or reach, the police would be justified in searching the area or container under this exception.

There are some limits to police action within the grabbable reach or area of control. For example, a court is unlikely to uphold a search where the officers actually place the container within reach in order to have a basis for a search. *See, e.g., United States v. Perea*, 986 F.2d 633, 643 (2d Cir. 1993) ("arresting agents are not allowed to simulate circumstances warranting application of the incident-to-arrest exception merely by bringing the item they wish to search into the area near the person arrested, or vice versa.")

From the defense perspective, the first basis for argument will be the legality of the search of itself. If unsuccessful on that front, the focus then turns to the scope of the incident to arrest search. Did the officer go beyond the permissible area? Was the area really within the reach and control of the defendant?

Although the courts have abandoned any particularized need to prevent destruction of evidence or ensure the safety of the officers, the argument should not be abandoned by defense counsel. It is useful for defense counsel to remind the judge of the reason why search incident to arrest was an exception to the Warrant Requirement in the first place. Placing the search within the framework of safety and destruction of evidence provides a context for the judge when assessing the scope of a permissible search. The

Supreme Court has made clear that the search is automatic and can be for anything within that grabbable area, see *United States v. Robinson*, 414 U.S. 218, 235, 94 S. Ct. 467, 477, 38 L. Ed. 2d 427, 440 (1973), but counsel will want to show how officer behavior had nothing to do with these concerns, especially if there is a dispute as to what was actually the "grabbable area."

Defense counsel should be prepared to argue how the search was not within a reasonable distance from the defendant that would justify an exception to the Warrant Requirement. Ultimately the defense position will be that the officers should have obtained a warrant to do a search if the area or containers are too far from the defendant even though recovered at the time of the arrest.

Counsel on both sides will need to be aware of the limits that have been recognized in a particular jurisdiction. For example, the Second Circuit invalidated the search of a machine gun and ammunition hidden under a mattress in the middle of a box spring over two feet from where the defendants were handcuffed. *United States v. Blue*, 78 F.3d 56, 60-61 (2d Cir. 1996). Similarly, the Sixth Circuit invalidated a search where the defendant was 30 feet from the car at the time of the arrest and was the driver of a car where the search was done of the passenger compartment. *United States v. Straham*, 984 F.2d 155, 159 (6th Cir. 1993).

Timing Issues and the Contemporaneous Requirement

Contemporaneous searches incident to arrest are likely to be upheld particularly if the searches are of the person being arrested such as pants and shirt pockets. A few minutes between an arrest and a search is permissible, particularly if the search is of the person and not a separate container. A container which was in the person's grabbable space at the time and was not searched at the time might not fall within the search incident to arrest exception if there was significant delay and relocation after the search. The search of a suit case that had been in the grabbable space thirty minutes before, for example, was not found to be a search incident to arrest. *See United States v. $639,558 in U.S. Currency*, 955 F.2d 712 (D.C. Cir. 1992).

If the search is done right before the formal arrest, it might be upheld, provided there was probable cause for the arrest without reliance on anything that was recovered as a result of the search. Although appearing to put the cart before the horse, the Supreme Court has allowed for this provided the arrest follows "quickly on the heels of the challenged search." *See Rawlings* 448 U.S. at 111, 100 S. Ct. at 2564, 65 L. Ed. 2d at 645.

When time elapses between the search and the actual arrest, it becomes harder to justify a search as incident to arrest, which ostensibly depends on the need for an immediate search for safety and to preserve evidence. The inherent exigency of the situation explains the real basis for the exception. If officers allow a long period of time between arrest and search without good cause it jeopardizes the legality of the search. Usually officers will have a ready reason for the delay between the arrest of the suspect and the search, such as the need to remove clothing for a full search and waiting until the person is taken to the station house for replacement clothing. *See, United States v. Edwards*, 415 U.S. 800, 805, 94 S. Ct. 1234, 1238, 39 L. Ed. 2d 771, 776 (1974).

Protective Sweep

Related to the search incident to arrest rationale is the need to ensure that other suspects who might pose a danger to officers are not in the area at the time of the arrest. A protective or security sweep is permitted without probable cause or even reasonable suspicion to believe anyone is present. It is routine and automatic for officer safety. Consider it a frisk or pat down of the area rather than of a person.

Officers conducting a protective or security sweep are permitted to look into spaces immediately adjoining the place of arrest from where there could be a person who could threaten officer safety such as in a nearby closet. *Maryland v. Buie*, 494 U.S. 325, 334, 110 S. Ct. 1093, 1098, 108 L. Ed. 2d 276, 286 (1990). Police may go beyond the immediate adjoining areas if there is some belief that would "warrant a reasonably prudent officer in believing that the area to be swept harbors an individual posing a danger to those on the arrest scene." *Id.*

The defense challenge will be to the scope of the search and the timing of the search. It is one thing to search in a tall closet but another to search in an underwear drawer or medicine cabinet where there is no possibility that a person could be hiding. The purpose of the search is not to investigate for evidence but to ascertain the security of the area. Obvious contraband in plain view during a protective sweep may be confiscated and used against the person, but only if it is indeed in plain view in a permissible area (obvious illegal drugs in a closet, but not drugs in that same underwear drawer or medicine cabinet.).

Typically drug cases involve the use of comprehensive security sweeps and the courts are almost always going to uphold a "pass through" as it is called through the entire house or apartment, especially if the defendant is believed to be part of a conspiracy. Such operations typically include lookouts, "steerers" and enforcers on site, thus police are almost always justified in believing others to be on the premises even if there is only one person in the area at the time of the actual arrest.

Some circuits have extended the security sweep to arrests outside the home. In those cases, the police may make a protective sweep of the house provided they have some reason to believe that evidence will be destroyed or safety concerns for the officers. *See, e.g., United States v. Hoyos*, 892 F.2d 1387 (9th Cir. 1989) (protective sweep of home after outside arrest justified where police had reason to believe evidence would have been destroyed or that officers might have been harmed).

Some Useful Cases

Rawlings v. Kentucky, 448 U.S. 98, 100 S. Ct. 2556, 65 L. Ed. 2d 633 (1980).

Chimel v. California, 395 U.S. 752, 89 S. Ct. 2034, 23 L. Ed. 2d 685 (1969).

United States v. Robinson, 414 U.S. 218, 94 S. Ct. 467, 38 L. Ed. 2d 427 1973).

CHAPTER TWELVE
PLAIN VIEW

A prosecutor summoning the plain view doctrine is something akin to the incantation "abracadabra" to make Fourth Amendment search and seizure problems disappear; a talismanic charm to justify a warrantless search. Presto—no constitutional violation. How many officers have uttered the magic words on the stand, "the evidence was in plain view," and opposing counsels have dejectedly put down their pens (and sometimes their heads) on counsel table and surrendered.

It is tempting for the defense to forgo the making of any significant counter arguments to a claim that the evidence was in plain view essentially believing that if the object was in plain view to the arresting officers, little can be done. Such presumed defeat is unwarranted. There are a number of defenses involving the so-called "plain view exception" to the Warrant Requirement that are not only available, but are often successful.

Litigators must be aware of the various layers to the doctrine to ensure that viable defense arguments are not overlooked. Prosecutors must also be cognizant of these issues to prepare for the defense challenges. Indeed, the plain view doctrine requires the prosecution to show more than just an initial legitimacy with the search, even in cases when a search is executed pursuant to a warrant. Indeed, it is a comparatively burdensome exception to the Warrant Requirement from the prosecution's perspective, provided the defense holds the prosecution to the requirements of the exception.

Plain View Generally

There are two separate notions of plain view that must be understood when litigating the doctrine. Property put out in plain view of the public that is obvious contraband may be seized by officers without a warrant. Period. The Supreme Court has held that visual observation is no search at all. *Dow Chemical v. United*

States, 476 U.S. 227, 106 S. Ct. 1819, 90 L. Ed. 2d 226 (1986). Specifically, there is no legitimate expectation of privacy involved for contraband in public view, though there is a possessory interest at issue in the thing seized where interference is justified by the officer's probable cause as to the object's obvious illegality.

Similarly, the viewing of objects displayed on the inside of a home by outsiders, including law enforcement, could be used to obtain a warrant or to allow the officers to act under any applicable exception to the warrant requirement such as exigent circumstances. "The Fourth Amendment protection of the home has never been extended to require law enforcement officers to shield their eyes when passing by a home on public thoroughfares." *See California v. Ciarolo*, 476 U.S. 207, 106 S. Ct. 1809, 90 L. Ed. 2d 210 (1986). This type of viewing does not necessarily allow the officer to seize the contraband, but the officer is permitted to use the information to obtain the necessary warrant.

Observing contraband in public view is somewhat different than observing something that is in "open view" within private premises though plainly visible to someone on those premises. There is a fundamental privacy interest at stake inside a dwelling. Leaving a kilogram of cocaine in front of an open window is contraband in public view. Keeping a kilogram of cocaine in one's closet shelf is a different matter. That is not to say that evidence within a home or premise cannot be in plain view unless it is visible through a window to passersby. If the officers who view the object are legitimately on the premises in that they have a warrant or an exception to the Warrant Requirement, and the officers have a right of access to the evidence whose incriminating nature is immediately apparent, that object may be seized under the plain view doctrine, even if its not the evidence for which the officers were searching. Conceptually the plain view doctrine is not so much an exception to the Warrant Requirement, as it is an extension of any legitimate basis for the search and seizure. *See Horton v. California*, 496 U.S. 128, 110 S. Ct. 2301, 110 L. Ed. 2d 112 (1990).

There are certain requirements that must be met before the plain view doctrine can justify a seizure of evidence. The officers must be legitimately on the premises. The officers must have a right of access to the evidence. Finally, the illegality of the evidence seized must be immediately apparent.

Legitimately on the Premises

The first requirement of the plain view doctrine is that the officers be legitimately on the premises also known as a "lawful vantage point." *See id.* The officer could legitimately be on the premises as a result of having come in hot pursuit, by invitation of the home owner or an authorized third party, in response to an emergency situation, when executing a search or arrest warrant or some other lawful means.

If the officers are not on the premises lawfully, the fact that contraband evidence might be in plain view, does not authorize a warrantless seizure of the contraband under the plain view doctrine. For example, if the officers secure access through an unlawful ruse that there is a fire in the building and they have to call the fire department, the fact that the officers view vials of crack in plain view while borrowing the phone, does not justify seizure without a warrant.

It is essential for lawyers to review the basis for the officers being on the premises. If the officers were not lawfully on the premises, then the plain view doctrine may not be invoked no matter how obvious the contraband. Defense counsel must be satisfied that the officers were indeed at a lawful vantage point, otherwise that is the first point of attack. The prosecution is likely to counter that the officer's location does not matter because the evidence was in plain view thus the officer had a right to confiscate it. Simply because the evidence is in plain view does not cure the unlawfulness of the officers' position, and seizure of the evidence would be unlawful.

Lawful Right of Access to the Evidence

The second requirement necessary for the plain view doctrine is that the officers must have a lawful right of access to the evidence. This second requirement is a corollary of the first and some circuits might not even treat it as a separate requirement. Counsel should be aware of how their circuit or state has interpreted plain view and specifically the requirements of Horton. Even in jurisdictions where there is no marked difference, defense counsel should evaluate whether the officers, though legitimately on the premises, still may not have had a lawful right of access to the evidence itself.

There is a subtle difference between the first two plain view requirements which counsel should explore. Even if the officers are legitimately on the premises and the evidence is in plain view, the officers must still have a right of access to that particular evidence. If the plain view contraband is in another room or apartment that is outside the scope of the warrant, the evidence cannot be seized merely because it is in plain view if it is in a separate area where there is a separate reasonable expectation of privacy.

If the officers are executing an arrest warrant and they open up a dresser drawer and discover a kilogram of cocaine, the officers are legitimately on the premises but they do not have lawful access to the evidence since the search for a person would not lawfully include a dresser drawer. However, in making a security sweep and looking for the arrestee in a closet where a kilogram of cocaine was packaged in clear wrapping, the officers could take the cocaine because they have a lawful right of access to the apartment and the closet where the evidence was found because a person could be hiding in a closet.

In *Arizona v. Hicks*, 480 U.S. 321, 107 S. Ct. 1149 , 94 L. Ed. 2d 347 (1987), for example, the officers were legitimately on the premises when investigating a bullet shot through the floor below; however, the officer's movement of stereo equipment he suspected was stolen to enable him to take down identification numbers amounted to an improper search. The officer did not have lawful access to move the stereo based on the exigency caused by the investigation of the gunshot. In short, it was an improper extension of the exigency exception to the Warrant Requirement even though the officer was lawfully on the premises and the movement of the stereo was minimal.

Incriminating Character Immediately Apparent

A final requirement for the plain view doctrine is that the incriminating character of the evidence be immediately apparent. This means that the officers must have probable cause to believe that the object is contraband or constitutes evidence of a crime without further exploration. *Minnesota v. Dickerson*, 508 U.S. 366, 113 S. Ct. 2130, 124 L. Ed. 2d 334 (1993). In *Hicks*, not only did the officer fail to have a lawful right of access to the stereo, he lacked probable cause to believe that the stereo was stolen because the incriminating character of the stereo was not immediately apparent. That being said, officers do not have to "know" for certain or have an "unduly high degree of certainty" or "near certainty" as to the incriminatory character of the evidence under the plain view doctrine. *See, e.g., Texas v. Brown*, 460 U.S. 730, 103 S. Ct. 1535, 75 L. Ed. 2d 502 (1983). The standard is essentially whether there is probable cause to believe that the evidence is contraband based on what is observed by plain view, plain feel and even "plain hear" by the officer.

The "immediately apparent" test becomes an issue frequently in cases involving evidence that is not inherently contraband such as documents, money, tickets, photographs, tools, etc., as opposed to such obvious contraband as kilograms of cocaine and defaced firearms. Counsel should investigate what the officers relied on when determining plain view. This investigation should include physical viewing of the evidence to see what would, in fact, have been immediately apparent to the officers. If possible, the evidence should be viewed in the container in which it was recovered. Often officers will take pictures of the location of evidence, and in some cases the entire encounter will be videotaped. Counsel should request access to any photographs or videos.

Even in drug cases, the container might not immediately reveal contraband or the pat reveal drugs. Opaque containers and carrying cases generally provide the most fertile grounds for this defense argument. Experienced officers are fairly adept at getting around the opaque container. Typically the officer will testify that such containers are commonly used to transport drugs. For example, in *Texas v. Brown*, the officer testified that he knew that drugs, particularly heroin, were often transported in balloons. *Id.* If the carrying case is something innocuous like a camera case, the defense could have a better basis upon which to challenge the search. *See, e.g., United States v. Donnes*, 947 F.3d 1430, 1438-9 (10th Cir. 1991) (finding that a camera lens case did not subject its contents to the plain view exception despite officer's claim that they could be used to carry drugs).

Even with opaque containers the officer will often testify to observing other suspicious behavior with the container or opaque package such as the suspect trying to push it under a seat or throw it in the back. Practically, courts are likely to find that an officer could tell whether the object's incriminating character was immediately apparent if the officer observing the suspicious conduct is experienced. Part of the defense's argument might include challenging the officer's actual experience with narcotics and experience with this particular type of container, particularly if the officer is new to the job. It might also include challenging whether the other behavior was indeed suspicious or just became suspicious in hindsight to justify the search.

The question of "immediacy" and "apparent" might also provide fertile ground for defense arguments. Officers are allowed to use flashlights, binoculars, shift angles and look under cars. For example, the officer in *Texas v. Brown*, used a flashlight and shifted positions to see what was in the glove compartment where the balloons were stashed when the driver leaned over to get the registration.

May the officer ask the suspect to roll down the heavily tinted windows of the vehicle? May the officer open the door, tell the suspect to move to the other side of the passenger area, or lift something up to get a better view of the evidence? How far the officers may move or have the suspect move until it constitutes a search beyond plain view will depend on the circuit and the reasonableness of the officer's actions under the totality of the circumstances. Squeezing a container to ascertain whether it contains drugs takes the search out of the plain feel or plain view arena. *See, e.g., Bond v. United States*, 529 U.S. 334, 337, 120

S. Ct. 1462, 1464, 146 L. Ed. 2d 365, 369 (2000) (finding an unconstitutional intrusion where border patrol agent squeezed luggage in rack.)

Inadvertency No Longer Required

It used to be that in order for the plain view exception to apply, the viewing of the object had to be inadvertent. This requirement developed from the Supreme Court's decision in *Coolidge v. New Hampshire*. 403 U.S. 443, 466, 91 S. Ct. 2022, 2038, 29 L. Ed. 2d 564, 583 (1971). The requirement itself, however, was not adopted by a majority of the Court. Subsequently in *Horton*, the Supreme Court made clear that inadvertency is not required for plain view seizures. The Court recognized that inadvertence is often a characteristic of most legitimate "plain-view" seizures, but it is not a necessary condition. *Horton*, 496 U.S. at 136-37, 110 S. Ct. at 2307-08, 110 L. Ed. 2d at 122-23. If counsel finds cases in their circuit requiring inadvertence, likely they predate Horton and should not be used.

Plain Feel

The Supreme Court has extended the plain view doctrine to "plain feel" demanding the same three requirements as plain view. *See Dickerson, supra.* Although the Court recognized the plain feel doctrine, it still found the search in *Dickerson* unlawful because the officer had manipulated the lump found on the defendant during a pat down. *Id.* Because the lump's illegality was not immediately apparent but required manipulation, the Court found that this violated the "plain feel" doctrine because the officer exceeded the scope of the lawful patdown.

A patdown for weapons is limited to the objective of ensuring the officer's safety. A patdown is not meant to be a fishing expedition for evidence. Defense counsel must be vigilant to discover whether the officers were in fact looking for evidence under the guise of a security patdown and went beyond the limited scope of a patdown for weapons. This will require the defense to investigate the exact location of the evidence on the defendant and the packaging of its contents. If the package was found in a jacket pocket it is essential that the jacket be produced. The defendant should be asked what he was wearing at the outset and to retain those clothes in the event they are needed for a suppression hearing. Counsel should also obtain arrest day photographs showing clothing as well as descriptions from pedigree and arrest reports.

If the prosecution is relying on plain feel, defense counsel should be prepared to make any one of the following arguments applicable to their case: 1) the patdown was not supported by reasonable articulable suspicion that the defendant was armed and dangerous; 2) even if a patdown had been proper, the contraband's incriminating nature was not immediately apparent through a patdown; and/or 3) in order to determine the incriminating nature of the evidence the officer was required to go beyond the scope of a proper *Terry* frisk.

Plain Smell

The Supreme Court has not specifically extended the plain view doctrine to "plain smell," although a number of circuit courts have upheld warrantless searches based on the smell of marijuana. *See, e.g., United States v. Roby*, 122 F.3d 1120, 1124-25 (8th Cir. 1997). Counsel should check their particular jurisdiction for its position on the issue. For example, the Second Circuit would not extend a "plain smell" exception to the Warrant Requirement when the marijuana had been placed inside a plain cardboard box, sealed with tape and put inside a van with its windows painted over and plywood placed behind the drivers' seat clearly evincing an evident desire to keep the contents private. *See United States v. Dien*, 609 F.2d 1038 (2d. Cir. 1979).

Counsel should be mindful that "plain smell" is different than a trained narcotics dog sniff. The dog sniff has been defined as not constituting a search at all because it is of very limited intrusiveness and the fact that the dog can only detect the evidence of contraband and not innocent materials distinguishes it from plain smell cases. *See United States v. Place*, 462 U.S. 696, 103 S. Ct. 2637, 77 L. Ed. 2d 110 (1983). Although in many cases there will be no intrusion when the officers smell the odor of marijuana, it certainly goes beyond the canine dog sniff and would require at a minimum the elements of the plain view doctrine that the officers have a lawful advantage, a lawful access to the evidence and that its incriminating nature be immediately apparent. The officer's qualifications to recognize marijuana would need to be established as well.

Some Useful Cases

Dow Chemical v. United States, 476 U.S. 227, 106 S. Ct. 1819, 90 L. Ed. 2d 226 (1986).

Horton v. California, 496 U.S. 128, 110 S. Ct. 2301, 110 L. Ed. 2d 112 (1990).

Texas v. Brown, 460 U.S. 730, 103 S. Ct. 1535, 75 L. Ed. 2d 502 (1983).

Arizona v. Hicks, 480 U.S. 321, 107 S. Ct. 1149, 94 L. Ed. 2d 347 (1987).

Coolidge v. New Hampshire. 403 U.S. 443, 91 S. Ct. 2022, 29 L. Ed. 2d 564 (1971).

CHAPTER THIRTEEN
EXIGENT CIRCUMSTANCES

Exigent Circumstances Generally

One of the most commonly invoked exceptions to the Warrant Requirement is the exigent circumstances exception. An officer may enter a dwelling or other area where there is a reasonable expectation of privacy without a warrant in order to respond to an exigent situation. In short, firefighters do not need a warrant to enter a burning building. The rationale for the exigency exception is that if warrants were required in such situations, officers would be delayed while obtaining the warrant, which could put people at risk and result in the irretrievable loss of evidence. Permitting officers to make warrantless entries to respond to exigent circumstances is a balancing of the public need against the privacy interest. As with most Fourth Amendment issues, the standard is objective based on the totality of the circumstances.

A common example of an exception to the Warrant Requirement that is rooted in exigent circumstances is the automobile exception. An officer with probable cause may arrest a suspect in a vehicle and search the vehicle without a warrant due to the inherent exigency arising from the mobility of the car. The automobile exception is a bright line rule and no further showing of exigency is necessary beyond that inherent in all vehicles, although there is some room to argue that if the car was towed to a secure police compound there is no longer an inherent exigency and the police are required to get a warrant. *See Coolidge v. New Hampshire,* 403 U.S. 443, 91 S. Ct. 2022, 29 L. Ed. 2d 564 (1971). *See also, Chapter Fourteen: The Automobile Exception.*

The Supreme Court has allowed for very few exigent circumstances when a warrant may be dispensed with when invading the sanctity of the home. Absent exigent circumstances or consent the "firm line at the entrance to the house ... may not reasonably be crossed without a warrant." *Payton v. New York,* 445 U.S.

573, 590, 100 S. Ct. 1371, 1382, 63 L. Ed. 2d 639, 653 (1980). Whether the officers can dispense with the knock-and-announce requirement even when executing a warrant is also dependent upon the exigencies of the circumstances. *See Chapter Six: Warrants.*

The Supreme Court has recognized exceptions when there is a reasonable belief of the imminent destruction of evidence; there is a fleeing suspect or hot pursuit of a suspect; or the need to act for the safety of officers or the public. *See Welsh v. Wisconsin,* 466 U.S. 740, 104 S. Ct. 2091, 80 L. Ed. 2d 732 (1984). The burden is on the prosecution to show that exigent circumstances exist to justify the lack of a warrant, and the burden is considered a "heavy one." *Id.*

The specific scope of exigency has not been defined by the Supreme Court, but rather left to the lower courts to assess within the context of individual case facts. Attorneys should become familiar with the law of their circuit and jurisdiction because many courts lay out specific factors, usually non-exhaustive, they consider when assessing whether the exigencies justify a warrantless intrusion. For example, the Second Circuit uses six "illustrative guides" to aid in determining whether the need for quick law enforcement action permits a warrantless entry: (1) the gravity or violent nature of the offense with which the suspect is to be charged; (2) whether the suspect is reasonably believed to be armed; (3) a clear showing of probable cause to believe that the suspect committed the crime; (4) strong reason to believe that the suspect is on the premises being entered; (5) a likelihood that the suspect will escape if not swiftly apprehended; and (6) the peaceful circumstances of the entry. *United States v. MacDonald,* 916 F.2d 766, 769-70 (2d. Cir. 1990) (en banc). Even if counsel is in a jurisdiction that has not adopted specific factors, judges often rely on other courts' decisions in assessing exigent circumstances within the totality of the circumstances facing the officers. Counsel should study those other cases in crafting arguments, and possibly urge the court to adopt another standard that is favorable if it is an open question in their particular jurisdiction.

In many cases the exigencies will overlap. For example, in addition to a fear of destruction of evidence, there might also be a fear that the suspects will escape or that an innocent bystander would be in danger if the suspects are armed. Any one of the exigencies will suffice for a warrantless entry, and certainly an accumulation of exigencies will strengthen the prosecution's position.

Nature of the Offense

The nature and seriousness of the offense are important in litigating a warrantless search. Certainly chasing an individual into a home because of a traffic offense or a misdemeanor marijuana possession would be much harder to justify than in a serious narcotics case where evidence could be easily destroyed.

The Supreme Court has approved the consideration of the seriousness of the offense in exigent circumstances cases:

> In a leading federal case defining exigent circumstances, for example, the en banc United States Court of Appeals for the District of Columbia Circuit recognized that the gravity of the underlying offense was a principal factor to be weighed. Dorman v. United States. Without approving all of the factors included in the standard adopted by that court, it is sufficient to note that many other lower courts have also considered the gravity of the offense an important part of their constitutional analysis....[We] hold that an important factor to be considered when determining whether any exigency exists is the gravity of the underlying offense for which the arrest is being made.

Welsh, 466 U.S. at 751-2, 104 S. Ct. at 2098-99, 80 L. Ed. 2d at 744 (citations and footnotes omitted).

Because the Supreme Court has embraced the seriousness of the offense as an important factor, both counsels must address this factor in their argument. If the offense is a misdemeanor or a non-violent, white-collar type felony such as tax evasion, the courts are less likely to find exigency; whereas, cases involving firearms, narcotics and crimes of violence are more likely to be viewed as compelling exigency in the situation to allow the warrantless intrusion.

Although the offense is minor, the prosecutor can argue any other exigencies in the case, such as the suspect's prior history of violence justifying the officer's belief that the person was likely to present a danger to the public or observations showing that the defendant was about to destroy evidence or carried a weapon. The defense can attempt to counter the seriousness of the offense in drug and weapons cases when there are no specific facts demonstrating any threat, particularly when the defendant was not believed to be armed

Destruction of Evidence

A reasonable belief in the imminent destruction of evidence is probably the most common justification offered for a warrantless entry. A frequently used standard is that set out by the Seventh Circuit, which has been adopted by a number of other circuits:

> In determining whether agents reasonably feared imminent destruction of the evidence, the appropriate inquiry is whether the facts, as they appeared at the moment of entry, would lead a reasonable, experienced agent to believe that evidence might be destroyed before a warrant could be secured.

See *United States v. Young*, 909 F.2d 442, 446 (11th Cir. 1990) citing with approval *United States v. Rivera*, 825 F.2d 152, 156 (7th Cir. 1987).

The officer must have probable cause to believe that such evidence exists. Even if exigent circumstances exist, those exigencies do not alleviate the need for probable cause. A warrant itself could only be issued upon probable cause under the Fourth Amendment, thus a warrantless entry under an exception to the Warrant Clause must meet the same standard.

The officers must also have a reasonable basis for believing that the evidence will be removed or destroyed. A hunch or a mere assumption that evidence will be destroyed will not be enough. Courts ordinarily require an officer to articulate objective reasons why he believed the evidence would be destroyed, *e.g.*, the sound of someone opening a window, the slam of a bathroom door, running water or a toilet flushed, people running and slamming doors, statements made by the occupants about getting rid of evidence, the fact that the suspects were aware of police presence, etc. The officers' observations must also have a nexus to the possibility of destruction. For example, the sound of an adding machine through a closed door in an illegal lottery case was insufficient to support exigent circumstances because it was not evidence of destruction of evidence or the flight of the suspects, only that the suspects were in the midst of their illegal operation. *See McDonald v. United States*, 335 U.S. 451, 69 S. Ct. 191, 93 L. Ed. 153 (1948).

Although exigent circumstances justifying a warrantless seizure to avoid destruction of evidence often arise in narcotics cases, the mere fact that the case involves narcotics is not enough to demonstrate exigent circumstances to avoid obtaining a warrant. Courts have consistently rejected a *per se* exigency in narcotics cases (as they have in murder cases) although they have recognized that the doctrine is particularly "compelling" in narcotics cases because drugs can be easily destroyed. *See, e.g., Young*, 909 F.2d at 446. The prosecution, who bears the burden of proving exigent circumstances, must detail objective factors in the individual narcotics case to justify a warrantless entry or search and seizure. Practically speaking, judges are much more likely to find exigency in drug cases where evidence is easily destroyed, but the defense still must hold the government to the particularities of its burden.

Unlike hot pursuit or public safety issues, in destruction of evidence exigencies the officers are involved in what the Supreme Court has described as the "often competitive enterprise of ferreting out crime." *See Johnson v. United States*, 333 U.S. 10, 14-15, 68 S. Ct. 367, 369, 92 L.Ed. 436, 440-41 (1948). In other words, the purpose is to preserve evidence to convict, not save a person from a burning building. The defense is in a better policy position to seek suppression than when the officers are responding to a life or death situation on behalf of public safety and happen to come across obvious contraband in plain view.

The key for both sides in challenging or defending exigent circumstances exceptions related to destruction of evidence is recreating for the judge what was going on at the time right up to the entry. Both sides should be attempting to answer these types of questions through their witnesses and arguments:

- What did the officers know that gave them probable cause?

- Did the probable cause include the belief that the evidence would be in the location?

- What lead the officers to believe that the evidence would be destroyed?

- Was it reasonable to rely on that evidence?

- When did they reasonably believe the evidence would be destroyed?

- Could the officers have obtained a warrant in advance?

- If the officers could have obtained a warrant in advance, why was there no warrant?

- If the officers could not have obtained a warrant in advance, what prevented them?

- Did the officers make any attempt to obtain a warrant?

- What were those efforts?

- Did the officers do anything themselves that caused the exigency?

- What did they do?

The defense should be vigilant in demanding that specific, individualized, objective articulable reasons are stated for why the officer believed the evidence was there and might be destroyed before a warrant could be obtained. The defense should argue that the failure of the officers to obtain a warrant in advance in the context of advanced technologies that have made obtaining a warrant much easier and quicker is not justified. Telephonic warrants are available in federal cases pursuant to FRCrP 41(c)(2). The officer can readily call in the information under oath and the magistrate judge would then authorize the warrant if it were sufficiently supported by probable cause. The defense should argue that failure to obtain such a warrant when there is sufficient knowledge and time requires suppression. (Not all states permit telephonic warrants; counsel should find out what warrants are permissible in their jurisdiction to contextualize the sense of urgency for warrantless actions by law enforcement. Prosecutors ordinarily would be aware of the requirements to obtain a warrant in a particular district, but it is essential for the defense attorney to know the requirements and any local rules pertaining to the issuance of warrants.)

Telephonic warrants and anticipatory warrants are particularly suited to narcotics cases where the agents often know in advance what is going to transpire at a given time or location, particularly in federal cases involving undercover sting operations or the use of confidential informants in an ongoing investigation. The Eleventh Circuit decision in *United States v. Santa*, 236 F.3d 662, 673-4 (11th Cir. 2000) is instructive. In *Santa*, it was early afternoon when the DEA learned of the location and approximate time of the planned drug transaction. The parties had agreed that the sale would take place at the apartment that evening after the informant had delivered the drugs, and the informant had promptly imparted this knowledge to the federal agents. This same informant had provided reliable information to the agents in the past, and the agents had independent confirmation of most of the informant's information on audiotape. The court concluded:

> We see no reason why agents, with this information, could not have gone before a magistrate to obtain a search warrant. In the age of telephonic warrants, we doubt that it would have been impossible (or even difficult) to obtain a warrant by telephone on that Wednesday afternoon. If we were to condone the warrantless entry of Ramirez and Santa's apartment under the circumstances presented here, we would effectively allow officers to create exigencies by failing to procure a warrant while there was time to do so. Every situation would become an eventual emergency; the practice of obtaining a warrant would soon fall by the wayside, and the exception would swallow the rule. Thus, we hold that in circumstances such as those presented here, where law enforcement agents have ample time and information to secure an anticipatory search

warrant, lack of time to obtain a warrant *after* delivery of the contraband is insufficient to justify a warrantless search.

Id.

The prosecution should be prepared to argue in their case that the agents did not have sufficient time to obtain a telephonic warrant and the need for the agents to act quickly to preserve evidence that would otherwise be destroyed justified a warrantless entry. The prosecution can also argue that the officers are not required to get a warrant at the earliest possible moment. The prosecution is assisted by a Supreme Court plurality opinion in *Cardwell v. Lewis*, 417 U.S. 583, 595-96 , 94 S. Ct. 2464, 2478, 41 L. Ed. 2d 325, 337-38 (1974) observing that the fact that the officers could have obtained a warrant earlier does not preclude a warrantless search based on exigent circumstances that arose at a later time. The defense can counter that the officers could have secured the location and sought a warrant once they were certain that no one else was on the premises to destroy the evidence, rather than conducting a warrantless search after the premises were vacated or the suspects apprehended.

The prosecution's argument will be made easier if the agents acted diligently during any intervening time period and if the officers made some attempt to get a warrant but were unable to do so in a time. Moreover, there is an undercurrent of good faith in the analysis of warrantless searches to avoid destruction of evidence. If the officers were erroneous but well intentioned in their belief that they would not have been able to get a warrant in time, the prosecution can argue that the exclusionary rule's deterrent value is not enhanced by suppressing the evidence. The prosecution should focus on the lack of improper conduct or any indication that the officers were trying to circumvent the Warrant Requirement. The defense should focus on the unreasonableness of the officer's belief and the lack of due diligence in seeking a court issued warrant suggesting that the reason for entry without a warrant was not exigency but inconvenience, particularly when the officers control the timing of entry.

Fleeing Suspect and Hot Pursuit

When an officer is in hot pursuit of a suspect the officer may be justified in pursuing the suspect into a private dwelling without a warrant. The first requirement is that the officer have the necessary probable cause to arrest the individual in the public area. Officers who have probable cause to arrest a person in public do not need a warrant. *United States v. Watson*, 423 U.S. 411, 96 S. Ct. 820, 46 L. Ed. 2d 598 (1976). If the officer could have arrested the suspect in a public area and the suspect flees the area, the officers are permitted to chase the defendant and make an arrest even if it means entering a dwelling, provided that there is sufficient exigency. Although some sort of a chase is required in a hot pursuit case, it need not be "an extended hue and cry... about the public streets." *See United States v. Santana*, 427 U.S. 38, 42, 96 S. Ct. 2406, 2409-10, 49 L. Ed. 2d 300, 305 (1976) (upholding a warrantless arrest on hot pursuit grounds where the defendant had been standing in the doorway of her apartment in public view and went back into the vestibule of her apartment).

In hot pursuit or cases where there is a reasonable belief the suspect will escape, a number of circuit courts have required the prosecution to demonstrate a high level of urgency to justify the warrantless invasion of a home including evaluating the seriousness of the offense, the quality of probable cause for the arrest, the likelihood that the defendant was in the house, the likelihood of escape, a reasonable belief that the suspect was armed, and the manner of police entry. *See, e.g., Dorman v. United States*, 435 F.2d 385 (D.C. Cir. 1978). Some courts have distinguished between "true hot pursuit" cases and a fleeing suspect. Hot pursuit involves the notion of chase, whereas a fleeing suspect can also encompass both hot pursuit and the fear of the suspect's escape when there is, in actuality, no chase or flight. *See, e.g., Santana*, 427 U.S. at 42, 96 S. Ct. at 2409-10, 49 L. Ed. 2d at 305, n. 3.

Although many circuit courts have delineated various factors in assessing such exigency, the analysis of exigent circumstances is still within the totality of the circumstances and the presence or absence of a particular factor will ordinarily not be dispositive. Each side should assess the factors such as seriousness of the offense or the likelihood that the defendant is armed to make a case for their position.

In addition, both sides should be aware of the law on exigency in their particular jurisdiction, but also to argue within the totality of the circumstances analysis to their advantage when a specific factor is absent or strongly present which supports their position. The Supreme Court has not fully detailed the requirements of exigency leaving it to the lower courts to consider the issues within the particular case facts, so that the most useful analogies are going to be to state, district and appellate court decisions.

Public Safety

The public safety exception to validate a warrantless entry is one of the easier ones for prosecutors to justify at the outset, because the officers are on the premises in response to a medical emergency or a public safety issue. On the other hand, the fact that the officers are on the premises to respond to an emergency does not itself justify scouring the place in the hopes of finding evidence of criminal conduct. Although officers can seize evidence in plain view they must meet the requirements of that exception. The officers must be legitimately on the premises. The officers must have a right of access to the evidence. Finally, the illegality of the evidence seized must be immediately apparent. *See Chapter Twelve: Plain View*.

The Supreme Court's decision in *Mincey v. Arizona*, 437 U.S. 385, 98 S. Ct. 2408, 57 L. Ed. 2d 290 (1978) provides a useful example of the distinction between public safety exigency and evidence gathering. *Mincey* involved an undercover drug deal that went awry resulting in the fatal shooting of a police officer. Law enforcement officers were on the scene for the undercover drug operation and heard gunshots coming from the bedroom where an undercover officer had gone. The officer emerged from the bedroom fatally wounded. Other officers entered the bedroom where they found the defendant also wounded. The officers then conducted a security sweep of the area for the assailant and any victims. The officers discovered a wounded woman in the bedroom closet and three other people in the living room, one of them with a head injury. The officers requested emergency assistance but did no further investigation of the scene; instead they guarded the suspects and the premises pursuant to department policy. Subsequently, a homicide team arrived and engaged in four days of intensive forensic investigation in the apartment, including ripping up the carpets, ultimately seizing over 200 pieces of evidence. No warrants were obtained for the homicide unit's searches.

In finding that the evidence obtained by the homicide unit should have been suppressed, the Supreme Court made clear that they did not question the right of the police to respond to emergency situations since the Fourth Amendment does not bar police officers from making warrantless entries and searches when they reasonably believe that a person is in need of immediate assistance. They also approved of the police's action when coming upon the scene of a homicide to make a prompt warrantless search of the area to see whether there were other victims or whether a killer was still on the premises. What was problematic in Mincey, was the homicide team's four-day search of a home without the benefit of any warrant. The Court rejected a *per se* homicide investigation exception to the Warrant Requirement and held that the homicide team had gone beyond the initial exigency which permitted warrantless entry and action, and, thus, a warrant was required as it would have been in any offense be it homicide, rape, burglary, etc. *Id.*

Mincey is an important case for the defense because it involves arguably the most exigent of circumstances–a life or death situation–and involved the death of a police officer, yet the Supreme Court found that the evidence should have been suppressed. Had there been separate concerns of destruction of evidence providing a separate exigency, the detectives might have properly searched without a warrant. No such exigencies existed. The only exigencies in the case that permitted the warrantless entry justified the initial law enforcement actions, not the subsequent search by the homicide team.

Police Created Exigencies

The police cannot create or manufacture their own exigent circumstances to circumvent the Warrant Requirement such as deliberately alerting the suspects to their presence resulting in the possible destruction of evidence, the flight of the suspects or the danger to the public. When the police control the timing of the situation ordinarily they should be in a position to seek and obtain a warrant.

If the exigency is created by police action that is beyond their control courts will usually uphold the warrantless entry. Two Fifth Circuit cases are illustrative. In *United States v. Hultren*, 13, F.2d 79, 87-88 (5th Cir. 1983), the court found exigent circumstances arose "naturally" when the confidential informant's transmitter suddenly failed during the drug buy, and upheld the warrantless entry. In *United States v. Scheffer*, 463 F.2d 567, 574-75 (5th Cir. 1972), the court rejected the prosecution's claim that agents lacked time to obtain a warrant when the agents controlled the timing of when to send the cooperating defendants into a residence to consummate a drug deal.

Scope of the Search

The extent of the intrusion should not exceed the need occasioned by the emergency. Provided there is sufficient justification for the search or seizure occasioned by the probable cause and the basis for the entry, officers may effect the search or seizure without a warrant. An exigent entry to assure that no evidence of narcotic distribution, for example, is destroyed, would permit an extensive search given the nature of the evidence, *e.g.*, the drugs themselves, records, paraphernalia, etc. In addition, any evidence in plain view while an officer is on the premises for the purposes of responding to the exigent circumstances may be seized if it meets the specific criteria of the plain view exception. *See Chapter Twelve: Plain View.*

In *Arizona v. Hicks*, 480 U.S. 321, 107 S. Ct. 1149, 94 L. Ed. 2d 347 (1987), for example, the officers were legitimately on the premises when investigating a bullet shot through the floor below; however the officer's movement of stereo equipment he suspected was stolen to enable him to take down identification numbers amounted to an improper search. The officer's actions constituted an improper extension of the exigency created by the public safety concern. Similarly, if the search is for a person as a result of a hot pursuit, but there is no reason to believe the person possessed weapons, the officers are limited to a search for the person; looking in areas where a person could not hide (such as a bureau drawer) would be impermissible without a warrant.

Separating the Exigency from the Evidence Gathering

The exigency exception to the Warrant Requirement arises not so much because there is a challenge to the action taken by the officers meant to ensure public safety or catch a criminal in hot pursuit, but because once in the dwelling or private area the officers observe and seize evidence that is subsequently introduced against the defendant at trial. Litigators must understand this distinction. Judges are often of the mind that if they rule in favor of the defense it would handcuff or stifle the police from acting on behalf of public safety. Prosecutors are likely to argue how important it is for the officers to be able to respond to emergency situations unfettered or delayed by the need to get a warrant. The defense attorney must make it clear to the judge that excluding the evidence from trial will not prevent police officers from acting to save a person from a burning building, but rather to prevent officers from circumventing the Warrant Requirement for searches and seizures for the purpose of obtaining incriminating evidence by misusing the emergency situation. The defense must convince the court to separate the exigency from the evidence gathering in analyzing whether there is a Fourth Amendment violation.

Exigent Circumstances Policy Arguments

The exigency exception strikes at the heart of law enforcement concerns with respect to searches and seizures and the exclusionary rule. How can officers be expected to get a warrant when they are in the midst of trying to catch the suspect or prevent the evidence from being flushed down the toilet?

Properly used, the exigent circumstances exception provides an important balance in the tensions between law enforcement needs and protection of Fourth Amendment rights. It is when the exigent circumstances exception is misused to circumvent judicial review through a warrant by officers presuming or overstating exigency, all in the name of crime control, that vigilance on the part of both the prosecution and the defense is required to preserve the integrity of the Warrant Requirement. Otherwise, if the need for law enforcement itself becomes an exigent circumstance, no warrant would ever be obtained rendering the Warrant Requirement in the Constitution essentially irrelevant.

Although the Warrant Requirement has been seriously diluted with ever mounting exception and the trend toward reasonableness analysis and away from a hard and fast requirement of a warrant, when a dwelling is at stake the courts take the Warrant Requirement far more seriously. The defense attorney can use this to her advantage in arguing against the unnecessary application or extension of exigent circumstances. The poignant observations of Justice Douglas in his majority opinion in *McDonald* are as pertinent today as in 1948:

> We are not dealing with formalities. The presence of a search warrant serves a high function. Absent some grave emergency, the Fourth Amendment has interposed a magistrate between the citizen and the police. This was done not to shield criminals nor to make the home a safe haven for illegal activities. It was done so that an objective mind might weigh the need to invade that privacy in order to enforce the law. The right of privacy was deemed too precious to entrust to the discretion of those whose job is the detection of crime and the arrest of criminals. Power is a heady thing; and history shows that the police acting on their own cannot be trusted. And so the Constitution requires a magistrate to pass on the desires of the police before they violate the privacy of the home. We cannot be true to that constitutional requirement and excuse

the absence of a search warrant without a showing by those who seek exemption from the constitutional mandate that the exigencies of the situation made that course imperative.

McDonald v. United States, 335 U.S. 451, 454, 69 S. Ct. 191, 192-3, 93 L.Ed. 153, 158 (1948).

Some Useful Cases

United States v. MacDonald, 916 F.2d 766, 769-70 (2d. Cir. 1990) (en banc).

United States v. Young, 909 F.2d 442 (11th Cir. 1990).

Johnson v. United States, 333 U.S. 10, 68 S. Ct. 367, 92 L. Ed. 436 (1948).

United States v. Santa, 236 F.3d 662 (11th Cir. 2000).

Mincey v. Arizona, 437 U.S. 385, 98 S. Ct. 2408, 57 L. Ed. 2d 290 (1978).

McDonald v. United States, 335 U.S. 451, 69 S. Ct. 191, 93 L. Ed. 153 (1948).

CHAPTER FOURTEEN
THE AUTOMOBILE EXCEPTION

Ten years of federal criminal practice has revealed two critical lessons: never commit a crime on federal property and never commit a crime in a car. The courts generally agree that people have a far reduced expectation of privacy in automobiles. For that reason, automobile searches are not subject to the same Fourth Amendment limitations that other types of searches are.

Officers must have probable cause to search a car, but are generally not required to obtain a warrant to conduct the search. This "automobile exception" is further justified by the mobility of cars and the ease with which they can transport contraband from area to area. In other words, automobiles create exigent circumstances. Cars are also heavily regulated by the government. As a result, society's ordinary expectations of privacy and possessory rights are mostly suspended for cars in favor of law enforcement needs.

Automobile Searches Generally

Because of the mobility of the car and its heavy regulation, the police need not actually go and get a warrant if they have probable cause to believe a vehicle contains contraband or evidence of a crime. If the police have probable cause to search an automobile, the automobile exception allows them to do so without a warrant and they may search to the same extent a warrant would allow. *See Carroll v. United States*, 267 U.S. 132, 45 S. Ct. 280, 69 L. Ed. 2d 543 (1925).

The automobile itself carries a certain inherent exigency such that the police need not find any additional exigency other than the fact that the evidence or contraband is in an automobile. *Maryland v. Dyson*, 527 U.S. 465, 119 S. Ct. 2013, 144 L. Ed. 2d 442 (1999). Rather than require a factual determination of the actual exigency and mobility of the vehicle to justify an exception to the warrant requirement, the courts have adopted a fairly bright line. If evidence or contraband is in a car it is an exception to the warrant requirement even when there is no possibility that the car could in fact be mobile or the evidence lost. Moreover, even if the police do not have probable cause to believe that the car contains contraband, if they believe the car itself is contraband, they may take it into custody and search it pursuant to an inventory search without a warrant. *Florida v. White*, 526 U.S. 559, 119 S. Ct. 1555, 143 L. Ed. 2d 748 (1999). *See also, Chapter Fifteen: Inventory, Regulatory, and Border Searches.*

Automobile Searches Incident to Arrest

When the police arrest a person for whom they have probable cause to arrest, they may also search the passenger area of the car as a search incident to arrest. This is called a "Belton search" pursuant to the Supreme Court's decision in *New York v. Belton,* 453 U.S. 454, 101 S. Ct. 2860, 69 L. Ed. 2d 768 (1981). The police may search incident to arrest even if the arrest is for a minor traffic violation and the police used the minor offense as a pretext to search for more serious contraband. *See e.g., United States v. Robinson*, 414 U.S. 218, 94 S. Ct. 467, 38 L. Ed. 2d 427 (1973). Such searches are also justified by the significant number of police shootings that occur at traffic stops, and the officer's need to protect his safety by searching the car for weapons. *Id.* at 234, 94 S. Ct. at 476, 38 L. Ed. 2d at 440. Although the search in *Robinson* was not of the vehicle, since the drugs were found on the defendant's person after he got out of the car, *Belton* would allow for such a vehicle search even if pretextual. The Court made clear more recently in *Whren v. United States*, 517 U.S. 806, 116 S. Ct. 1769, 135 L. Ed. 2d 89 (1996) that officers may arrest and search the passenger area of the vehicle incident to arrest on a minor traffic offense, such as failure to signal, even if the officer's ulterior motive is to discover drugs.

Containers within Automobiles

Whether officers were permitted to search containers within cars used to be quite confusing depending on whether the probable cause was for a specific container or the car generally. Now containers within cars may be searched even if the police lack probable cause to believe that the particular container holds contraband or evidence of a crime, providing there is probable cause to believe that the car contains such evidence or contraband, and the container could hold the object of such a search, *e.g.*, drugs. *California v. Acevedo*, 500 U.S. 565, 111 S. Ct. 1982, 114 L. Ed. 2d 619 (1991). It is no longer a rule that the officers must hold the container and obtain a warrant. *Id.* overruling *United States v. Chadwick*, 433 U.S. 1, 97 S. Ct. 2476, 53 L. Ed. 2d 538 (1977) and *Arkansas v. Sanders*, 442 U.S. 753, 99 S. Ct. 2586, 61 L. Ed. 2d 235 (1979).

Because of the exigent circumstances arising in automobile cases, a container that would otherwise not be subject to a search without a warrant does not carry the same expectation of privacy once the owner places it into a vehicle. If counsel finds cases requiring a warrant to search a container found in a car, they no doubt predate *California v. Acevedo* and should not be used.

Passengers

If officers have probable cause to believe there is evidence of a crime or contraband in a car, the officers may also search the property of passengers without separate probable cause to believe those passengers are carrying contraband or evidence. *Wyoming v. Houghton*, 526 U.S. 295, 119 S. Ct. 1297, 143 L. Ed. 2d 408 (1999). The facts of *Houghton* provide a strong lesson on the Supreme Court's thinking on the scope of automobile searches and the reduced expectation of privacy in a car.

During a routine traffic stop, a Wyoming Highway Patrol officer noticed a hypodermic syringe in the driver's shirt pocket. The driver confessed that he had used it to take drugs. The officer searched the passenger compartment of the car as well as the passenger's purse, though he had no specific probable cause to believe the purse contained contraband. The officer found drug paraphernalia in the purse and arrested the passenger on drug charges. The Court described how containers within cars are subject to search even if the containers are owned by passengers. Like the driver, passengers in a vehicle have a reduced expectation of privacy in the car. *Houghton*, 526 U.S. at 301-02, 119 S. Ct. at 1301, 143 L. Ed. 2d at 416. Additionally, the Supreme Court recently held that drugs and money found in an armrest of a car provided a sufficient basis to arrest all three passengers of the car. The Court inferred that all three had knowledge and dominion over the drugs. *See Maryland v. Pringle*, 124 S. Ct. 7956, 157 L. Ed. 2d 769 (2003).

Although an officer may search the effects of a passenger within the car, the police are not permitted to search the body of a passenger without specific probable cause to arrest that person. The rationale for this rule is that the invasion of a container is far less intrusive than a body search, which must be justified by the appropriate level of reasonable suspicion or probable cause for a patdown or search.

What's Left to Argue?

Automobile searches still require probable cause to arrest the driver or passenger, or probable cause to search the automobile. If the officers lacked probable cause, the fact that the search was of a car will not cure the problematic search. Defense counsel may attempt to attack the basis for the probable cause by claiming that there was no fair probability to believe evidence of a crime or contraband was concealed in a car. However, if the officer arrests the driver for a minor traffic offense, he may conduct a full search of the passenger area without specific probable cause that there is evidence of a crime or contraband in the car.

Defense counsel might also be able to argue that the scope of an automobile search was unreasonable. If the probable cause is not for the car generally, but a specific package or container in a specific part of the car, the police may not search other areas of the car beyond where they have probable cause to believe the package is located. For example in *Acevedo*, the police had probable cause to believe that the paper bag in the trunk contained marijuana. That probable cause would allow a warrantless search of the paper bag. The police did not have probable cause to believe that contraband was hidden in any other part of the automobile and a search of the entire vehicle would have been without probable cause and unreasonable under the Fourth Amendment.

Some Useful Cases

Whren v. United States, 517 U.S. 806, 116 S. Ct. 1769, 135 L. Ed. 2d 89 (1996)

Wyoming v. Houghton, 526 U.S. 295, 119 S. Ct. 1297, 143 L. Ed. 2d 408 (1999)

California v. Acevedo, 500 U.S. 565, 111 S. Ct. 1982, 114 L. Ed. 2d 619 (1991)

New York v. Belton, 453 U.S. 454, 101 S. Ct. 2860, 69 L. Ed. 2d 768 (1981)

CHAPTER FIFTEEN
INVENTORY, REGULATORY, AND
BORDER SEARCHES

There are a number of searches that are done for what can be called collectively administrative reasons and not specifically for criminal investigation, though the results of the search are often used in criminal prosecutions. The purpose of these administrative searches is ostensibly non-criminal; to effect a regulatory goal such as monitoring entrances and exits at borders, cataloguing and safekeeping defendants' property, or installing sobriety checkpoints to protect the public from drunken drivers.

Administrative searches ordinarily do not require a warrant, probable cause or even reasonable suspicion, provided they are properly administered. Defense counsel may challenge searches which fail to adhere to the regulatory standards. If the administrative procedure is used as a pretext for criminal investigation or the officer overstepped the regulatory or administrative guidelines to effect a criminal search, this could preclude introduction of the evidence at trial as violative of the Fourth Amendment.

Inventory Searches

An inventory search may be conducted upon the arrest of an individual or impounding of property including a vehicle. The searches are conducted for administrative, security and liability purposes and are not supposed to be criminal investigation searches. The purpose is to catalogue and account for a defendant's property, safeguard the property and to ensure that the property does not contain explosives or other harmful items. In short, the rationale is to make sure that the defendant does not claim later that the cops stole his twenty-six dollars in cash or to confirm there is no bomb in the backpack.

Because it involves cataloguing evidence, the scope of an inventory search is broad. That being said, defense counsel should be on the lookout for any actions taken by the police that were not done in the spirit of the administrative procedure but smack of criminal investigation, *e.g.*, dusting property for fingerprints. Defense counsel should also make sure that the search did not extend beyond the scope of the purposes of an inventory search, particularly when that search occurs well after the property should have been catalogued or accounted had the real concern been to avoid liability issues.

Inventory searches must be conducted pursuant to established standardized procedures. *Illinois v. Lafayette*, 462 U.S. 640, 644, 103 S. Ct. 2605, 2608, 77 L. Ed. 2d 65, 70 (1983). In other words, the procedures cannot be ad hoc. These procedures must be in place and regularly followed. Although the procedures do not necessarily have to be in writing, they must still be standardized and the burden would be on the prosecution to prove the regularity of the procedures.

Defense counsel should obtain a copy of any written procedures, any internal memoranda, documents or manuals regarding the procedures, to determine whether they were in place at the time, whether they are standardized and whether they were followed in the individual case. If the procedure was written the day before the suppression hearing in the case, defense counsel needs to know this. Interviewing administrative personnel in addition to the officers (engaged in the often competitive business of ferreting out crime) might provide critical and more neutral information on the administrative procedures as compared with police officers. For example, defense should consider interviewing the evidence custodian or locker clerk.

Defense counsel must always get a copy of the evidence voucher listing the items taken from the defendant or from the defendant's car or home and read it carefully. Prosecutors do not usually turn this document over unless they are using it in their case in chief or it is specifically requested by the defense. Defense counsel should always ask for it. Information on that form is frequently useful in the theory of defense. How could this have been a reverse buy if the defendant only had $20 with him at the time of the arrest as logged in the evidence voucher? Where is the key to the locked apartment which the cops claim the defendant was on his way up to when they arrested him; they had to use a battering ram to get in, how would the defendant have gotten in without a key?

Ultimately the main argument for the defense is that the investigatory search was used as some kind of ruse or pretext to make an end run around the Warrant Requirement. If the procedures touch on criminal investigation issues—testing money for the presence of narcotics, fingerprinting items or taking down cell phone numbers, the defense should challenge that aspect of the search as non-inventory and, thus, requiring a warrant.

Regulatory Searches

Regulatory searches such as sobriety checkpoints are ordinarily permissible under the Fourth Amendment. The touchstone is reasonableness within the balancing of law enforcement needs against personal intrusion. Curtailing drunk driving outweighs the minimal infringement on liberty at such a checkpoint. If the detention is not random, there could be a defense challenge to the search as unreasonable and requiring articulable suspicion. Similarly, if the detention is for a lengthy period of time and involves searches beyond reasonable investigative steps to determine the sobriety of the driver, looking in the trunk for example or subjecting the driver to extensive sobriety tests, could be problematic.

If the purpose of the search is criminal investigation, the roadblock loses its regulatory status and reasonable suspicion is ordinarily required; the purpose must be a regulatory or administrative one rather than to catch criminals. Courts have routinely found roadblocks and checkpoints violative of the Fourth Amendment if an administrative search is being used for general crime detection or interdicting drug couriers. *See, e.g., United States v. Morales-Zamora*, 974 F.2d 149, 151 (10th Cir. 1992) (roadblock to check driver's licenses and vehicle registrations was pretextual set up for sole purpose of subjecting all stop vehicles to canine sniff and violated Fourth Amendment.) However, if a car is stopped at a legitimate checkpoint and contraband or other criminal activity is observed in plain view, the officers are permitted to investigate and act on that information if it provides reasonable suspicion or probable cause.

The Supreme Court clarified the issue of general crime detection versus observed criminal behavior in a recent checkpoint case, *Illinois v. Lidster*, 124 S. Ct. 885, 157 L. Ed. 2d 843 (2004) where the police set up a road block and stopped each motorist to inquire about a recent hit and run accident. During the stop of the defendant, the officers determined he was driving under the influence and arrested him. The Supreme Court explained that the arrest in *Lidster* was not contrary to the Court's decision in *Indianapolis v. Edmond*, 531 U.S. 32, 121 S. Ct. 447, 148 L. Ed. 2d 333 (2001), which found that a checkpoint station set up to stop vehicles and look for crime in the vehicles violated the Fourth Amendment in the absence of reasonable, particularized suspicion. In *Lidster*, persuasive to the Court, the primary object was to obtain information about a crime presumably unrelated to the motorists stopped for questioning. In such cases, defense counsel should determine whether the checkpoint was really a pretext for drug or general crime interdiction rather than as a regulatory checkpoint and request internal memoranda, documents and manuals regarding the checkpoint.

Although checkpoints for regulatory purposes have been upheld, officers still need a warrant to search buildings for most regulatory violations. The warrant need not be a search warrant as would be issued in a criminal case, but can be an administrative warrant accounting for the regulatory and administrative purpose, provided the need is balanced against the level of invasion to determine whether the search is reasonable. *See Camara v. Municipal Court of San Francisco*, 387 U.S. 523, 538, 87 S. Ct. 1727, 1735, 18 L. Ed. 2d 930, 940-41 (1967). These "lighter" warrants are not properly issued if the primary reason for the search is criminal investigation rather than regulatory inspection. Indeed, in closely regulated industries (banks, stock exchanges, etc.) no warrant is required at all given the intense regulation and reduced expectation of privacy in those industries. *See New York v. Burger*, 482 U.S. 691, 702-03, 107 S. Ct. 2636, 2643-44, 96 L. Ed. 2d 601, 613-14 (1987).

Border Searches Generally

Routine, warrantless searches of persons entering the country are considered reasonable and may be conducted by law enforcement officers without any suspicion whatsoever. *See United States v. Montoya de Hernandez*, 473 U.S. 531, 537-39, 87 L. Ed. 2d 381, 389-91, 105 S. Ct. 3304, 3309-3310 (1985) ("[N]ot only is the expectation of privacy less at the border than in the interior, the Fourth Amendment balance between the interests of the Government and the privacy right of the individual is also struck much more favorably to the Government at the border.") These inspections include cargo, containers, clothing, purses, luggage and the like and may include some physical touching such as patting or lifting of clothing. The officers may also ask questions about citizenship and immigration status at these checkpoints.

After a person has cleared a border search and is no longer present at the border, reasonable suspicion would be required for an officer to seize him a second time for an investigatory stop. Reasonable suspicion would also be required for "roving border patrols" if the person was not at a fixed checkpoint. However, if the person cleared customs but was still physically at the border, an additional routine search or secondary search would ordinarily be permissible without reasonable suspicion. *See, e.g., United States v. Nieves*, 609 F.2d 642, 648 (2d Cir. 1979).

If the search goes beyond routine, it may impact the Fourth Amendment. The setting, the length of detention, the methods employed, the location of the detention, the existence or lack of any exigency, the effect of the search such as leaving children unattended, etc., all impact reasonableness and both parties should consider these types of issues in the viability of challenges to any detentions and searches at the border. Certainly a detention for any significant period of time without access to judicial review or counsel should be challenged as unreasonable by the defense. Even if the motion is ultimately unsuccessful, it could provide valuable discovery to the defense of the facts of the case.

What Constitutes a Border?

"Border" is a more fluid location than might be assumed. For example, checkpoints such as those at airports, which are the equivalent of a border, can fall under the same standards for searches as borders. On the other hand, a checkpoint that is merely near a border might not fall under the same standards. Search of a car 20 miles from the border without probable cause was considered a violation of the Fourth Amendment. *See Almeida-Sanchez v. United States*, 413 U.S. 266, 272-73, 93 S. Ct. 2535, 2539-40, 37 L. Ed. 2d 596, 602-03 (1973).

Neither party should assume that the border is truly a border without thorough investigation of the location; both the border itself and the actual location of the search relative to the checkpoint station, for example. If a search is not directly at a border checkpoint station, defense should challenge the use of the border standards for searches.

Car Searches at the Border

The lesser expectation of privacy at the border coupled with the lesser expectation of privacy in a car, as well as the government's need to protect its borders, has rendered almost any car search at the border "reasonable." The Supreme Court recently reviewed the issue of whether a border officer needed reasonable suspicion to disassemble a gas tank. *United States v. Flores-Montano*, 124 S. Ct. 1582, 158 L. Ed. 2d 311 (2004). The Ninth Circuit had held that this was not routine and therefore required reasonable suspicion. The Supreme Court determined that the issue did not hinge on the notion of routine, but whether such a search was reasonable. The Court emphasized the lessened expectation of privacy and the fact that contraband is frequently carried over the border in gas tanks.

The Supreme Court in *Flores-Montano* left open the possibility that there could be some car searches that were so intrusive as to require some suspicion, perhaps drilling into car doors or engines, but frankly gave every indication that anything less than a junk yard compressor would survive scrutiny. The question of reasonableness of any significant destruction of property such as drilling into the car should still be assessed given that the issue was left open by the Supreme Court.

Body Searches

The Court in *Flores-Montano* also left open the possibility that more personal searches, for example body cavity, strip, full pat down and involuntary x-ray searches, might also be so intrusive as to require some level of suspicion. A number of circuits have upheld strip searches where the officer has reasonable or "real" suspicion that the person at the border is carrying drugs on the body. *See, e.g., United States v. Vance*, 62 F.3d 1152, 1156 (9th Cir. 1995); *United States v. Okeyan*, 786 F.2d 832, 837 (8th Cir. 1986). The Supreme Court, in its decision in *Montoya de Hernandez*, approved of detaining a border suspect where there is reasonable suspicion that he or she is smuggling contraband in a stomach or alimentary canal.

Circuits with a large number of border cases have adopted procedures for handling these kinds of cases. For example, in the Second Circuit, which has two international airports, a suspect may be detained until the person consents to an x-ray or until his body "dispels" the suspicion; however the agents must notify a federal prosecutor within 24 hours of detaining a "suspected swallower," who must then notify a magistrate judge and defense counsel. *See United States v. Esieke*, 940 F.2d 29, 36 (2d Cir. 1991).

Counsel must be aware of the procedures required, if any, in the particular district with respect to swallower cases and other prolonged detention cases. How far can law enforcement go? Is it okay to give the person laxatives with or without a court order, for example? The focus, again, will be on reasonableness balancing governmental need versus intrusion.

CHAPTER SIXTEEN
WIRETAPS AND ELECTRONIC
SURVEILLANCE

The commentary on wiretaps and electronic surveillance is treated in its own chapter given that litigation of wiretaps and certain electronic surveillance involves specialized strategies beyond a typical warrant or standard Fourth Amendment issues.

This chapter provides a brief, workable outline for litigating wiretaps and electronic surveillance; however, this area of the law is extensive and complex. Attorneys are advised to consult any number of specialized treatises that have been written on electronic surveillance, such as *Electronic Surveillance: Commentaries and Statutes*, James A. Adams and Daniel D. Blinka (NITA, 2003).

Furthermore, technological advances bring new Fourth Amendment challenges and judicial interpretations such that the law is constantly changing—seemingly daily. Passage of the "Uniting and Strengthening America by Providing Appropriate Tools Required to Intercept and Obstruct Terrorism Act" known as the USA PATRIOT Act, or simply the Patriot Act, which significantly affected the application and scope of this area of law enforcement investigation, is a notable example.

Effect of the Patriot Act

The passage of the Patriot Act has had a dramatic effect on electronic surveillance, with the government's ability to invade electronic communications being greatly expanded. Although a detailed discussion of the Patriot Act is beyond the scope of these commentaries, counsel must be aware that previous limitations on surveillance may have been broadened considerably under this new legislation. Moreover, although the focus of the act is terrorism and international surveillance, the provisions of the Patriot Act often can be used for general surveillance.

Under the Act, for example, the powers of the Department of Justice have been augmented to allow it to track and gather information by (1) permitting pen registers and trace orders for electronic communications (tracing email addresses for example); (2) authorizing nationwide execution of court orders for pen registers, trap and trace devices and access to stored email or communications records (not content); (3) treating stored voice mail like stored email, falling under the Stored Communications Act, rather than as phone conversations which would mandate the special federal wiretap laws, and (4) allowing officers to intercept communications to and from a trespasser within a computer system (with the permission of the system's owner).

The Patriot Act has also eased restrictions on foreign intelligence gathering in the United States by: (1) permitting roving surveillance without identification of the particular instrument where the target is likely to "thwart identification with particularity"; (2) allowing application for a Foreign Intelligence Service Act surveillance or search order when gathering foreign intelligence is a "significant" reason rather than the sole reason for the request; and (3) authorizing pen registers and trap and trace device orders for email information as well as telephone information.

Title III Surveillance in General

Wiretap and electronic surveillance are covered in a separate statute by Congress: Title III of the Omnibus Crime Control and Safe Streets Act, 18 USC §§ 2510-2522, known in the criminal law community simply as "Title III" or the federal wiretap law. Title III is essentially an eavesdropping statute that authorizes the "seizure" of wire, electronic and oral communications provided certain requirements are met. *See* 18 USC § 2511.

The statute is detailed and formulaic. It must be read carefully. There are a number of rather "picky" requirements that can mean the difference between suppression and admissions, *e.g.*, whether the Attorney General or other listed official has authorized the surveillance. *See, e.g.*, 18 USC § 2516(1). Due to the specialized requirements, much of the litigation in electronic surveillance involves Title III issues and the majority of this chapter is devoted to those litigation strategies which go beyond the standard Fourth Amendment issues discussed in other chapters of this book.

Title III requirements apply when law enforcement seeks to intercept "the aural or other acquisition of the contents of any wire, electronic, or oral communication through the use of any electronic, mechanical, or other device." 18 USC § 2510(4). This means a listening device (the guy with the big headphones in the unmarked van down the street), but also can include interception of electronic communications over a digital-display paging device. *See* 18 USC § 2511(1)(a); § 2510(12); § 2518.

Title III does not apply to stored electronic communications such as pen registers and trap and trace devices where the contents of a message are not revealed. Electronic mail or "email" is covered by a separate statutory scheme at 18 USC §§ 2701-2711 as discussed below. Pen registers and trap and trace devices, which record the numbers dialed by or to a telephone without revealing the actual contents of a phone call, are covered by a separate statute as well: 18 USC § 3121 et. seq. A pen register order may be issued if the information sought is merely relevant to an ongoing criminal investigation, though there are procedures similar to Title III which must be followed. Mobile tracking devices are not covered under Title III but rather 18 USC § 3117. Section 3117 simply states that a court is empowered to issue a warrant or other order for the installation of a mobile tracking device.

Title III protections do not apply to conversations or communications where one of the participants has consented to the interception, referred to as "consensual recordings." Such consensual recordings do not violate the Fourth Amendment. *See United States v. White*, 401 U.S. 745, 751-53, 91 S. Ct. 1122, 1126-27, 28 L. Ed. 2d 453, 458-59 (1971). This means that law enforcement need not seek a special wire tap order or any authorization for an officer or an informant to wear a recording device or "wire" during a drug deal, for example.

Surveillance done in the ordinary course of business, including the ordinary course of business in law enforcement, does not require Title III authorization. Typical course of business surveillance would be an alarm company surveillance, surveillance at prisons, or surveillance at a police station like the recording of 911 calls.

Title III does not specifically address video surveillance, which is generally analyzed under ordinary Fourth Amendment principles. In some circumstances a warrant for such surveillance may be required and some courts have demanded that the warrant meet the more rigorous standards of Title III. *See, e.g., United v. Biasucci,* 786 F.2d 504, 508 (2d Cir. 1986) (applying Title III requirements to video surveillance warrant including minimization and time limitations).

Surveillance of cellphones is somewhat complicated because in some instances cellphones can be used as tracking devices by virtue of locating and tracking cell-data as opposed to surveillance of actual conversations. When used as a tracking device, and to the extent they provide information to which someone does not have a reasonable expectation of privacy, such as location on a public highway, there is no Fourth Amendment violation. If a beeper is used to track devices or people within a home or other area where there is an expectation of privacy, the Fourth Amendment is implicated.

Similarly, if information that would be obtained from a cellphone involves an expectation of privacy and implicates the Fourth Amendment, prior court order would be required in order to install a tracking device. When the surveillance is of the content of the phone call itself, Title III is implicated as electronic surveillance of oral communications. Indeed, certain Title III legislation was compelled by the advent of cellphones and cordless phones which, technologically, are far easier to intercept than a standard phone line. *See Bartnicki v. Vopper,* 532 U.S. 514, 523-24, 121 S. Ct. 1753, 1759-60, 149 L. Ed. 2d 787, 799 (2001). Title III was specifically amended in 1994 to cover remote or cordless phones. The Supreme Court has definitely recognized that surveillance of cellphone and cordless phone conversations fall under Title III. *Id.*

The Application for Electronic Surveillance under Title III

Generally speaking, electronic surveillance of telephone conversations is usually referred to as a wiretap, and electronic surveillance to record conversations in a place (*e.g.* a room or a car) is usually referred to as a "bug." Because both types of interception are considered "seizures," Fourth Amendment principles apply.

Before an order to intercept communications under Title III can be issued, very specific procedures must be followed by government attorneys; for example, a specified Justice Department official must grant an approval even to make the application for electronic surveillance, and there are a number of subsequent security measures with which the government must comply.

As a defense attorney, the first thing you must do when you learn that there has been electronic surveillance in a case is to request discovery so that you can determine whether you have a basis to challenge the interception/seizure of your client's communications. You should specifically ask for the applications for the electronic surveillance orders and any applications for extensions of those orders. These applications should contain a recitation that the statutory requirements have been complied with. The sections below will help you understand what to look for when you review these applications.

Attorney General Approval. As mentioned, the statute requires that an application for electronic surveillance be authorized by the Attorney General or other deputy Attorney General as listed in 18 USC § 2516(1). In reviewing the application, you should look for the Attorney General's approval and make sure the appropriate official signed the approval.

Identification. The government must "identify the person, if known, committing the offense and whose communications are to be intercepted." 18 USC § 2518(1)(b)(iv). Basically this means that the government has to list the people who are the targets of the surveillance (those believed to be engaged in the criminal activity) and whose conversations will be intercepted. The government can list "possible interceptees" and others "unknown."

If a person is discovered during the surveillance who was not previously listed but who is determined to be engaged in criminal activity through the interceptions, that person will be listed in subsequent applications for extensions of the surveillance order, and the interception will ordinarily be upheld. Identification issues rarely result in suppression of the communications if there is probable cause to believe the person is involved in criminal activity as a result of the interceptions.

Duration. Court orders authorizing a wiretap are usually for an initial period of 30 days—the initial maximum period allowed. The government typically will then make a series of applications for extensions of the order. If a person not previously named as a target is intercepted during the first 30 days, but is not named as a target in the extension, this omission could provide a basis for challenging the interception of that person's later conversations.

Necessity. Title III requires a "full and complete statement as to whether or not other investigative procedures have been tried and failed or why they reasonably appear to be unlikely to succeed if tried or to be too dangerous." 18 USC § 2518(1)(c). This is one of the more fruitful areas of defense litigation. Title III applications should not be routine, and should be thought of as a "last resort," where traditional investigative techniques have been unsuccessful or are too dangerous to attempt. The purpose of the alternative investigative techniques provision "is to guarantee that wiretapping or bugging occurs only when there is a genuine need for it." *Dalia v. United States*, 441 U.S. 238, 250, 99 S. Ct. 1682, 1689, 60 L. Ed. 2d 177, 188 (1979). Strict compliance with § 2518(l)(c) is essential "to assure that wiretapping is not resorted to in situations where traditional investigative technique would suffice to expose the crime." *United States v. Kahn*, 415 U.S. 143, 153 n.12, 94 S. Ct. 977, 983 n.12, 39 L. Ed. 2d 225, 236 n.12 (1974).

Typically, a section of the application is titled "Alternative Investigative Techniques Have Been Exhausted." Applications rarely list more than the same boilerplate language used in every application. The defense attorney should review this section carefully to determine whether the government ever attempted, let alone exhausted, alternative investigative techniques such as the use of informants, pen registers, search warrants and grand jury subpoenas, to name just a few. For example, did the government rush to conduct the most drastic invasion of privacy first, before even trying to obtain consensual recordings of the targets' conversations with informants?

Probable Cause. The government must show that there is probable cause to believe that: 1) an individual has committed an enumerated crime; 2) communication relevant to the offense will be intercepted; and 3) the facilities to be surveilled are or were being used in furtherance of criminal conduct. 18 USC § 2518(3)(a). The standard is totality of the circumstances and challenges to probable cause for wiretaps are the same as for any other warrant. *See Chapter Five: Probable Cause and Chapter Six: Warrants.*

Remember that to obtain a search warrant the government must establish that evidence of a crime is likely to be found in a particular place; to obtain a wiretap or bug, the government must show that conversations about a crime are likely to occur over a particular telephone or in a particular place. It is not enough for the government to show that the targets of the investigation often communicate by telephone; the government must also provide probable cause to believe that the targets communicate over the particular telephone to be tapped or the place to be bugged. In short, probable cause is required as to "person, crime, conversation, and place or facility of communication." *See United States v. Bianco*, 998 F.2d 1112, 1121 (2d Cir., 1993), cert. denied, ___ U.S. ___, 114 S. Ct. 1644. Compliance with all prongs of this test is essential under both 18 USC §§ 2518(a)–(d) and the Fourth Amendment.

An exception to the particularity-as-to-place requirement for probable cause occurs when the government establishes, pursuant to 18 USC §2518(11) that "there is probable cause to believe that the person's actions could have the effect of thwarting interception from a specified facility." In such cases, the government applies for something called a "roving bug," which allows officers to eavesdrop on conversations that they have probable cause to believe will occur, but they do not know, at the time of the application, when or where. Counsel should be aware that a roving wiretap must be authorized by a senior Justice Department official at the level of Assistant Attorney General or higher; other wiretaps only require a designated Deputy Assistant Attorney General.

A typical situation requiring a roving bug occurs where there is a wiretap and it appears that that the targets are conscious of surveillance, so they do not talk openly over the telephone but instead arrange meetings at frequently changing locations. The government monitors the telephone conversations to ascertain the place and time of the meetings, and, pursuant to a "roving bug" warrant, the government is authorized to "bug" the meeting site without prior authorization as to the specific place. Although such warrants have been upheld, defense counsel should still consider challenging the surveillance as a kind of prohibited general warrant that the Supreme Court criticized in *Berger v. New York,* 388 U.S. 41, 59, 87 S. Ct. 1873, 1883-84, 18 L. Ed. 2d 1040, 1052 (1967)—the general seizure of "conversations of any and all persons coming into the area covered by the device ... indiscriminately and without regard to their connection to the crime under investigation."

With respect to cell phones, the surveillance order typically authorizes surveillance of a specific telephone identified by its serial number, regardless of whether the telephone number is changed. The order will state that it applies to any changed number subsequently assigned to or used by the instrument identified by its serial number. This order does not constitute a "roving wiretap" because the location is fixed in the sense that the phone is identified even if the telephone number is changed.

Enumerated Offenses. The list of offenses for which an electronic surveillance order can be issued is lengthy and includes most major federal crimes. In reviewing the application, the defense attorney should compare the crimes mentioned in the surveillance application to those listed in the statute, *see generally*, 18 USC § 2516, to ascertain whether electronic surveillance is authorized to investigate the offenses mentioned in the application.

The list of offenses includes just about any federal offense a defendant can be charged with in federal court, with the notable exceptions of tax evasion, certain interstate racketeering acts such as transportation of gambling paraphernalia and certain health care frauds. Check the list in every case.

The requirement that the offense be one listed as an enumerated offense is very specific and clear in the statute. Although some federal courts have found that if the offense under investigation is related to an enumerated offense it is authorized, other courts have rejected such an argument. Similarly, some courts have applied the good faith exception of Leon for warrants involving non-enumerated offenses, while others have rejected good faith since the warrant is arguably facially invalid and a law enforcement officer should be familiar with the enumerated offenses when applying for and executing any warrant. Counsel must familiarize themselves with the law in their individual jurisdictions on these issues.

A court may not authorize a wiretap to investigate a crime not enumerated under § 2516; however, communications regarding a non-2516 crime gathered pursuant to a valid wiretap may be used by the prosecution in certain jurisdictions if a court finds that the original wiretap warrant was sought "in good faith and not as a subterfuge search, and that the communication was in fact intercepted incidentally during the course of a lawfully executed order". *See, e.g., United States v. McKinnon*, 721 F.2d 19, 22 (1st Cir. 1983); *United States v. Vento*, 533 F.2d 838, 855 (3d Cir. 1976). To use these incidental communications as evidence, the government must obtain authorization by applying to a court for an order pursuant to the provisions of 18 USC § 2517(5).

Jurisdiction

A federal district court judge may enter an *ex parte* order "authorizing or approving interception of wire, oral, or electronic communications within the territorial jurisdiction of the court in which the judge is sitting." 18 USC § 2518(3). (Magistrate Judges are not permitted to make such determinations under the statute, but given the broadening of Magistrate Judge roles, it is likely that Magistrate Judges may soon have that authority just as they are now able to take guilty pleas for felonies.)

For the district judge in Brooklyn, for example, wiretap jurisdiction is the Eastern District of New York. The key, however, is what constitutes "interception" for the purpose of jurisdiction, which is a two-way street. Jurisdiction exists where the interception is received or where the conversation takes place. So as long as the interception is received in the Eastern District of New York, there is jurisdiction even though the communications occur in an entirely different district.

Minimization

Of great concern in electronic surveillance is the interception of conversations that are for benign or innocent purposes. Law enforcement is required to avoid such interceptions or "minimize" such intrusions as it is called. Thus, even though an application has been judicially approved, the government must still comply with the various "minimization" requirements under Title III. *See* 18 USC § 2518(5). Primarily, minimization means that the government must ensure that innocent communications or conversations that do not fall within the scope of the Title III warrant are not intruded upon.

Courts are fairly indulgent with respect to otherwise innocent conversations where the officers believed the interceptees were using codes, such as "shoes" for drugs or "bread" for money. The degree of minimization required depends on the facts of a specific case and the context of the conversation. If the calls are brief and involve ambiguous language, the courts will uphold the interceptions even though they are eventually determined to be outside the scope of the order.

The Supreme Court has cautioned that interception of "non-pertinent calls" is less tolerated in the later stages of the investigation, after surveillance has been conducted for some time. Once surveillance has been going for a while, the monitoring agents should be able to recognize speakers and codes, and have less of an excuse for listening to obviously non-pertinent conversations. *See Scott v. United States*, 436 U.S. 128, 140, 98 S. Ct. 1717, 1724, 56 L. Ed. 2d 168, 179 (1978).

If communications are in a foreign language, they can be intercepted and interpreted at a later time without undermining the warrant. Minimization must still be accomplished, however, in the translation process. Section 2518(5) permits after-the-fact minimization of conversations conducted either in code or in a foreign language, where an expert is not reasonably available during the interception. Under those circumstances, however, the invasion of privacy is mitigated by the fact that the coded or foreign language conversations are not comprehensible to those initially recording them. When a person with the expertise to understand the conversations subsequently listens, minimization is required, and the interpreter or expert must stop listening to a tape once she determines that the conversation is beyond the scope of the investigation. *See United States v. David*, 940 F.2d 722, 730 (1st Cir. 1991).

The defense attorney should check to make sure the wiretap application contains a provision for minimization procedures and that the orders themselves direct minimization. The problem with minimization motions, however, is that the remedy for the defense is suppression of non-pertinent conversations, unlikely to be offered into evidence by the prosecution anyway. If, however, the defense can show that lack of minimization was so systemic that the government essentially violated the court's order regarding minimization, then a broader suppression motion can be made. The point of minimization is that it prevents the eavesdropping warrant from becoming a "general warrant."

Extensions and Amendments

The statute requires that a wiretapping order authorize interceptions for a period "no longer than is necessary to achieve the objective of the authorization, nor in any event longer than thirty days." Typically, the government applies for a series of thirty-day extensions of the order. Each extension requires a separate application and a showing of continued probable cause. If new targets are ascertained during the previous thirty days, they are added to the application.

The extension applications are useful because they summarize the previous thirty days of interceptions and disclose the government's view of the incriminating nature of the conversations. Some courts order that the government file "ten-day reports," summarizing the interceptions at ten-day intervals. These reports will often become the substance of the extension application.

A court order can amend an application if it determines that other offenses not included in the original application were involved. The contents of such conversations cannot be disclosed until the court approves an amendment of the original order. This requirement ensures that the wiretap application is not some sort of subterfuge for other offenses and that the other crimes were intercepted incidentally during the course of a valid wiretap authorization.

The defense attorney should review each and every extension or amended application to make sure all of the statutory requirements have been maintained and that there is probable cause to continue the surveillance or to amend the authorization. The government cannot just apply for an extension on the basis that they have not intercepted anything interesting yet, but they are sure it will turn up. If no pertinent conversations are intercepted during any thirty day period, that is a pretty good basis to conclude that probable cause is lacking either because no crime is being committed or because the particular telephone is not being used for criminal purposes, and the surveillance should be terminated.

Finally, defense counsel should check to make sure that the extension orders are contiguous in terms of time; if there are time gaps, then any monitoring that occurred after one order expired and before another took effect was unlawful. Similarly, if authorization must be amended, it needs to be done "as soon as practicable." 18 USC § 2517(5).

Other Discovery

In addition to the affidavits and applications discussed above, defense counsel should make sure to ask the government for the ten-day reports. Again, these can provide information as to whether the government is complying with the requirements of the statute. Prosecutors often resist providing the reports and judges will ordinarily not require disclosure at the time in the absence of a particularized reason.

Defense counsel should also ask for "line sheets" which are the agents' contemporaneous summaries of the interceptions. These are useful in order to locate conversations that do not seem to be minimized—defense counsel can then listen to those specific conversations to make a minimization argument.

Post-Surveillance Requirements

Sealing. Title III requires that, upon expiration of a wiretap order, the tapes be given to a judge for immediate sealing. *See* 18 USC § 2518(8)(a). In order to disclose surveyed conversations, the statute requires that there either be a seal or a "satisfactory explanation for the absence" of one. *Id.* The rationale behind the sealing requirement is to ensure the "integrity" of the tapes and limit the government's ability to alter them. *See United States v. Ojeda Rios*, 495 U.S. 257, 263, 110 S. Ct. 1845, 1849, 109 L. Ed. 2d 224, 234 (1990).

The meaning of "immediate" is often a source for litigation. One or two days are ordinarily acceptable. Anything beyond that should be considered too long and the defense should make a motion to suppress on the basis of lack of immediate sealing. Take a careful look at the dates when the interceptions ended and the dates of the sealing orders which you should receive as part of discovery.

Whether a delay will be upheld will usually depend on the reason for the delay and whether there was any "flouting" of the requirements. The flouting is generally easy for a prosecutor to avoid with a careful explanation of the reason for the delay, although it will depend on the amount of time elapsed. Explanations for delays such as heavy prosecutor workload or unavailability of a judge have been upheld. However, where the delay is a matter of months without explanation, the court has suppressed. *See, e.g., United States v. Gigante*, 538 F.2d 502, 507 (2d Cir. 1976) (suppression where there was more than an eight month delay and no satisfactory explanation).

Inventory Notice. Once a wiretap has been terminated or an extension application has been denied, an "inventory notice" must be served within 90 days upon the persons named in the warrant or others determined to be necessary by a judge. 18 USC § 2518(3)(d). The notice sets forth (1) the fact of the application; (2) the dates of the surveillance or the denial; and (3) whether interceptions occurred. The rationale underlying the notice is to "assure the community that the wiretap technique is reasonably employed..." *United States v. Donovan*, 429 U.S. 413, 439, 97 S. Ct. 658, 674, 50 L. Ed. 2d 652, 675 (1977). Failure to provide the inventory is not ordinarily grounds for suppression unless the target can show prejudice. *Id.* at 438-39, 97 S. Ct. at 673-74, 50 L. Ed. 2d at 674-75.

Disclosure

Disclosure of intercepted communications is permitted under Title III by law enforcement officials under specified circumstances, most commonly in the investigation and prosecution of enumerated federal offenses. Any other disclosure not provided for in the statute could constitute grounds for imposition of a civil penalty under § 2520 of the statute. Counsel should review the permissible disclosures if there is any indication that disclosure was made beyond the criminal case, *see generally*, 18 USC § 2517, although improper disclosure is very rare.

Suppression

Title III specifically provides for suppression of an intercepted communication in violation of Title III by an "aggrieved person." 18 USC § 2518(10). An "aggrieved person" is one who "was a party to any intercepted wire, oral, or electronic communication or a person against whom the interception was directed." In other words, all the participants in the conversations and the targets named in the electronic surveillance orders have standing to challenge the surveillance. In reality, the standing provision has been held synonymous with the ordinary Fourth Amendment standing requirements. *See Alderman v. United States*, 394 U.S. 165, 175-76 n. 9, 89 S. Ct. 961, 968 n. 9, 22 L. Ed. 2d 176, 188 n.9 (1969).

Those who own premises subject to a telephone wiretap or a bug have standing even if they were not part of the conversations and may also challenge the legality of the entry to install the electronic device. Targets who are named in the orders and whose communications were intercepted, but who do not have privacy interests in the premises or the telephone used, may challenge the probable cause underlying the warrant, but would not generally have standing to challenge minimization of conversations other than their own.

A motion to suppress must be made pretrial or prior to any proceeding where the evidence will be used unless the basis for the motion was unknown to the movant. 18 USC § 2518(10). Failure to make the motion can constitute a waiver.

Title III lists three grounds for suppression:

(i) the communication was unlawfully intercepted;

(ii) the order of authorization or approval under which it was intercepted is insufficient on its face; or

(iii) the interception was not made in conformity with the order of authorization or approval.

18 USC § 2518(10)(a).

Unlawful interception as a grounds for suppression requires that the violation be of a Title III provision that plays "a central role" in the statutory framework. *See United States v. Giordano*, 416 U.S. 505, 528, 94 S. Ct. 1820, 1832, 40 L. Ed. 2d 341, 360 (1974). For example, if law enforcement failed to obtain the necessary authorization suppression would be proper. If the authorization was not supported by probable cause suppression would be proper. However, if the officers omitted the name of a person on an application where there was probable cause to believe that person would be on the call, suppression would not be imposed. Identification errors are usually not a ground for suppression.

Insufficient on its face means that the warrant can be determined to be illegal without resorting to extrinsic facts. A non-enumerated offense could constitute facial invalidity. In determining whether a warrant is insufficient on its face, the court looks to the warrant itself and not to extrinsic factors in determining whether it is or is not sufficient.

Lack of conformity is a scope issue for the most part. Did the interception go beyond the area or persons approved. Did the officers fail to minimize as required by the authorizing warrant. If an eavesdropping warrant specifies minimization procedures and hours of interception, any surveillance conducted without minimization procedures in place or outside the authorized time frame would not have been done in conformity with the order, providing a basis for suppression.

Exclusion of the evidence is the remedy for a violation of Title as provided in the statute: *see*, 18 USC § 2515: "no part of the contents of such communication…may be received in evidence." The statute also creates a fruit of the poisonous tree exclusion: "no evidence derived therefrom may be received in evidence." *Id.* If a wiretap is determined to be illegal, evidence derived from the warrant would be precluded. For example, if extensions or amendments were obtained as a result of information derived from the original warrant, conversations taken through those extensions and amendments would be inadmissible.

If the evidence is not derived from the unlawful authorization or was independently obtained, the evidence may be received despite the tainted authorization. The burden is on the government, as with other "fruit" issues, to show that the evidence is untainted. Although derivative evidence is precluded from use in court it can sometimes be used by law enforcement for specific duties, *see, e.g.,* 18 USC §§ 2517(1)&(2), including such things as witness preparation.

18 USC § 3504(a)(1) provides that when an aggrieved party challenges evidence in a proceeding that was derived from an illegal wiretap, the government must "affirm or deny the occurrence of the alleged unlawful act." The prosecution will not be required to respond to such a request if it is determined to be based on mere suspicion.

For additional discussion on exclusion of evidence, *see Chapter Seven: The Exclusionary Rule.*

A Title III Checklist

In every wiretap case, the defense attorney should go through a checklist of things to look for in the discovery materials. At a minimum, that check list should include:

1) **The Attorney General's Authorization:**

    a) was there prior approval?

    b) did the proper official approve the application?

2) **Applications:** The electronic surveillance application usually consists of affirmations by a prosecutor and a law enforcement agent and should be checked for the following:

    a) is there probable cause as to an offense enumerated in the statute?

    b) is there probable cause that conversations would occur over a particular telephone or in a particular place?

    b) were alternative investigative techniques exhausted?

    c) is there a provision addressing minimization procedures so that the eavesdropping warrant does not become a "general" warrant?

3) **Extensions:**

    a) is there continuing probable cause?

    b) have the previous interceptees been named as targets in the extension applications?

4) **The Orders:**

    a) what procedures were required and were they complied with?

    b) were there any limitations?

5) **Reviewing the Tapes:** Of course, defense counsel must also review the tapes and transcripts of the tapes for minimization, compliance with the terms of the Orders and to determine whether the government represented the substance of the conversations accurately in the extension applications.

6) **Sealing Orders:**

    a) was sealing accomplished?

    b) was there a delay?

If, in reviewing the materials, any irregularities appear, there might be a basis to challenge the orders and suppress the fruits of the surveillance.

The Internet and Email

Electronic mail or "email" is covered by a separate statutory scheme at 18 USC §§ 2701-2711 known as the "Stored Communications Act." The formal requirements of Title III do not apply when law enforcement wishes to intercept or obtain email from a service provider. To obtain the contents of an email ordinarily requires a warrant or a special court order under the Stored Communications Act.

A warrant is required for emails stored with a service provider for less than 180 days. For emails stored for more than 180 days, if no prior notice is given to the subscriber a warrant is required. If prior notice is given to the subscriber, a lesser warrant may be obtained such as a grand jury subpoena or a court order if the governmental entity offers "specific and articulable facts showing that there are reasonable grounds to believe that the contents are relevant and material to an ongoing criminal investigation." 18 USC § 2704(d). A governmental entity may request that such records be preserved pending the issuance of a court order up to 180 days. 18 USC § 2704(f)(2). The government can obtain subscriber information (not email contents) including name, address, telephone number, length of service, and payment information through lesser showings including administrative warrants. *See, e.g.,* 18 USC § 2704(c).

Email messages that have not been sent and are kept on a personal computer in a home are protected by the Fourth Amendment and subject to general analysis under this amendment. However, email that has been sent to a third party and received by that third party (in other words not still stored solely with the server) generally does not implicate the Fourth Amendment because there is usually no expectation of privacy once the email is sent and received by a third-party. It will depend on whether efforts are made to retain the privacy of the communication and whether the expectation of privacy is a reasonable one.

Use of the Internet (a term in this chapter to mean generally the Internet system and the World Wide Web together) to display or search a Web site even from a home computer, does not ordinarily implicate the Fourth Amendment because there is generally no expectation of privacy on readily accessible public sites. If a Web site on the Web is secured and there are notifications regarding security and confidentiality an expectation of privacy may be created at least with respect to the information kept in that Web site.

Information transmitted to a third party through the Internet such as a bank or a business ordinarily loses its expectation of privacy once transmitted depending on the circumstances. Information on a home computer obtained by a private source such as a hacker, does not implicate the Fourth Amendment without some proof that the private person is acting as an agent of the government.

Ordinarily there is some privacy expectation in an office computer, but it will depend on whether there are office policies and practices that would diminish that privacy interest. For example, privacy disclaimers or notices of employer audits of computer use would subject a person to searches of computer files and use of the Internet without a warrant even if the employer were the federal government if the search had to do with work related violations.

The actual "surfing" of public Web sites would not usually implicate the Fourth Amendment. Indeed, many Web sites place markers or "cookies" on a computer in order to track that user on other Web sites owned by that site or to provide an easy marker for the user to return to a site. The legal question that is typically litigated with respect to these cookies is whether placing such cookies violates the "Electronic Communications Protection Act" or "ECPA" which makes it a crime to intentionally intercept electronic communications without authorization or consent. Cookies that do not result in interception of an electronic communication are not violative of the ECPA by definition. Internet Service Providers are not permitted to reveal subscriber information to the government without proper warrant or court order; however, they are ordinarily permitted to reveal such information to non-government entities unless precluded by contract or other agreement.

If the user consents to the cookies (sometimes done implicitly through use of the site or explicitly) there is no violation of the ECPA even if the result of the cookie is to intercept information. If there is no consent and there is interception as defined under the ECPA, the question becomes whether there is tortuous intent to intercept electronic communications. In sum, the "cookies" issue is less one of Fourth Amendment import, unless the cookies were being planted by government sites with the intent to obtain information that would otherwise require a warrant, than whether the site placing the cookies (usually done for business purposes anyway) violates the ECPA subjecting the site to criminal and civil sanctions. Indeed, nearly all of the litigation involving cookies is brought through civil actions seeking restraining orders and monetary damages.

CHAPTER SEVENTEEN
FOURTH AMENDMENT ISSUES AND
CLIENT/AGENT INTERVIEWS

Fourth Amendment concerns should be addressed at the initial client and agent interviews. The sooner the agent and client are questioned about these issues the better. Memories fade and minor details might be forgotten later which could turn out to be crucial, such as what the officer said exactly, his tone of voice and where he was standing. Even if the defense lawyer is uncertain whether there was evidence taken or any reason to move to suppress evidence, she should gather the facts from the client at the first opportunity to have in her file, since most motions to suppress ordinarily are not filed until much later after the arrest. Defense attorneys should also advise their client (if the client is literate and able to write) to sit down and recollect everything he or she can about the incident. This information is protected by the attorney client privilege and is not available to the prosecution as impeachment material even if the client testifies. *See* FRCrP 26.2(a).

It is also important for prosecutors to interview arresting officers for similar information to assess whether any search or seizure raises Fourth Amendment concerns. Case agents typically file a report, known in federal circles as a 302, and this information will become available to the defense if the agent testifies. Any other written statement about the events made by a prosecution witness who will testify will also become available to the defense for the purposes of impeachment and cross examination, under 18 USC § 3500, the Jencks Act. Prosecutors should avoid having agents "create" such Jencks material unnecessarily by confining the details of the arrest and any search to the report. *See also, Chapter Twenty One: Fourth Amendment and Discovery Issues.*

In some cases, particularly where there was a stop of a vehicle, the officer may have videotaped the interaction, and counsel can more easily assess what occurred. However, given that only some cases will have a videotape and the tape will still not capture everything that transpired or all of the words, it is still critical to interview about the events as soon as possible.

Client/Agent Interviews Generally

Before interviewing, it is a good idea for counsel to review *Chapter Two: Search and Seizure Law and Chapter Five: Issues of Standing.* Knowing the legal framework will help when eliciting the necessary facts during the interview to assess the viability of Fourth Amendment claims and to support or challenge the search or seizure.

Through the client or agent the lawyer should, at a minimum, discover the following list of information. (This list is certainly not meant as a script and is certainly not exhaustive. However, it is a good starting place with topic areas designed to assist the attorney in discovering the actual facts necessary to make such Fourth Amendment determinations.)

Seizure Issues:

How was the defendant stopped?
What did the defendant do before and during the stop?
What did the officers do?
Where was the defendant stopped?
How long was the stop?
Other facts showing whether a person would reasonably believe he was free to leave.

Search Issues:

Was anything taken by the officers?
How did the officers get those things?
Did they have a warrant?
When were the things taken relative to the arrest?
Where were the things when they were taken?
Did the defendant have a reasonable expectation of privacy in the area searched?
Did the defendant have a reasonable expectation of privacy in the thing seized?

Interviewing Tips

Formatting questions. There are many ways to ask a question to get at a particular answer. For example, when asking a client about *Miranda* warnings the questions might be:

a) Did the officer give you *Miranda* warnings? or

b) Did the officer read you your rights? or

c) Did the officer tell you that you had a right to remain silent, a right to an attorney and that if you could not afford one, one would be provided to you? or

d) What did the officer say to you after he placed you in hand-cuffs?

Each of the above questions is aimed at assessing whether the defendant was advised of her *Miranda* warnings but the answers given might be very different, depending on the level of sophistication and legal knowledge of the client. Some of the questions assume knowledge on the part of the client which might not always be accurate. In general, open but directed questions are best to avoid misleading responses such as the questions asked in "c" and "d."

In most cases, the attorney should avoid questioning the client and even the agent using technical or legal language. It is the rare client who will be able to answer whether the officers had "probable cause" or whether the client had a "reasonable expectation of privacy." Even clients who think they know such answers are unlikely to have gone to law school and recently practiced as criminal lawyers, thus, their answers to technical legal questions should not be relied upon despite any professed expertise. Similarly, arresting officers are not necessarily well-versed in Fourth Amendment jurisprudence (which is subject to change) and might have honestly believed there was probable cause even if the information relied on by the officer was, under the law, insufficient.

Both prosecutors and defense lawyers need to get at the actual facts through directed open ended questions to assess the answers in a Fourth Amendment context, rather than rely on the client or agent to make a legal determination which he or she might not be qualified to make. Even when a sophisticated client or agent with great knowledge of the law is interviewed, it is still the duty of counsel to obtain the factual information and make his or her own legal conclusions as the attorney on the case.

Interviewing Techniques. The key is for the client or agent to provide the facts of any search and seizure as neutrally and accurately as possible. One technique is to advise the client or agent to tell the lawyer what happened as if there had been a video camera strapped to her. Questions should be directed but open. "I want to know what you saw and what you heard when the officers seized your bag." "I want to know what you and your fellow officers said when the bag was seized."

Tell the client or agent to avoid conclusions. "He violated my rights" is not very helpful to the lawyer. "He walked up to me and took my purse away," is more helpful. If the client or agent starts to use conclusory statements, it is essential for the lawyer to go back to those conclusions and get the underlying facts. "Now you said the officer violated your rights, what did he do?" Even non-conclusory language will often need more detail. "You said the officer walked up and took your purse away, what did he say before he took your purse? How did he take your purse? Show me."

When questioning officers the focus is from the other direction but the openness of the questions is the same; "you say you had probable cause to arrest, what did you observe that showed probable cause to arrest?" and "what did you say to the suspect before taking her purse?"

Attorneys might be tempted to "lead" the client or agent to a particular answer. "You never told him he could look in your bag, did you?" "The suspect told you it was okay to look in her purse, didn't she?" Aside from obvious ethical problems with this strategy, practically such tactics cause bigger problems than they solve. Importantly, the lawyer will lack the actual facts of the case from one of the few people who was present. On a basic interviewing level, suggesting answers is confusing to the interviewee.

The client or agent might try to "help" the case and give worse answers than the actual facts. It is far better to obtain a neutral but accurate picture than an ostensible "helpful" spin that turns out to be unfounded in fact.

That being said, there is nothing unethical in advising the client that the prosecution must obtain evidence lawfully, and that if the officers lacked a warrant there might be a basis to keep the evidence from trial. It is also appropriate for the prosecutor to advise the arresting officer that it is important that the seizure and subsequent search be lawful. Contextualizing the information can assist the client and the agent in understanding why the facts are important and why they should not leave out seemingly minor details.

The lawyer must strike a balance between asking for enough context to show the importance of certain facts and having the client or agent focus too much on a particular issue, rather than giving all of the facts as neutrally and accurately as possible. The more specific and detailed the facts, the easier it will be for the lawyer to sort through them for the ones that could raise Fourth Amendment issues. "I need to know exactly what the officer said and how he said it when he asked for your license." "I need to know exactly what you said to the suspect and how the suspect responded when you asked for the license."

It is usually advisable to let the client or agent go through generally what happened without much interruption at the outset. Interrupting can throw the narrator off and cause him or her to forget or skip over key parts. Once the client or agent has gone through the whole situation, the lawyer can then go back to the particular areas which require more detail or expansion.

If the narrative is particularly long, it is often helpful to interject at the end of a particular area or "chapter" of the narrative (what happened before the arrest, for example) to seek specific details, but then allow the narrator to continue with his version on the next section of events so as not to loose too much flow or important details with interruptions. Criminal case narratives often fall into easy chapters for retelling, such as: what happened before the officers arrived, what happened when the officers encountered the defendant, what happened at the time of the arrest, what happened after the arrest, etc. Counsel can even suggest retelling the events with those divisions in mind.

Finally, it is also useful at the end of the interview to have the client or agent think of anything else that happened that did not come out during the interview even if the client or agent might not think it is important. It is surprising how often this question brings out useful information. "Oh, I forgot, there was another officer with a police dog who came up to the scene right before I was handcuffed."

Interviews and Specific Seizure Questions

How was the defendant stopped?

The mechanics and details of the stop or encounter are essential. In order to constitute a seizure the person must have reasonably not felt free to leave. An officer may approach someone on the street and ask questions even asking to search the person. It is not a seizure if the person is free to disregard the police and continue "going about one's business." *See Illinois v. Wardlow*, 528 U.S. 119, 125, 120 S. Ct. 673, 676, 145 L. Ed. 2d 570, 577 (2000). But if the officer, through a show of authority or use of physical force, restrains that person's liberty, she has been seized for Fourth Amendment purposes. *See Terry v. Ohio*, 329 U.S. 1, 20, 88 S. Ct. 1868, 1879, 20 L. Ed. 2d 889, 905, n.16 (1968); *see also, Chapter Eight: Investigatory Detentions.*

Focusing on "the stop" or the encounter with officers rather than "the arrest" is important when questioning the client as well as when questioning the agent. A stop where someone does not feel free to leave requires at least reasonable suspicion and possibly probable cause if the intrusiveness of the seizure amounts effectively to a formal arrest.

If the attorney asks the client whether he was under arrest, such a question technically calls for a legal conclusion. Either a yes or a no answer will be of little value without the underlying reasons. If the attorney's questions focus solely on "how were you arrested?" the client might dwell on the moment handcuffs were snapped on or rights administered and not other essential factors that could show a seizure well before the client was handcuffed. The lawyer could lose vital information surrounding the stop.

The term "stop" might also need clarification. If this was a pull-over in a car, the client is likely to understand the question, how did the police stop you? Or the client might respond that they were already "stopped" in that they were standing on the corner, meaning they were not physically moving. The follow up question could then be, "When did you first encounter the police officers. Tell me what happened? When did you first see them?"

The more effective means of obtaining information from the client, in order to assess Fourth Amendment seizure issues, is to tease out all of the facts of the initial stop up to the formal arrest. It might have been that an officer came up to the defendant on a street and inquired whether he could ask some questions and then placed the defendant up against a wall. It might be that the officer had an arrest warrant, knocked on the door, the defendant stepped out and the police put on handcuffs. It might be that the defendant was pulled over by the officer while driving in his car along the highway and a patrol car stopped in front of his car and another pulled up from behind.

What did the defendant do before and during the stop?

A police officer may come up to a person on the street and ask questions as any ordinary citizen without any suspicion at all. The police may also detain someone for investigative purposes if they have reasonable suspicion as to criminal activity by that person. The police may also place someone under arrest officially or perform the functional equivalent of a formal arrest if the police have probable cause to believe the person committed a crime. Counsel must ascertain what facts were known to the officer at the time of the seizure including what conduct by the defendant was observed by the officers, which could have formed reasonable suspicion or probable cause.

A common response from the client as to what he was doing before the officer came up might be, "nothing." Counsel should not end the interview there satisfied that the officers clearly lacked probable cause or even reasonable suspicion. "Nothing" could mean nothing of significance, nothing illegal or nothing worth mentioning. You ask a teenager what he did all three months of summer vacation and the answer is often "nothing."

The response of "nothing" means very little until counsel explores what happened factually. That does not mean that counsel should aggressively challenge the client's veracity. Counsel's job is to get at the facts and then determine whether it really was "nothing" in terms of reasonable suspicion and probable cause. Follow-up questions to get at the facts of what really happened could include:

- Before the officer walked up what were you doing with your hands?
- Your feet?
- Your head?
- Your eyes?
- What were you wearing?
- Were you carrying anything?
- What was it?
- How was it packaged?
- What did you do with it?
- Were you with anyone else?
- What were other people around you doing with their hands? feet? head? etc.
- Was anyone else carrying anything?
- Did you say anything?
- What did you say?
- How loud did you say it?
- Did anyone else say anything?
- Did you go anywhere else?
- Where did you go?
- How did you get there?

The purpose of this type of questioning is to get a visual picture of what might have sparked the officer's interest, particularly when the officers knew nothing about the defendant prior to the encounter. It could be that four kids were in a car sharing a cigarette and passing it back and forth. This could have appeared to the officers to be a marijuana cigarette based on the manner in which the cigarette was handled. Keying in on the movement rather than the conclusions as to whether the defendant and his pals were doing anything wrong, will often get at the facts necessary for accurate Fourth Amendment assessments.

Agents are likely to answer questions about what they observed in police legalese conclusions. "He was acting suspicious." "Suspicious" is a conclusion. Counsel needs the facts to determine whether it was indeed suspicious and to what degree. The questions for the client are instructive for the agent as well. What did the suspect do with his hands, feet, head, eyes, etc. What did the informant tell you he had seen in the apartment?

What did the officers do during the stop?

What the officers did during the stop should be viewed broadly. The lawyer, whether defense attorney or prosecutor, needs to know basically everything that went on with the officers since it is primarily their actions that affect whether a person would reasonably feel he or she was not free to leave. Certainly the courts focus more on police behavior than the subjective feelings of the defendant.

Again, the questions should be open but directed, like a good direct examination. The who, what, where, when and how type questions are most effective, particularly if the questions are directed at a specific issue. For example, rather than asking "Did you take the identification?" (too directed) or "What happened next?" (not directed enough) it is more useful to direct the client or agent to the important information needed but still keep it open to get as much information in the answer, *e.g.*, "What did the officer do after he asked for your identification?"

The following is a starter list of sample follow-up questions to help when eliciting information for assessing whether the defendant was seized under the Fourth Amendment. Again, the list is not meant to be a script or exhaustive, but rather to assist the attorney in crafting an effective interview and understanding conceptually what issues should be covered. Ideally these more directed questions will follow general questions about what happened using who, what, where, when, and how:

- How many officers?
- How did the officers get there?
- Were they in a vehicle?
- What kind of vehicle?
- Were there sirens or lights?
- Where did they park?
- How did they approach the defendant?
- Where were they standing relative to the defendant?
- What were they wearing?
- Were they wearing badges?
- Were they in uniform?
- What were they carrying?
- Did they carry a gun, billyclub, handcuffs, etc.?
- Did they display their badges, gun, billyclub, handcuffs, etc.?
- How did they walk?
- What did they say?
- How did they say it?
- What did they say next?
- How did they say it, etc.?
- What did they do with their hands?
- What did they do with their feet?
- How close were they to the defendant?
- What did they say to the defendant?
- Did they put their hands on the defendant?

- Did they ask for identification?

- Did they tell the defendant he was free to leave?

- Did they tell the defendant he was not free to leave?

- Did they tell the defendant he was under arrest?

- When did they tell him that?

- How did they say it?

- What did he say to them?

Where was the defendant stopped or encountered by the officers?

The place where the interaction between the officers and the defendant occurred is important because it can affect whether a reasonable person in the defendant's position would have felt free to leave. "[W]hat constitutes a restraint on liberty prompting a person to conclude that he is not free to 'leave' will vary, not only with the particular police conduct at issue, but also with the setting in which the conduct occurs." *Michigan v. Chesternut*, 486 U.S. 567, 573-4, 108 S. Ct. 1975, 1979, 100 L. Ed. 2d 565, 572 (1988). The following questions provide the type of information the attorney needs to make those assessments. The questions themselves can be asked in a more open style: *e.g.* please describe the area where you were arrested with these questions as follow-ups. The point is to make sure that it is clear whether the area was open to the public:

- Was this an area open to the public?

- Were there other people around?

- Was there public transportation nearby?

- Was there a pay phone nearby?

- How was it lit?

- What time of day was this?

- Was the defendant moved to another location?

- How was he moved?

- What did the defendant do or say at the time he was asked to move?

- Did he agree to be moved?
- How did he agree?
- What was said by the officers regarding the move?
- How was it said?
- What was said by the defendant regarding the move?

The defense will have a better argument that the defendant did not feel free to leave if he was taken to a closed room, away from public view, into a police car, etc., and the request was essentially a command in a tone that appeared to demand acquiescence to authority. The prosecution, on the other hand, will have a better argument that the defendant was free to leave if the encounter was in an openly public place and the officer asked in a non-threatening manner if the suspect would accompany them, told the suspect he did not have to accompany them and the suspect agreed to accompany the officers "voluntarily in a spirit of apparent cooperation." *See Sibron v. New York*, 392 U.S. 40, 63, 88 S. Ct. 1889, 1903, 20 L. Ed. 2d 917, 935 (1968).

How long was the defendant stopped?

The longer the stop the greater the likelihood that the court will find some type of seizure. If the encounter was short it is more likely to be considered purely consensual and no requirement of reasonable suspicion or probable cause is required. If the seizure is minimal, the police may be able to justify a seizure with mere reasonable suspicion. If the seizure amounts effectively to an arrest, the police would need probable cause.

Although there is no bright line test as to the amount of time of a stop that converts an otherwise consensual encounter into a seizure or even in effect an arrest, over an hour has been considered prolonged for certain investigative detentions. Specifically, in *United States v. Place*, 492 U.S. 696, 709, 103 S. Ct. 2637, 2645, 77 L. Ed. 2d 110, 122 (1983) where the officer detained the defendant for ninety minutes in an airport to await a narcotic detecting canine, the Court found that the "length of the detention of respondent's luggage alone precludes the conclusion that the seizure was reasonable in the absence of probable cause."

Other factors causing a person to reasonably believe he was not free to leave

The above issues highlight the major concerns the court will consider in assessing the degree of seizure, but there can be countless other factors in the totality of circumstances analysis.

- Whether the defendant's property or car was held pending the questioning.

- What the defendant was wearing that might make him more vulnerable to seizure such as a swimming suit or being barefoot.

- Whether the defendant spoke or understood a different language than the one used by the police officers.

- Whether the defendant was near his home or his work place.

- Whether the defendant was separated from the rest of his companions.

- Whether the defendant was told to get out of the car or to step away from the sidewalk.

When counsel has a potential seizure issue, in addition to reviewing the chapters in this book on search and seizure law, it is very helpful for the lawyer to take a look at seizure cases in her own jurisdiction for other factors to which the courts might have looked in assessing seizure. This review will give the lawyer not only a sense of which factors the courts in that jurisdiction have tended to rely on as particularly persuasive in seizure analysis, but the other individual factors used by the courts in determining the degree of any seizure and whether the officers had a legal basis to make such a seizure.

Interviews and Specific Search Questions

Was anything taken by the officers?

Although the most obvious question in assessing Fourth Amendment search issues could be, "Did the officers do a search?" that particular question will be less fruitful at the outset than asking the client or agent whether anything was taken. The term "search" has many meanings from ransacking through every drawer in a house, to a small movement of a stereo to look for numbers on the back.

Agents in particular might work off erroneous conceptions of legal definitions and say there was no search when in fact actions were taken which could constitute a search under the law. Think of the minor movement of the stereo in *Arizona v. Hicks,* 480 U.S. 321, 107 S. Ct. 1149, 94 L. Ed. 2d 347 (1987) to record serial numbers from the back and that officer's likely response if asked immediately afterwards whether he had conducted a search. Similarly, defendants might think of a search as an action verb only; a search occurring only if the police actively looked around for something. Defendants might not think to include descriptions of police taking property directly from the defendant's person or taken from under the bed or obtained with the defendant's consent since the officers did not need to "search" meaning "hunt" for the evidence.

The term "taken" is also problematic though less so than "search," and counsel must consider how to address these issues in follow-up questions. Agents might assume that "taken" means vouchered and defendants might assume that "taken" means it was never given back and fail to list property released to the defendant after arrest, which might have been unlawfully procured yet used to support the arrest.

Counsel should stress that "taken" includes anything removed from the person of the defendant, removed from any vehicle, house, or container at any time even if it was ultimately given back or left where it was found or taken from a place which the defendant did not own or could not access. It should also include property taken even though the defendant said they could take it.

If counsel asks whether "evidence" was taken, the client or agent might assume counsel is interested in incriminating evidence or something that has legal significance. Counsel should make clear that anything taken means exactly that, anything, even a paper clip no matter where it went or why.

By asking whether something was taken or removed, counsel can work backwards to determine how the item was obtained and will be more likely to get the facts necessary to assess Fourth Amendment issues accurately. Getting at the facts rather than a description or opinion of the facts is better for the interviewing lawyer because it will avoid answers which contain misleading assumptions and unsupported conclusions; answers counsel might rely on to the detriment of the case or client.

Did the officers have a warrant?

Given the relative ease of getting a warrant including telephonically or by facsimile transmission, it is always surprising how few searches are conducted pursuant to a warrant. Use of a warrant issued by a neutral and detached magistrate judge answers nearly all Fourth Amendment concerns and there is very little to argue against, particularly given the good faith exception to the warrant requirement under *United States v. Leon*, 468 U.S. 897, 104 S. Ct. 3405, 82 L. Ed. 2d 677 (1984).

If there was a warrant, the issues for the interview will focus on how the warrant was executed and whether the information seized was within the scope of the warrant. Other warrant issues including particularity (does the warrant set forth the places to be searched and the things to be seized) are usually resolved through an examination of the warrant itself and the supporting documentation where the officer or defendant's testimony would ordinarily not be as crucial. *See also Chapter Six: Warrants and Chapter Nineteen: Fourth Amendment Issues at the Initial Appearance.*

The following questions are helpful in assessing the execution of the warrant. Again, the questions themselves can be asked in a more open style: *e.g.* please describe how the officers entered the apartment; the point is to make sure that it is clear about the timing and the use of force or a battering ram and whether there was any damage, as listed below. This information will assist in determining whether the warrant was executed reasonably and whether the evidence taken was within the scope of the warrant.

- How was the area entered?

- Was there a knock and announce?

- Was there an answer to the knock?
- Was there anything said after the knock?
- How much time between the knock and announce and the entry by officers?
- Was a battering ram used or other device?
- Were firearms drawn?
- Was any property destroyed?
- Was there any physical damage to the dwelling or door as a result of the entry?
- Did the officers have the warrant with them?
- Did the officers show the suspects the warrant?
- How many officers were involved in the execution of the warrant?
- What was taken?
- Where were the things that were taken?
- What happened to the things that were taken?

Beyond the facial challenges discussed in *Chapter Six: Warrants,* there is little that can be done with respect to a warrant in terms of interviewing the client and agent with the exception of ensuring that the probable cause that was relied upon for the warrant was not misleading or false. Counsel should go over the information in the supporting documents carefully with the agent or client to ensure that it is truthful and accurate. If the information relied upon by the neutral and detached magistrate was misleading or false, there is no good faith exception and a *Franks* hearing and motion to suppress might be available. *See Chapter Six: Warrants.*

If there is no warrant, much of the interview will concern how the officers took the property they recovered and whether the defendant had a reasonable expectation of privacy in the area searched or the thing seized. In some cases the attorney will have access to police reports, which will usually detail how a search was conducted, however, counsel must still interview the client or agent as the report may not be exhaustive or contain inaccuracies.

Likewise with videotaped searches, which will not include everything that occurred during the search.

How did the officers get the things which were taken?

Counsel should be looking for the most basic information in terms of how the officers obtained what was taken. It is not helpful for the agent to respond that the cocaine was found pursuant to a lawful search incident to arrest. Such a scenario might, in fact, be what happened, but the lawyer must assess the facts to determine the lawfulness of the search and ultimate seizure of the drugs. Moreover, the subjective belief of the officer is not controlling. The more helpful facts would be something in this colloquy:

Q: "What did you do when you first approached the suspect?"

A: "I stopped the suspect, patted him down and discovered a hard, brick shaped item in his right coat pocket."

Q: "How did you discover the brick shaped item?"

A: "Just by a standard pat down."

Q: "Show me."

Q: "What did you do after you felt the hard brick shaped item?"

A: "I knew it was contraband so I took it out of the pocket."

Q: "How did you know it was contraband?"

A: "From my five years experience as a narcotics interdiction officer, that is the way powder cocaine is packaged."

Clearly the concern in this questioning is whether the officer manipulated the package to determine it was contraband beyond the permissible pat down if there is reasonable suspicion to believe the suspect is armed.

Defendants might claim that the officers took the package without any reason. Counsel must get at the facts underlying this statement such as in the following colloquy:

Q: "Where was the package?"

A: "In my jacket pocket."

Q: "How did the officer know it was in your jacket pocket?"

A: "They patted me down and then took out the package."

Q: "How did they pat you down?"

A: "With their hands like this."

Q: "What did they do when they got to the package?"

A: "They felt around it and said, 'you've got drugs in there don't you?'"

Q: "When you say they felt around, what exactly did they do? Show me."

Q: "Did you do anything when they said 'you've got drugs in there don't you?'"

A: "I reached in and gave him the package."

Q: "Did the officer tell you to give him the package?"

A: "No."

Q: "What did he say to you?"

A: "He didn't say anything."

Q: "Why did you give him the package?"

A: "I knew I was busted."

Q: "You are certain he didn't say one word to you."

A: "Oh, he might have said, if you give us the stuff now we'll go easier on you."

The concern in this exchange is whether the package might have been improperly manipulated and whether the defendant might have voluntarily given over the package or whether he was acquiescing to authority.

Another issue under this topic is whether the defendant gave consent to the search and if so, whether he did so voluntarily. The following questions are helpful in assessing consent issues, keeping in mind that more open questions should be asked at least at the outset, but making sure to include this information as well:

- How many officers approached?
- Where were they located?
- How far from you were they?
- What were they wearing?
- Were they in uniform?
- Were they armed?
- Did they display their weapons at any time?
- How did the officers ask if they could search?
- What tone of voice was used?
- What were they doing when they asked?
- What were they wearing?
- What else were they saying?
- How did the defendant respond?
- Did the officers tell the defendant he had a right to refuse?
- Did the officers tell the say anything about what would happen if he did not consent?
- What was the defendant doing when he said they could search?
- Was the defendant under arrest when he said they could search?
- Were there third parties who told them they could search?
- What was their relationship to the property? To the defendant?
- What did the third parties say to the officers?
- What did the third parties do during the search?

When and where was the property at the time the officers took it?

It is also important to determine where the property was when the officers took it relative to any seizure or arrest. Was it visible to the officer as he stood in the doorway? Was it in a container? Was it in a home? Was it in a car? Was it is in a purse? Was it is a closet? Was it in a locked closet? Learning only that it was in the house is a start but not the end of the inquiry. There could be containers within containers and each one might require a separate expectation of privacy and separate basis for a legitimate search. Counsel should also get good descriptions of the containers. Were the containers locked? How did the officers get into the containers? Did the defendant give them permission? Give them the key, etc.

Throughout the interview counsel should bear in mind the exceptions to the Warrant Requirement, *see Chapter One: List of Exceptions to the Warrant Requirement*, page 8 and the subsequent chapters, to determine whether any exception might exist in the case, *e.g.*, plain feel during a *Terry* stop, plain view while legitimately on the premises, etc. If the evidence was potentially taken in a search incident to arrest, it is important to ferret out the facts of the taking vis-à-vis the arrest including location and timing.

Did the client have a reasonable expectation of privacy?

Conceptually it might seem odd to leave to the end whether the client had a reasonable expectation of privacy when it is a threshold inquiry for the court in determining whether there was even a search, and for the defendant to claim standing to make a Fourth Amendment claim. However, if counsel begins an interview assuming what evidence was seized and where it was seized, essential information might be lost as to how that evidence was obtained. By establishing seizure issues and search issues first with directed but open questions, the lawyer can be assured of knowing most of the facts of what evidence got into police hands, how it got there and to some extent why. Once all of the physical property is accounted, the lawyer can then determine if the defendant had a reasonable expectation of privacy in the thing seized or the area searched.

To make a determination of whether the defendant had a reasonable expectation of privacy requires a thorough interview of the defendant, and sometimes the agent to the extent the agent might know the defendant's interest in a particular area or object. (Of course the prosecution does not have a right to question the defendant without permission of defense counsel who will almost always advise the defendant to invoke his Fifth Amendment rights against self incrimination and refuse an interview.) However, since it is the defense's burden to show that the defendant had a reasonable expectation of privacy as a threshold matter to meet the burden of going forward, *see Chapter Five: Issues of Standing*, it is less important for the prosecution to discover at the outset, than it is for the defense attorney.

The following questions are helpful in assessing expectations of privacy:

- Did the defendant own the house, the car, the container?
- If not, did the defendant have permission or authority to use?
- What was the extent of that permission or authority to use?
- What was the relationship of the defendant to the owner?
- Could the defendant exclude or invite others?
- Had the defendant been given a key to the house, the car, the locker?
- How long was the defendant on third party property?
- Did he stay overnight?
- Did the defendant have personal property in the home or area searched?
- Did the defendant own the thing taken by the officers?
- If not, what was his relationship to the thing taken by the officers?

- What efforts had the defendant undertaken to keep the property private?

- Was the property enclosed in a bag or purse or other opaque carrying case?

- Was the property wrapped in opaque paper or other covering?

- Locked in a box or hidden in a sock drawer?

- Who else had access to the property?

- Did the defendant expect that the property would be kept private from others?

Counsel must assess whether the defendant had a reasonable expectation of privacy. However, little will be gained by merely asking the defendant if he had a reasonable expectation of privacy outright since these are legal concepts open to interpretation. Moreover, a lay person's notion of privacy could be very different from the law. A lay person might not consider the inside of a home private, but only the inside of the medicine cabinet, a locked drawer or a personal diary.

Although the defendant must assert a subjective belief that he had an expectation of privacy, the meat of the issue is whether that expectation was reasonable. Counsel should obtain as much information about the container or area as possible in order to assess whether the way the package was wrapped or the location or nature of the package was such that society would recognize the expectation of privacy in the object or area as reasonable. *See Chapter Five: Issues of Standing.*

Some Useful Cases

United States v. Place, 492 U.S. 696, 103 S. Ct. 2637, 77 L. Ed. 2d 110 (1983)

CHAPTER EIGHTEEN
THE INITIAL APPEARANCE AND PRELIMINARY EXAMINATION

Warrant Versus Non-Warrant Arrests

A formal arrest is clearly a seizure for Fourth Amendment purposes. Although the Fourth Amendment does not require that all seizures be executed by warrant, the courts are consistent that a formal arrest requires probable cause. The Fourth Amendment mandates that an arrest warrant be supported by probable cause, thus, a warrantless arrest must meet the same standard; otherwise, the preference for a warrant would be entirely eviscerated.

There are generally three means by which a defendant is arrested and brought into court on charges: (1) by an officer's determination of probable cause without a warrant (probable cause for a felony or an officer actually witnesses a misdemeanor or other non-felony); (2) pursuant to an arrest warrant issued by a judicial officer on the basis of a complaint or other sworn information; or (3) pursuant to an arrest warrant based on a grand jury's indictment. In most jurisdictions, defendants are usually arrested as a result of an officer's determination of probable cause at the scene rather than pursuant to an arrest warrant, although at the federal level with the higher incidence of white collar crimes and more complex ongoing investigations, many defendants are arrested pursuant to indictment, where probable cause has already been determined by a grand jury.

When a person is arrested without a warrant and is taken into custody by law enforcement, ordinarily he must be brought before a neutral and detached magistrate within at least 48 hours for a judicial determination of probable cause. *See County of Riverside v. McLaughlin*, 500 U.S. 44, 56, 111 S. Ct. 1661, 1670, 114 L. Ed. 2d 49, 63 (1991). Some state jurisdictions mandate an even shorter period, such as New York, where defendants must be arraigned within 24 hours of arrest unless a satisfactory explanation for the delay is given. *See People ex rel. Maxian v. Brown*, 77 N.Y.2d 422, 570 N.E.2d 223, 568 N.Y.S.2d 575 (1991); *See also Natali, Parsons, Statsinger & Wolfe, Practice Commentaries to Federal Rules of Criminal Procedure, Commentary* to Fed. R. Crim. P. 48 (2002-2003).

In federal cases, the defendant is brought before the magistrate judge for a proceeding known as an initial appearance under FRCrP 5, where the judge will advise the defendant of certain rights, including the right to remain silent and the right to an attorney and consider issues of bail. State jurisdictions have similar proceedings though they might be known by some other name. (Indeed, the initial appearance in federal court is commonly referred to by court personnel and parties as an "arraignment" although it is not technically an arraignment unless the defendant actually pleads at the time of the initial appearance).

If the defendant is arrested pursuant to an arrest warrant issued by a neutral and detached magistrate based on a sworn affidavit or indictment, a judicial or grand jury will have already found probable cause for the arrest based on the warrant. However, under FRCrP 41, federal officers are still required to bring the defendant before a magistrate judge for an initial appearance. The Federal Rules require that the officers bring the defendant before the magistrate judge without *unnecessary delay* as discussed in detail below. See FRCrP 5; *see also Natali, Parsons, Statsinger & Wolfe, Practice Commentaries to Federal Rules of Criminal Procedure, Commentary* to Fed. R. Crim. P. 5, 5.1 and 41 (2002-2003).

Challenging Probable Cause in a Warrant Affidavit at the Initial Appearance

The defense may challenge the magistrate judge's determination of probable cause when a defendant is seized pursuant to a warrant based on a sworn affidavit from a law enforcement officer or prosecutor. If there is a viable challenge to the warrant, the defense should make its argument as to the insufficiency of the probable cause ideally at the initial appearance. (Allegations of false or misleading information in the affidavit, or challenges alleging that evidence was obtained as a result of a warrant not supported by probable cause, ordinarily will be litigated at separate pretrial hearings and not at the initial appearance.)

However, unless there is an obvious and blatant lack of probable cause in the affidavit, meaning the affidavit fails to make out *prima facie* probable cause, usually there is little to be gained in challenging an arrest by warrant at the initial appearance. Certainly it should not be done as a matter of course. A judge presiding at the initial appearance is very unlikely to disagree with another judge's determination of probable cause. This is particularly true when the judges are at the same court level; magistrate judges usually issue warrants and the initial appearances are typically held before magistrate judges. (It might even be the same judge who approved the warrant before whom the defense is appearing at the initial appearance. Defense counsel should always check the judge's signature to ensure that counsel knows which judge signed the warrant before pounding the table and implying that the issuing judge was "off his rocker" on the probable cause issue.)

Where there is no clear lack of probable cause on the face of the affidavit, a defense challenge to a court-issued warrant will typically be viewed by the court as frivolous and obstructionist. Such a challenge is highly unlikely to succeed and more likely to result in defense counsel's loss of credibility with the court—credibility better spent trying to get the defendant out on bail. Defense lawyers must carefully weigh the advantages and disadvantages before a particular judge in deciding whether to mount a challenge to the warrant at the initial appearance.

Some challenges are appropriate and often fruitful. There are times when issuing magistrate judges do not in fact review the supporting information carefully in a warrant application at the time of issuance and act more like the proverbial "rubber stamp" for law enforcement and prosecutors than a neutral and detached judge. If the allegations in the supporting affidavits are conclusory, *e.g.*, "I observed the defendant committing the crime of money laundering," or "there was probable cause to believe that Ms. Jones applied for a false passport," and fail to detail the facts demonstrating what the defendant was doing, a challenge should be made by the defense. The argument to the court in such a case is that the officer (or prosecutor) essentially made the determination of probable cause to arrest rather than presenting the facts for review by a neutral and detached judicial officer.

Similarly, many warrants contain "boilerplate" language used in every such warrant and often do not contain specific information tailored to the individual case. If the warrant contains boilerplate conclusions, "based on my training and experience, drugs and guns are kept in closets, locked containers, etc." without specific information linked to that individual case, the defense should challenge the warrant as lacking in particular probable cause that weapons or drugs would be found in certain containers. Otherwise, warrants could be issued simply based on the fact that the case involves drugs without individualized probable cause.

In some cases there clearly exists probable cause for the arrest of the main defendants in the warrant application, but the affidavit might not detail sufficient evidence for lesser-involved defendants. Prosecutors tend to submit the same affidavit for all co-defendants. Where there is an obvious lack of probable cause contained in the supporting information, defense attorneys should make a challenge allowing for the possibility that the court might have misread the information, did not have sufficient time to consider the application, or focused more on the main defendants and less on the minor players.

The defense challenge to a warrant at the initial appearance is properly based on the facial invalidity of the supporting affidavits. In cases when the defense challenge goes beyond an evaluation of the facial validity of the sworn documents, the judge will either deny the challenge outright or simply await any preliminary examination or grand jury indictment if the judge is satisfied that the initial warrant is properly supported on the face of the allegations.

On the other hand, challenges to the affidavits might prompt the prosecution to reveal additional information to satisfy the judge that even if the officers might have "arguably" lacked probable cause at the time, there is sufficient evidence at present to hold the defendant on the charges. These prosecution proffers will usually provide valuable discovery for the defense. Of course, such proffers are unlikely to be made where probable cause is set forth clearly in the supporting affidavits.

Finally, there are judges who will refuse to entertain any challenge to the warrant and require the defense to make whatever challenges in pretrial motions. (If the arrest warrant was issued pursuant to an indictment, the defendant would not have a right to challenge the issuance of the warrant because the grand jury's determination of probable cause is by itself a sufficient finding, provided the grand jury is properly constituted).

Regardless of whether there might be a viable challenge to the affidavit, any sworn information supporting an arrest warrant or any accompanying search warrant should always be obtained by defense counsel at the initial appearance and carefully reviewed. At a minimum, it provides important discovery on the case and a sworn statement by an officer who is likely to be a witness in future matters including any suppression hearing and trial.

Both sides will often use the information contained in any affidavit at the bail argument, which usually occurs at the initial appearance. The defense might be able to argue that the lack of detail in the supporting documents indicates that the prosecution does not have a strong case against the defendant compelling, at a minimum, that the defendant be released on his own recognizance or a modest bail. In those cases when the review reveals that the affidavits were insufficient to support a judicial finding of probable cause, a defense challenge might be warranted.

Challenging Probable Cause in the Complaint at the Initial Appearance

Generally. When there is no warrant for the arrest of the defendant, a sworn statement must be filed at the initial appearance that satisfies probable cause. The arresting officer typically will swear to a complaint—usually written by the assigned prosecutor—that sets out the basis for the apprehension of the defendant. The judge will review the complaint at the initial appearance, assessing whether the complaint sufficiently demonstrates that there was probable cause. Although the issue of probable cause might be formally reviewed at a subsequent preliminary examination, the court still must assess whether the complaint that was filed to support the warrantless arrest of the defendant sufficiently sets forth probable cause. This document offers defense counsel an opportunity to argue that it fails to do so.

A defendant arrested without a warrant and on the basis of an officer's determination of probable cause is in a better position to claim a lack of probable cause on the face of the complaint than if a warrant is issued by a neutral and detached magistrate in advance of the actual arrest. When a case proceeds by complaint at the initial appearance, it is a judicial officer's first review of the facts, whereas with a warrant, another judge has already made the decision that there was probable cause.

The typical complaint filed in federal court contains information to demonstrate probable cause justifying the bringing of charges against the defendant and any co-defendants. It is also an important source of information for the court to consider in deciding whether the defendant should be detained during the pendency of the case, or whether the defendant should be released on his own recognizance or on bail. Although most of the culture of federal court criminal practice is to keep information "close to the vest," because prosecutors know that the judge relies heavily on the complaint in evaluating the strength of the government's case and the legitimacy of the arrest, federal complaints tend to be quite detailed. Such complaints are typically a treasure trove of information about the facts leading up to the arrest, the manner of the arrest, and the evidence obtained. State complaints might or might not be detailed depending on the jurisdiction and the type of offense.

Discovery. When a defendant is arrested without a warrant, defense counsel should scrutinize the complaint for a possible challenge that there is insufficient evidence to support a finding of probable cause. In addition to assessing the sufficiency of the probable cause, counsel should review the complaint for additional discovery and consider the strength of the prosecution's case as it affects any application for bail.

Beyond what was known at the time of the arrest, other facts might come to light from the complaint, such as post-arrest statements, physical evidence found on the defendant in the search incident to arrest, or statements given by a cooperating witness. If these facts were not included in the original complaint, the prosecutor often proffers the information in open court to supplement the complaint. Hearsay may be used to support probable cause, and a judge will assume all facts to be true in assessing the facial validity of the complaint.

Given that at this stage the judge is not supposed to be concerned with the legality of the arrest itself, most judges will accept the proffered information and use it to determine whether to hold the defendant for a preliminary hearing (or examination). Still, it is helpful to advise the court of search problems because if it is a close case on whether there is probable cause, a judge may be persuaded to dismiss the complaint without prejudice due to the fact that it is probable that the evidence will be suppressed.

If the proffered facts are necessary to establish probable cause, the defense should insist that the officer take the stand and swear to proffered facts as if it were a supplemental complaint. The defense should also request that the judge give the defense an opportunity to cross examine the officer. Because this is not a preliminary examination, the judge is unlikely to allow for cross-examination, but the judge might be persuaded to have the officer assert the additional facts under oath. These additional sworn facts provide useful discovery to the defense and material for a possible impeachment of that witness in the future. If, from the comments of counsel, it becomes clear that the issue is more the credibility of the officer or the other witnesses than a facial challenge to the complaint, the judge will usually await the preliminary hearing before making any findings.

Effect on Bail. Challenging the sufficiency of probable cause can also set up the defense's argument that the defendant should be released on bail because the prosecution's case is so weak. One of the facts a federal judge is required to consider in determining whether the defendant should be released is the weight of the evidence against the defendant. *See* 18 USC § 3142(g)(2).

Although the defense might lose its request to have the complaint dismissed, the defense could persuade the judge that, despite a finding of probable cause, the case is weak and would be unlikely to result in a conviction, and that therefore bail should be set. *See Chapter Twenty: Fourth Amendment Issues and Investigations.*

Dismissals. It is important to remember that the issue for the court at the initial appearance is not whether the evidence was obtained lawfully or whether the officer had sufficient probable cause at the point of arrest—these will be litigated at different pretrial hearings. Rather, the court must decide whether there is sufficient probable cause to hold the defendant on the charges as he stands before the judge in court that day.

The standard for probable cause is a low one. It is not a preponderance of the evidence, but a matter of a reasonable likelihood that a crime has been committed and that this defendant committed it. It is unusual for the court to dismiss a complaint for lack of probable cause because the standard is so low. Moreover, by this point in the proceedings, the prosecutor has screened the case and prepared the complaint containing the arresting officer's allegations. Judges typically give deference to the prosecution's view on whether charges should be brought. Even so, judges will now and again dismiss insufficient complaints at the initial appearance.

Dismissals at the initial appearance happen most often in large conspiracy cases where there is probable cause to believe a conspiracy took place, but a particular defendant's participation and agreement to conspire might not be sufficiently detailed in the complaint. If the judge finds that the complaint fails to set out probable cause as to a specific defendant, the complaint against him will be dismissed without prejudice to the prosecution to recharge the defendant at a later time within the statute of limitations. Thereafter, in order to prosecute that defendant, the prosecution would have to file an amended complaint or obtain an indictment, which does not require judicial review.

Although a dismissal of the complaint at the initial appearance is without prejudice to the prosecution to bring the charges again provided it does so within the statute of limitations, there are many advantages bestowed on the defendant from such a dismissal. First, the judge sends a strong signal to the prosecution as to the weakness of the case, and this is likely to prompt fruitful negotiations. Second, a dismissal will require additional work by the prosecution to bring the charges again and this might also prompt more generous plea offers. Finally, in some cases, a dismissal convinces the prosecution that it is not worth pursuing the defendant at all when a judge considers the case insufficient to meet such a low standard of proof as probable cause, and therefore could decline to reinstate the charges, particularly where there are other defendants.

Unnecessary Delay Concerns

Once a defendant is arrested, he must be brought "without unnecessary delay" before the nearest available magistrate judge or local judicial officer. *See* Fed. R. Crim. P. 5, 9. Although the term is not defined in the Federal Rules, the 1944 Advisory Committee Notes provide that unnecessary delay must be "determined in light of all the facts and circumstances of the case." The requirement to be brought before a magistrate judge applies whether the defendant is arrested by warrant based on an indictment or complaint, or by the arresting officer's own determination of probable cause. The analysis of unnecessary delay, however, depends on whether the officer was proceeding with a prior judicial or grand jury determination of probable cause or by the officer's own observations.

At the initial appearance, defense counsel should ensure that the court inquire on the record the date and time the defendant was arrested. The present date and time should also be noted so that any delay can be calculated from the record. If the delay seems at all unreasonable—even a delay of a few hours could be undue if the defendant was arrested, say, outside the agency office—defense counsel should ask the judge to have the prosecution set down the reasons for the delay.

Since there is no set time at which a delay becomes unreasonable, defense counsel must individualize why the delay is unreasonable under the circumstances. The Supreme Court provides for a safe harbor from challenges of undue delay if there is a probable cause determination within 48 hours of arrest. This rule pertains to an arrest proceeding by complaint under FRCrP 4. *See McLaughlin*, 500 U.S. at 56, 111 S. Ct. at 1669, 114 L. Ed. 2d at 62. If the defendant was brought to court after 48 hours, the defense should request a full hearing on the matter to determine the reason for the delay. Ultimately, the defense should request dismissal of the charges pursuant to FRCrP 48. *See Natali, Parsons, Statsinger & Wolfe, Practice Commentaries to Federal Rules of Criminal Procedure, Commentary* to Fed. R. Crim. P. 48 (2002-2003). State jurisdiction might have shorter time periods for safe harbor.

When the defendant is arrested by warrant based on an indictment or information, a sufficient determination of probable cause will have already occurred, and thus the 48-hour rule is not binding. Nonetheless, the rule can provide a context for the defense to argue that the delay was unnecessary. Defense counsel should request that a hearing be held to determine what transpired during the extended delay (often it is interrogation of the defendant), and why the delay occurred. Defense counsel should also insist that the arresting agents take the stand under oath on the matter, rather than allow the prosecution to proceed by proffer. However, most judges (nearly all former prosecutors) will allow the prosecution to proceed by proffer rather than require an agent to take the stand on the issue.

Unnecessary delay arguments are very difficult to win where there is a warrant supporting the arrest. Indeed, delays of as long as five days have been upheld when the warrant was supported by indictment. *See, e.g., United States v. Purvis*, 768 F.2d 1237 (11th Cir. 1985) (holding that the five days it took for defendants to be brought in front of a magistrate from the time of their arrest was not unreasonable given that they were arrested 350 miles offshore). Nevertheless, many of the cases finding no unnecessary delay can be distinguished, and the role of defense counsel is to individualize the prejudice to a particular client and show that the reasons for the delay proffered by the prosecutor are insufficient in the instant case.

The remedy for a finding of unnecessary delay is not necessarily dismissal of the indictment or information. While some federal circuits approve of dismissal, others have considered the remedy too drastic or unavailable under the specific language of the Speedy Trial Act, 18 USC § § 3161 et. seq. and FRCrP 48. Thus, counsel for both sides should be aware of the position of their respective jurisdiction. *See also Natali, Parsons, Statsinger & Wolfe, Practice Commentaries to Federal Rules of Criminal Procedure, Commentary to Fed. R. Crim. P. 48 (2002-2003).*

Generally, if evidence is obtained during an unnecessary delay, the remedy will be suppression. Where statements have been taken from the defendant during the time period between arrest and appearance before a magistrate, the defense should move for suppression on the independent grounds of unnecessary delay, aside from any other Fifth or Sixth Amendment considerations.

Effects on Bail

One of the issues a federal judge is required to consider in determining whether the defendant should be released on bail is the weight of the evidence against the defendant. *See* 18 USC § 3142(g)(2). As discussed above, even an unsuccessful challenge to the sufficiency of probable cause could lay the foundation for the defense's argument that the defendant should be released on bail because the prosecution's case is so weak. Although the judge might be persuaded that the prosecution has met the minimal standard of probable cause, the judge could be concerned about the strength of the prosecution's case and release a defendant out on bail on account of that weakness.

Although a violation of a defendant's Fourth Amendment rights is not ordinarily a concern of the judge's at the initial appearance (the defense must ordinarily challenge the taking of the evidence through pretrial motions), it could have some impact on the judge's determination as to whether to set bail. Since federal judges consider the strength of the prosecution's case, evidence deemed inadmissible could weaken the prosecution's case to the point that the case may not be able to be prosecuted at all. *See also, Chapter Twenty: Fourth Amendment Issues and Investigations.*

Negotiation Considerations at the Initial Appearance

In some jurisdictions, prosecutors make plea offers at the initial appearance, particularly at the state level. Defense lawyers typically focus on whether the plea is a good one assuming the guilt of the defendant, based on what is known about the prosecution's case, and comparing the plea offer with the likely sentence after trial. Unfortunately, there tends to be less focus at this stage on Fourth Amendment issues. Frequently what appears to be an excellent plea offer at the outset might not be such a good one if, in fact, the prosecution's evidence was obtained in violation of the defendant's Fourth Amendment rights and therefore would be inadmissible at trial. Early plea offers look less like bargains when there are problems with the search or seizure in the first place. Indeed, too-good-to-be-true offers might be extended to the defense because of the prosecution's concern that the evidence could be tainted.

Certainly, potential Fourth Amendment issues spotted at the outset should be used by the defense in negotiations. Empirically it is difficult for the defense to prevail on motions to exclude evidence from trial, but such motions, even if unsuccessful, require prosecution witnesses to testify and the prosecutor to spend time briefing responses. If there is a clear issue as to the admissibility of the evidence, this will give the defense some leverage in negotiations. For that reason, the defense should always interview the client, review the complaint and any other affidavits or available reports to ascertain whether there may be potential motions to suppress evidence before counseling a client whether to accept a plea bargain. *See also, Chapter Twenty Two: Fourth Amendment Issues and Negotiations.*

Preliminary Examinations

A federal defendant charged with any offense other than a petty offense (defined in the federal system as a crime of six months or less maximum imprisonment) is entitled to a preliminary examination unless waived, or unless an indictment or information has been filed. *See* FRCrP 5(c), 5.1. At the preliminary examination, the prosecution presents evidence and witnesses to support probable cause, and the defense may cross-examine the witnesses in addition to presenting its own evidence and witnesses. (In actuality, the defense rarely puts on a case at these hearings and would only be permitted to do so if it would aid the court in determining probable cause.)

The purpose of the preliminary examination is for the prosecution to present evidence in open court to allow the magistrate judge to make a finding as to whether there exists probable cause to hold the defendant on the charges. The judge does not determine credibility, but whether the evidence, if believed, would make out a prima facie case of probable cause to bring the charges against the defendant.

In many jurisdictions, preliminary examinations are rarely held because such hearings are negated if the prosecutor obtains an indictment before the time of the preliminary examination. Furthermore, the defendant typically waives the preliminary examination when the case is being resolved by guilty plea. As a result, challenges to probable cause are typically made at the initial appearance on the basis of the facial deficiency of the supporting affidavits and complaints.

In federal court the preliminary examination must occur within 10 days if the defendant is in custody or 20 days if the defendant is not in custody. *See* FRCrP 5. This time period may be extended upon the consent of the defense and a showing of good cause. If the defense does not consent to a continuance, an extension can only be imposed upon a showing of "extraordinary circumstances" and that such delay is "indispensable to the interests of justice." *Id.* In practice, preliminary hearings are often continued on consent to allow time for negotiations. If a disposition can be reached, the defendant may waive the preliminary hearing and waive his right to have charges proceed by indictment to avoid having to be under federal indictment during the case.

Although an indictment is simply the formal charges being brought, and it has been said that the grand jury would indict a ham sandwich if asked to do so by a prosecutor (incidentally said by a former Chief Judge of the New York Court of Appeals who himself was indicated and convicted on stalking charges), an indictment is generally viewed by the lay public as a very bad thing. Some defendants, typically those who have a stake in their community and are concerned about their reputation, want to avoid being indicted even if they know that they will ultimately plead guilty to the charges.

A preliminary hearing offers the defense the opportunity to observe government witnesses on the stand and to obtain discovery about the facts of the case. Prosecutors usually want to avoid preliminary hearings whenever possible to preclude additional sworn testimony by a potential trial witness. Prosecutors prefer, whenever possible, to seek indictments in secret grand jury proceedings they essentially control where the defense attorney is not usually permitted to attend rather than put witnesses on the stand at a preliminary hearing subject to defense counsel's examination.

At the preliminary examination, although the defense is entitled to cross-examine the government witnesses, typically the questions will be open-ended ones aimed at eliciting information about the case or pinning down the officer's testimony for future impeachment. If such questions are not related to probable cause, judges are likely to limit the extent of the examination by the defense especially if the judge suspects the proceeding is being used for discovery purposes rather than to attack probable cause. *See also Natali, Parsons, Statsinger & Wolfe, Practice Commentaries to Federal Rules of Criminal Procedure, Commentary to Fed. R. Crim.* P. 5 and 5.1 (2002-2003).

If the court determines on the basis of the evidence presented at the hearing that there is no probable cause to hold the defendant, the remedy is dismissal of the charges against that particular defendant. This dismissal is ordinarily without prejudice to the prosecution to refile charges. In many cases, the prosecution will simply proceed by indictment or information (in non-felonies) that will provide the basis for an arrest warrant under FRCrP 9. If the dismissal does not state whether it is with prejudice or without prejudice, it will be presumed that it is without prejudice.

CHAPTER NINETEEN
BAIL HEARINGS

Seizure in many aspects of Fourth Amendment litigation is often a term of art both abstract and academic. "Class, if the officer stands this close to the suspect with this expression and for this many minutes does it amount to a seizure requiring reasonable suspicion or probable cause?" But for any person who has been handcuffed, fingerprinted and placed in a holding cell, seizure is far from abstract. Whether the defendant will be "seized" on a more permanent basis, i.e., kept in custody while the case is pending, is one of the most important issues that must be handled by a litigator, particularly a defense attorney.

Bail issues and hearings should never be treated as run of the mill by a defense lawyer, no matter how many cases she has and no matter how hopeless the chance of release. At a minimum, it is one of the first opportunities an attorney will have in a case to fight hard for a client, even if the result would be the same as if the defense had consented to detention. In some cases, it might be prudent to consent to detention at the outset, as discussed below, but fighting for the freedom of a client is where defense counsel can make a significant impact on establishing good attorney-client rapport, and sometimes, even in serious cases, get bail set.

An early victory on bail and the ability to have a client available "on the outside" to assist more fully in his defense (not to mention having a client come to the lawyer's office rather than enduring the ever changing rules of prison bureaucracies) is worth every extra amount of time and effort put into a bail application. Getting a client out not only sets a tone for defense counsel's commitment to advocating, but if an attorney is successful in getting bail for her client it signals to the court and the prosecution that this is the kind of case and client who might also warrant a more lenient outcome or sentence.

Statutes and Federal Rules on Bail

A federal practitioner must become well-acquainted with the Bail Reform Act to represent a defendant effectively in federal court. Rule 46 FRCrP and the Bail Reform Act codified in 18 USC §§ 3142-61 set forth the procedures of bail. Read them. Read them again. There are a lot of factors involved and a few sections can be very helpful to the defense, *e.g.*, 18 USC § 3142 (j) provides that nothing in the Bail Reform Act shall be construed as modifying or limiting the presumption of innocence. Attorneys should also know the main bail cases in their jurisdiction, especially any published decision upholding the granting of bail. (Realistically there are so few "defense friendly" cases that it will be easy to keep abreast.)

The federal bail laws encourage pretrial release in many cases (good news for the defense) and often the federal prosecutors will consent to bail and even consent to release the defendant on his own recognizance in non-violent, non-drug cases. *See Natali, Parsons, Statsinger & Wolfe, Practice Commentaries to Federal Rules of Criminal Procedure, Commentary to Fed. R. Crim. P. 46* (2002-2003). The Bail Reform Act requires judges in such cases to first consider releasing the defendant on her own recognizance (referred to as "ROR") or releasing the defendant on an unsecured personal recognizance bond (referred to as a "PRB"). See 18 USC § 3142(b). Only if this release is inadequate to ensure the defendant's presence in court and the safety of the community may the judge then consider adding restrictive conditions such as requiring the defendant to remain in a family member's custody, report to pretrial services on a regular basis or attend a substance abuse program. See 18 USC § 3142(c) for a list of conditions. Detention is the last resort except in certain serious offenses, discussed below.

In short, the court ordinarily releases a defendant unless it determines there are no conditions or combinations of conditions that would ensure the defendant's presence in court and the safety of the community. The factors the court looks to in making its determination are detailed at 18 USC § 3142(g) and include the nature and circumstances of the offense, the weight of the evidence against the defendant, the history and characteristics of the defendant including family ties, employment, financial resources, substance abuse, criminal record and whether the defendant's release would pose a danger to a person or the community.

Although a violation of a defendant's Fourth Amendment rights in terms of recovering evidence is not specifically a concern at the bail hearing, the possibility of suppression of evidence could have some impact on the judge's determination as to whether to set bail. If, from the complaint, there is a reasonably strong argument that the defendant's rights were violated, this could bear on the strength of the prosecution's case. It might be that after a motion to suppress, the evidence is deemed entirely inadmissible, making the prosecution's case much weaker or such that it cannot be prosecuted at all.

In cases with viable Fourth Amendment motions, the defense might be successful in getting the judge to release the defendant on bail at least pending the determination of the Fourth Amendment motion. The defense can argue that while the Fourth Amendment issue remains a viable one for the defense—especially where a favorable decision would result in dismissal of the case—the defendant has an incentive to stay and fight the issue. After any pretrial hearings on the issues, the district court judge could then revisit the issue of bail depending on the court's decision on the motion and whether the prosecution still seeks detention.

One of the "reforms" of the federal Bail Reform Act was to avoid the phenomenon where poor people were kept in custody simply because they did not have money. The Act specifically states that the "judicial officer may not impose a financial condition that results in the pretrial detention of the person." 18 USC § 3142(c)(2). Although the judge can justify financial conditions as necessary to ensure the defendant's presence in court and the safety of the community, once bail is set, if the defense can demonstrate an inability to meet a financial condition, often the judge will agree to a lower amount to avoid conflicting with § 3142(c)(2). Be aware, however, that some courts have allowed for very high bail that the defendant is unable to meet, if the case involves a serious risk of flight. *See, e.g., United States v. Jessup*, 757 F.2d 278, 389 (1st Cir. 1989).

The bad news for defendants charged with federal drug offenses and crimes of violence, is that they can be detained not only for risk of flight but also for potential dangerousness if the prosecution meets a clear and convincing burden. There is also a rebuttable presumption that the defendant is a risk of flight and a danger to the community for most of these offenses, discussed in more detail below. *See* 18 USC § 3142 (e)-(f); *see also United States v. Salerno*, 481 U.S. 739, 107 S.Ct 2095, 95 L. Ed. 2d 697 (1986).

Preparing for Bail

The issue of bail arises in most federal cases before the magistrate judge at the initial appearance held pursuant to FRCrP 5. If defense counsel has been retained or appointed in advance of the initial appearance there are important preparations to be done. Defense counsel should interview the client in-depth focusing on the release factors set out in 18 USC § 3142(g). Defense counsel should also determine all bail resources including cash, property (even jewelry and stocks) and financially responsible persons (referred to as "FRPs" or sureties) who would be willing to co-sign a bond or take custody of the defendant. If there is real property and the case is one where the posting of substantial security is anticipated, a recent assessment of the property might be required. Documentation on the property should be brought to court showing proof of ownership and value.

If defense counsel's first exposure to the case is the day of the initial appearance, similar interviews and investigation should be done to the extent possible given the time constraints of the court appearance. In cases where the prosecution is seeking detention it might be better to hold off the judge's determination of bail until resources and FRPs can be marshaled, even though the defendant will have to stay in custody during the meantime. This also provides additional time to try to work out a negotiated bail with the prosecution.

Ideally the FRPs should physically be in court with proof of their income and assets. If the judge orders the bond to be secured by FRPs, this can be accomplished more immediately if the sureties are in court. Perhaps even more importantly, having the FRPs physically in court visually demonstrates to the judge support for the defendant as well as ties to the community.

In federal court, the defendant no longer has to post the full amount of the bond through a bail bondsman. Instead, the federal court holds the bond and the defendant posts any requisite security. Some judges will even take wedding rings and other items of sentimental value to ensure the presence of the defendant. The defendant will be required to surrender all travel documents and should bring any passport or visas to the initial appearance.

In some cases it might be possible to have bail set and still have the defendant released even before all conditions are met. Judges will sometimes approve a premature release (usually if the prosecution consents and it is not a serious rebuttable presumption case) as long as a date is given when all bail conditions must be met or the defendant will be returned to custody or a bench warrant will issue for failure to appear. If the condition is a relatively minor one, such as surrendering a passport when the defendant has signed a substantial bond, judges are likely to give the defendant 24 hours to go home and get the passport. In other cases, usually rebuttable presumption cases, the defense might want to consent to detention without prejudice to bringing a motion for bail at a later date if defense counsel does not believe she will have enough time to marshal the resources necessary to overcome the presumption by the date of the detention hearing which must be held within five days.

The strength of the prosecution's case is an important area for the defense. It provides a basis for seeking as much information about the prosecution's case as possible at this initial stage in order for the court to assess the strength of the prosecution's case. It is also an area where any weakness in the prosecution's case, including the possibility of suppression of evidence, could give the defense a good argument for getting bail. To that end, the defense attorney should speak to the prosecutor and attempt to get as much information as possible about the strength of the case against the client. This is essential for bail issues but also for the beginning of negotiations.

Defense counsel might be tempted in cases where the client is charged with a serious drug offense involving a mandatory minimum, has a significant criminal record and/or is in the country illegally to consent to detention without prejudice because the attorney is convinced that there is no way the defendant will be released. Even in those cases it is usually better to have the detention hearing and at least hear the prosecution's proffers which could lead to discovery of important information about the case. The prosecution might have to call witnesses to support its assertions and those witnesses would be under oath and subject to cross-examination. Although judges may allow the prosecution to proceed by proffer, for certain assertions some judges will require live testimony. Defense counsel should request that witnesses be called. The prosecution would also have to turn over any statements of the witnesses pursuant to FRCrP 26.2. FRCrP 46(i). Prosecutors might want to consider consenting to some astronomical bail to avoid disclosing witnesses where that is likely. Again, for defense counsel, contesting bail provides an opportunity to fight hard for the client, discover case facts early on, as well as establish good client rapport even where release is highly unlikely.

Pretrial Services Interview

Before the initial appearance the federal defendant ordinarily will be interviewed by the Pretrial Services Office, a division of the Probation Department, in order to determine whether the defendant is a risk of flight and/or a danger to the community. The Pretrial Services Office issues a brief report setting forth the charges, the defendant's prior record (in some jurisdictions the "rap sheet" is attached to the report), bail resources and, importantly, a recommendation as to whether the defendant should be released, and, if so, on what conditions.

If counsel has been retained or assigned in advance of the interview it is often helpful to be present at the interview, particularly since counsel might have useful information on potential co-signers and be able to provide confirmation of the client's assets and resources. In many cases the interview is held without counsel but the substance of the report is confidential and is to be used solely for bail purposes. Although the statute provides that regulations may be promulgated allowing for release of the bail information to specified individuals such as probation officers, law enforcement agencies in limited circumstances and for criminal justice research, no such regulations have been promulgated to date. *See* 18 USC § 3153(c). Indeed, even in the wake of the events of 9/11 and passage of Patriot Act type legislation seeking access to more and more personal information, such information still remains confidential. In any event, information contained in the report is not admissible on the issue of guilt unless it is a crime committed to obtain pretrial release or for failure to appear. *Id.*

Although the parties are entitled to a copy of the pretrial services report, most jurisdictions require that the report be returned at the end of the bail hearing. Any information contained in the report helpful to the defense should be written down in the file. It is especially important to note whether the defendant tested positive for controlled substances and any incriminating statements. Should the prosecution attempt to use that information to establish the defendant's knowledge of narcotics, for instance, the defense should object that the prosecution is precluded from doing so under the Bail Reform Act. *See* 18 USC § 3153(c)(3).

Detention Hearings

In certain cases the prosecution is entitled to seek detention. However, unless it is a crime of violence, an offense carrying life imprisonment or death, a drug offense with a maximum of 10 years or more (essentially any federal drug felony), a felon with two violent or drug priors, or the case involves a serious risk of flight or obstruction of justice the prosecution is not entitled to a detention hearing and bail must be set even if the person is dangerous. *See* 18 USC § 3142(f)(1). Although section (f)(1) covers a wide range of cases both parties need to assess whether a detention hearing is required. For example, if the defendant is accused solely of having brought a firearm from another state, for example, and there is no risk of flight or obstruction of justice, the prosecution could not seek detention even though the case involved a firearm and the potential argument of dangerousness.

Once the prosecution establishes that it is entitled to seek detention the issue is whether the hearing will go forward immediately.
The defense may request a continuance for up to five days and the
prosecution can request a continuance for up to three days (these
time periods do not include holidays and weekends). 18 USC §
3142(f)(2). It is usually better for an attorney to be prepared fully
for the hearing rather than risk having the judge impose an order
of detention or release based on half a presentation and then have
to overcome that order later on.

In most cases the judge will ask at the outset what the prosecution's position is on bail. If the prosecution is seeking detention
the judge will inquire whether it is a rebuttable presumption case,
and, if not, whether the prosecution is proceeding on risk of flight
or dangerousness to the community or both. When the judge
neglects to ask, defense counsel should insure that the prosecutor states specifically for the record on what grounds it is relying
in seeking detention. A rebuttable presumption exists for serious
narcotics and firearm offenses as set out in 18 USC § 3142(e) and
(f). This means that there is a presumption that the person is a risk
of flight and/or a danger to the community.

Prosecutors prefer to proceed on risk of flight rather than danger
to the community because the burden of proof for risk of flight is
preponderance of the evidence, but for danger to the community
the burden of proof is by clear and convincing evidence. *See* 18
USC § 3142(f)(2). Similarly, judges usually will rule on risk of
flight in most cases and might not even reach the issue of danger
to the community. A judge who is asked to find a danger to the
community is likely to also find a risk of flight, where appropriate,
to insulate the bail order from review at the higher standard of
clear and convincing evidence.

In rebuttable presumption cases, some judges will require the
defense to go first once it is determined that the presumption applies, since in those cases the defense technically has the burden
to rebut the presumption. Defense counsel should request that
the prosecution set out all of the facts it relies on first so that the
defense can make a consolidated response. In addition to arguing that the presumption is rebuttable, defense counsel is usually

benefited by offering a concrete proposal or package complete with monies, bond co-signers, FRPs and restrictive conditions. Defense counsel should be aware of the "going rate" for the district as to bail in such cases. Asking for bail without offering a specific package can be dangerous because even if the judge is persuaded that bail can be set, the conditions the judge chooses to set might be impossible for the defendant to meet. The following is a typical defense response.

"Your Honor, although there is presumption of risk of flight and danger to the community, the presumption is rebuttable. As the Pretrial Services Officer observed in her recommendation, there are conditions or combinations of conditions that will ensure the defendant's presence in court and the safety of the community. Mr. Jones is a lifelong resident of the community. He is a 38-year old U.S. citizen, married with two children. His wife and mother are present in court today. Mr. Jones' immediate and extended family all live in the metropolitan area. A total of seven of them are in court today, having taken off from work to attend this proceeding.

Mr. Jones has worked for the postal service for 15 years. His only other brush with the law involved a misdemeanor simple possession of marijuana six years ago for which he received a suspended sentence. Although this offense involves the sale of narcotics, thus triggering the presumption, there are no allegations of actual violence or the presence of any weapons. Moreover, the evidence linking Mr. Jones to the offense relies solely on the uncorroborated testimony of a confidential informant and the evidence was seized during a search where the officers lacked a search warrant. If Your Honor will rely on the testimony of the confidential information in determining bail, the defense would requests that the confidential informant come before this Court and testify under oath subject to cross examination. In addition, as Your Honor is well aware pursuant to 18 USC § 3142 (j), nothing in the Bail Reform Act shall be construed as modifying or limiting the presumption of innocence.

The defense submits that a $200,000 personal recognizance bond co-signed by three financially responsible people, Mr.

Jones' father who is a retired school superintendent with a pension, Mr. Jones' mother who currently works as a nurse at the VA hospital and Mr. Jones' brother who is a sanitation worker with the city. All three are present in court with proof of income and are prepared to sign today. If necessary, Mr. Jones' father would put up his home which has an equity value of over $65,000. Mr. Jones would submit to strict pre-trial supervision, and, of course, surrender his passport."

If the defendant is released the judge will issue a release order including any special conditions and advising the defendant of the penalties for failure to appear and committing an offense while out on bail. *See* 18 USC § 3142(h). The judge must also advise the defendant of the crimes of witness tampering, obstruction of justice, etc. *See* 18 USC § 3142(h)(2)(C). Defense counsel should tell the defendant that if she is found guilty of bail jumping any jail sentence for that offense is required to be run consecutively and any crime committed while out on bail must also run consecutive to the original offense sentence. *See* 18 USC § 3146(b)(2); 18 USC § 3147.

If the defendant is detained, the court must issue an order of detention including findings of fact and statement of reasons for detention. 18 USC § 3142(i). These reasons will be helpful if counsel decides to reopen the hearing or appeal the order. The judge can also permit the temporary release of a person in custody for the preparation of the defense or for "another compelling reason." *Id.* In practice the compelling reason allowing for such a release is almost always when the defendant becomes a cooperating witness for the prosecution and must meet with the prosecution and case agents away from prison.

A defendant may be detained pretrial provided the detention does not amount to punishment. In a typical semantic side step, the Supreme Court has defined pretrial detention as having a regulatory purpose, rather than a punitive purpose, to avoid any conflict. *See Salerno*, 481 U.S. at 747-49, 107 S. Ct. at 2101-02 , 95 L. Ed. 2d at 708-10. That being said, the defendant is entitled to credit toward his sentence if he is convicted for his "regulatory" federal pretrial detention time. If the detention seems excessive, particularly if there is a delay because of the prosecution, the defense could bring a motion for release on the grounds that the pretrial detention violates the defendant's due process rights. Such motions are rarely granted provided the defendant is brought to trial within the requirements of the Speedy Trial Act. *See also Natali, Parsons, Statsinger & Wolfe, Practice Commentaries to Federal Rules of Criminal Procedure, Commentary to Fed. R. Crim. P.* 48 (2002-2003).

Special Conditions and Considerations

Pretrial Services administers a drug test by testing the defendant's urine at the pretrial interview. If the defendant tests positive for narcotics she will be subject to drug testing as a condition of bail. If the defendant did not test positive and there is no evidence of drug use the defense should object to the imposition of drug testing as a release condition. Where the defendant has a substance abuse problem, the defense might want to propose having the defendant submit to in house drug treatment as an alternative to detention.

If possible, the defense should try to get "regular" pretrial service supervision rather than "strict" pretrial supervision. Strict pretrial supervision usually means the defendant has to report daily to the pretrial office, sometimes in person. Regular pretrial supervision might only require a weekly telephone call or monthly reports mailed in. The defense should also try to get generous travel restrictions such as the ability to travel within the continental United States or even foreign countries if that is necessary for the defendant's employment. The standard condition when a bail is set is usually that the defendant remains in the jurisdiction or surrounding jurisdictions (Southern District of New York and Eastern District of New York, for example) unless receiving prior permission to travel beyond that jurisdiction.

Defense counsel should avoid offering real property to secure a bond unless it is absolutely necessary. Counsel might not want to include it in the first pitch to the judge and might offer it only if it will make the difference between release and detention. Judges require proof of the value of the property and some might insist on a current assessment which can be costly and the paperwork often delays release. Some prosecutors will demand deeds and signing over liens to the prosecution in advance. Defense counsel should object to actions by the prosecution that are more appropriate for a real estate agent in the sale of a house rather than an officer of the court seeking security for a bond. The argument by defense counsel is that the purpose of putting up the house is not to provide a real estate investment for the government. It is the risk of losing the property that compels the defendant's presence in court and the reason for requiring the property as security.

As a last resort the defense can offer that the defendant would wear an electronic monitoring device while in home detention. Electronic monitoring can be expensive to operate and prosecutors usually object because the defendant can still make it out of the state before the defendant is discovered missing. If electronic monitoring and home confinement is ordered, defense counsel should make certain that the defendant is still able to attend employment, medical, religious and legal appointments.

If the defendant is detained but requires medical or psychological treatment, defense counsel should ensure that the detention order or separate medical order includes specific treatment. This will help the defendant to get services from the Bureau of Prisons, and counsel can return to the judge to enforce the court's order if services are not provided.

Sureties and Securities

FRCrP 46(d) requires that every surety be justified by affidavit which could include detailing the property and encumbrances and liabilities of the surety. The requirement of an affidavit may be relaxed in some jurisdictions and a verbal representation in court or a proffer by counsel could be sufficient justification. Counsel should determine what the local practice is with respect to the justification of sureties.

Before offering a surety or FRP, defense counsel should interview the person as to their financial situation but also as to their relationship to the defendant and their knowledge of the facts of the case. Remember, this person will be interviewed by a prosecutor whose motives could include additional investigation into the facts of the case rather than just the financial responsibility of the FRP. In some instances it might be wiser for the defense not to proffer a particular FRP whose testimony might compromise the defendant and the merits of his case even if the FRP's bank account might ensure release. The better practice is to try to get the judge to approve the surety on the record at the bail hearing so that the prosecution does not have the opportunity to interview the sureties privately. Prosecutors should demand the opportunity to interview the FRPs before they are approved by the court.

Prosecutors have used the FRP interviews not only to further the investigation, but in some cases to discourage potential co-signers from signing in order to keep a defendant in custody when bail has been set over the prosecutor's objection. If there is a dispute as to the adequacy of the surety, the issue will be resolved by the judge. In most cases judicial intervention is unnecessary because the prosecutor will be successful in dissuading the FRP from signing, often by emphasizing that if the defendant fails to come to court the surety could lose her life savings, be unable to send her children to college and will owe the government hundreds of thousands of dollars, possibly for the rest of her life.

Prosecutors have been known to focus on a potential co-signer's immigration status he is a non-U.S. citizen and suggest that this status could be compromised by signing a bond. Once the FRP declines to sign, defense counsel has few options except to "debrief" the FRP on what the prosecutor said and to explain realistically what the consequences would be if the defendant were to fail to appear when the prosecutor has exaggerated those consequences. In some cases defense counsel might wish to have the judge explain to the potential FRP what the consequences would be if the defendant did not appear in court. Again, the better practice is to try to get the judge to approve the surety on the record at the bail hearing so that the prosecution does not have the opportunity to interview the sureties privately.

If the judge is convinced that the money or property used to secure bail was obtained from illegitimate sources, the judge may decline to accept it. Prosecutors should review the source of the monies carefully since a hearing to determine its legitimacy, known as a *Nebbia* hearing from *United States v. Nebbia*, 357 F.2d 303

(2d Cir. 1966), could provide discovery to the prosecution and an opportunity to put sureties on the stand and prevent them from signing a bond. *See also* 18 USC § 3142(g)(4). Conversely, defense counsel should know what monies will be used and the source of those monies before they are offered as bail. It is within the judge's discretion to hold a hearing; the prosecution is not entitled to a hearing on the source of the funding. *See, e.g., U.S. v. O'Brien*, 895 F.2d 810, 817-18 (1st Cir. 1990).

Sureties or FRPs should be advised that they will be jointly and severally liable for the full amount of the bond should the defendant fail to come to court as required. FRCrP 46(e) provides further details on the forfeiture of bond for failure to appear.

Appealing, Revoking or Amending a Bail Decision

There is a right to a prompt appeal to a district court for review of a magistrate judge's bail determination. 18 USC § 3145(b). If a bail decision is adverse to counsel's position and the attorney intends to seek district court review, counsel should ask for a stay of the bail order pending that review.

On appeal, district courts are permitted to reach their own decisions and need not defer to the magistrate judges. Usually the district court judges are less sympathetic to releasing defendants on bail. Magistrate judges hear thousands of cases on bail and have a sense of permissible bail cases. These same judges also do not want to put every defendant charged with drugs in detentions which would overwhelm the prisons, especially in districts with large metropolitan cities and high crime rates. Because District court judges oversee far fewer hearings, they consider these issues less often, and tend to think any defendant where the prosecution moves for detention is in fact a high risk.

A bail decision of the district court is appealable to the circuit court. 18 USC § 3145(c). The appeal is interlocutory (meaning it can be appealed before the end of the case); otherwise the issue of release would be moot once the defendant was convicted and sentenced under the original release or detention order. *See* 18

USC § 3731. The standard of review for an appeal of the district court decision is not set out in the Bail Reform Act and circuits differ on the level of deference, thus, counsel should familiarize themselves with the standard in their jurisdiction. For example, the standard in the Second Circuit is "clearly erroneous." *See United States v. Shakur*, 817 F.2d 189, 196 (2d Cir. 1985).

Often more useful and successful from a defense perspective than bail review or appeal, is the reconsideration of bail. A bail hearing may be reopened any time before trial if there is new information. 18 USC § 3142 (f)(2). New information could mean one more co-signer was found or an extra ten dollars discovered. In practice, it does not take much to get the hearing reopened. It might be that the magistrate judge has changed or the case is now with a particular district court judge who historically might be more likely to rule in a particular party's favor. The judge's decision on bail might depend on the posture of the case. If the defense has a strong motion to suppress defense counsel could argue that the defendant has little incentive to flee while the issue is pending. If the defendant qualifies for a substantial reduction under the drug guidelines she might have less incentive to flee. Once bail is granted and the defendant shows up, it is harder to justify detention even if the defendant loses the suppression hearing. Getting bail might take six bites of the apple and 10 FRPs before a judge will finally relent, but most defendants will appreciate the extra effort—they really want to get out of jail.

Bail orders may be amended on motion of the defense or the prosecution. 18 USC § 3142(c)(3). If the defendant commits other offenses or violates the conditions of bail the prosecution can move to have the bail revoked. The procedures and sanctions for violating the terms of release are set out at 18 USC § 3148.

Some Useful Cases

United States v. Salerno, 481 U.S. 739, 107 S.Ct 2095, 95 L. Ed. 2d 697 (1986).

United States v. Nebbia, 357 F.2d 303 (2d Cir. 1966).

CHAPTER TWENTY
FOURTH AMENDMENT ISSUES AND INVESTIGATION

As a result of the fact specific nature of totality of the circumstances analysis, investigation is an essential aspect of Fourth Amendment litigation. Unless an attorney can determine the relevant circumstances surrounding the search or seizure, counsel will be at a severe disadvantage when challenging or defending these issues in court.

Visit the Scene

Other than interviewing the client or agent in the case (*see Chapter Seventeen: Fourth Amendment Issues and Client/ Agent Interviews*), there is nothing more important than visiting the scene of the alleged crime. It is tempting to rely solely on the reports and descriptions from the client or agents or even pictures taken by an investigator rather than go and walk the area oneself. Two words: JUST GO. There is no substitute. Even if the investigator does exactly as told with respect to the important aspects of the case, a lawyer is losing out by not seeing the area and getting clues and case theories suggested by the physical layout. Most investigators and agents think only like police officers, not like lawyers who ultimately will be litigating these issues.

It is always surprising how infrequently prosecutors personally go to the area relying almost exclusively on the reports from the agent. In one case in the Southern District of New York, for example, the prosecutor failed to go personally to the scene where the issue was whether the defendant had been living in a particular apartment where drugs were found in that apartment's mailbox. The prosecution had no direct evidence that the defendant lived there; the only mail taken from the mailbox was an envelope addressed to a third party who remained unidentified during the trial. Had the prosecutor gone to the scene he would have observed that the names of the third party as well as the defendant had been written on tape on the bottom of the same mailbox. By failing to go and look at the mailbox himself, the prosecutor was unaware of direct, damaging evidence overlooked by the agent that he could have offered in his case in chief.

Take the client (if he is out on bail) or the agent to the scene. They were usually the ones there; the attorney was not. Without the client or agent input it is difficult to recreate the sequence of events and the location of critical junctures during the searches and seizures. Even if defense counsel has the police reports early in the case (unusual in federal court), agents may not have included many details or may have put facts down incorrectly.

Try to go to the scene at the same time of day (and ideally season) when the events took place. Keep in mind that if it is a different time of year from the date of the search or seizure the scenery might be quite different, for example, no foliage on the trees providing a better view of the scene than the officers may have actually had. Make sure to ask the client or agent in what ways the scene differs from the date of arrest.

Visiting the scene might also lead to the discovery of witnesses who observed the encounter between the defendant and the officers. The potential to find witnesses and observe the scene the same time of the year are reasons why one should try to get to the scene as close to the day of the search or seizure as possible. In case of witnesses, ALWAYS TAKE BLANK SUBPOENAS which can be filled out and given to witnesses to get them to court for the hearing or trial, especially for witnesses who may be hard to contact in the future. Serve a subpoena even if ultimately you decide not to call that person so that at least you have the option.

Bring an investigator to take pictures and describe the area in the event he or she needs to be called to establish the layout of the area. If you are the prosecutor, take the case agent for the same reason and to refresh his recollection if he is going to have to testify at hearing or trial.

Take Photographs

Take a ton of photographs of the scene. When the client is in custody, counsel should take comprehensive photographs of the entire area to use when meeting with the client to discuss Fourth Amendment issues so that the client can point out the areas where the events took place. Even if the client is not in custody, defense counsel should take lots of pictures to use in the investigation of the case, in assessing case theories and possibly introduce at a hearing or trial. This will also prevent having to take too many additional trips to the scene.

DO NOT TAKE PICTURES WITH THE DEFENDANT IN THEM if you are going to use them in court. It almost never helps the defense case to demonstrate unequivocally that the defendant was at the scene of the so-called crime on some prior occasion (even if in actuality it was after the alleged crime). It is particularly unhelpful when the damaging photo is introduced by the defense unwittingly. The prosecution should also take pictures to avoid having to come back to the scene for hearing or trial preparation and to assist when questioning and preparing witnesses. Such pictures may also be important to introduce into a case in chief or as rebuttal or impeachment.

The defense should also take pictures of the physical evidence recovered in the case such as any weapon, the narcotics, the wallet, etc. It is a hassle to go to government evidence custodians to review the physical evidence, only to remember the next day you forgot to get the serial numbers off the pager they claim the co-defendant called to contact your client.

You will have to get special permission to take photographs of the evidence and to bring a camera into a prosecutor's office. Get the permission. In federal court, and most states the defense is entitled to review and make copies of evidence necessary to present a defense under FRCrP 16. If the prosecution is uncooperative, seek a court order.

It is a good idea for the prosecution to take pictures of the physical evidence to use with officers and witnesses rather than having to trot down to the evidence locker for every witness. These pictures could also establish proof of the evidence vouchered in the unlikely but possible event that the evidence becomes misplaced or lost. (There have been cases when drugs in particular have disappeared from evidence lockers.)

The key photographs are the ones which support the theory of the case. If the challenge to the search of the vehicle is that the officer could not have seen what was on the console because of the tinted windows and the jacked up tires, pictures of the same vehicle (if possible) or at least a representative vehicle to show the impossibility would be crucial. If the police claim they saw what appeared to be a brick of cocaine in plain view in the closet during a security sweep, make sure to have pictures of the cocaine as well as the wrapping, since the defense may be that there was no way to tell that it was narcotics because the wrapping was opaque and the shape unremarkable.

Interview Police Officers

Prosecutors do not like defense lawyers interviewing the arresting officers or any police officer for that matter. The mentality of the prosecutor in many ways is that the police officer or agent is to the prosecution what the defendant is to defense counsel: privileged. Police officers and case agents are not "represented" by the prosecutor and are not a party to the action. There is no attorney client privilege and technically the defense is not required to ask permission from the prosecutor to speak to an arresting officer or case agent.

Police officers are often witnesses to the crime and will usually be called as a witness in the case. Often police officers will decline defense counsel's request for an interview for the above-stated reasons. Although they are not supposed to do it, prosecutors, particularly new ones, have been known to tell officers not to speak to defense counsel at all. Such an admonition is unethical.

A smart, seasoned prosecutor knows how to convey the message more delicately (and ethically): *the defense may ask you questions, you do not have to answer their questions; you are free to meet with them but you absolutely have a right not to meet with them; bear in mind that anything you say to them they will attempt to use against you on cross examination, etc.* Most officers already know the message or get it quickly: do not speak to defense counsel. This blue wall of silence is more prevalent in some jurisdiction than others.

Defense counsel can often use a refusal by the officer to be interviewed by the defense to impeach the officer when he does take the stand. The key is to set it up so that the defense can argue that the police officer has something to hide or wanted to be able to change his testimony or was biased in favor of the prosecution.

First and foremost, defense attorneys should NEVER represent themselves as anything but defense attorneys representing the defendant when communicating with any witness. Officers have been known to claim that they thought they were talking to a prosecutor or prosecutor's assistant; either directly accusing defense attorneys of misrepresenting their identity or implying such. Defense attorneys and defense personnel should always give the officer or any witness a business card and make it clear who they are. Explain why you are asking questions: *My name is Ms. Jones and I represent Mr. Smith, the defendant in this case. I would like to ask you questions about what you saw on the date Mr. Smith was arrested.* The purpose of making the object of the interview clear is to demonstrate to the judge or jury that it was not to trick the officer or only to hear helpful information for the defense case, but to get the officer's side of the story.

ALWAYS have a witness to an interview, like an investigator, who can observe the conversation and be called as a witness to that conversation should there be an issue as to what was represented or said. Otherwise, counsel would place herself in the awkward and unethical position of needing to call herself as a witness to impeach an officer on the stand if he denies that the lawyer told him she represented the defendant or made other statements that he subsequently changed on the stand.

An attorney may not be called as a witness and still represent the defendant. Even if the defense lawyer has to get a spouse or a boyfriend to listen in, do so. Importantly, defense counsel should introduce the person who will be observing the interview and why they are there: *Officer Johnson, this is Mr. Thompson, he is my investigator and is going to be sitting in and listening to this interview.* This is particularly important in phone interviews.

Officers may ask to have the prosecutor present during the interview or prosecutors may ask to be present. Ordinarily the defense should object. Interviewing witnesses is work product (the prosecutor is going to hear what questions you ask and that reveals case theory, etc.). Opposing counsel is not entitled to be part of the interview of a witness. Prosecutors do not allow defense lawyers in on any of their witness interviews. The request to be present by prosecutors is often based on the mistaken assumption that the prosecutors control or represent the officers. If the officer insists, defense counsel should raise the issue before the judge.

If the officer asks for the prosecutor to be present, defense counsel should ask why? If it is to have a witness to the conversation, the prosecutor is disqualified from such a role for the same reasons a defense attorney cannot be called to the stand to impeach a witness she has interviewed during the course of a case. In some instances, the fact that the officer asked to have the prosecutor present is very helpful to the defense because it could be argued that he needs to be coached or watched by a prosecutor; it certainly gives the appearance that he is controlled by the prosecution and not a neutral witness. At a minimum it suggests that he is very much a part of the prosecution team with a vested interest in obtaining a conviction.

If defense counsel is practicing in a jurisdiction where officers routinely refuse to speak to defense lawyers as part of the police culture (often they will admit it is the policy on their force) it will take separate litigation to crack through to the officers. One of the best techniques is to seek intervention from the court. Explain to the court that the officers are witnesses in the case and have categorically refused to meet with the defense.

What defense counsel must make clear when asking for court intervention on the issue is not to direct the officer to speak to the defense (the judge has no authority to do so), but to have the court advise the officer that although he is not required to speak to the defense, he is permitted to speak to the defense and he cannot be reprimanded nor can his job be jeopardized by speaking to the defense.

Defense counsel should make sure that the judge advises the police officer what the defense is asking by providing a script, for example: *Officer Johnson, do you understand that the defense has requested an opportunity to interview you on this matter? Do you understand that the defense has requested to hear your side of what happened on the day you arrested Mr. Smith; specifically they would like to know what you observed that day. Do you understand that as a witness in this case you are permitted to speak to the defense without being reprimanded or jeopardizing your job? Although you are not required to speak to the defense, do you understand that you have a right to speak to them without any adverse consequences from the government or your precinct.*

The prosecutor will typically assure the judge at the outset that this proceeding is unnecessary and a waste of the court's time because the prosecutor himself has conveyed that message to the officer and the officer still does not want to speak to the defense. Defense counsel's response should be that the message is being given by an interested party to the case, and someone who has the appearance of authority over the officer. The defense must express to the judge that it is essential that a neutral party convey the message. Ultimately what the defense hopes to achieve is that the officer will be embarrassed by refusing to speak to defense attorneys given these understandings.

Should the officer continue to refuse to speak to the defense after the judge's admonition, the defense attorney is in a position to use that information against the officer before the judge at a suppression hearing and before the jury at trial: *Officer Johnson the defense asked to interview you about this case two months ago? You were told that the purpose of the interview was to hear your side of what happened on the day you arrested Mr. Smith. Judge Marshall told you that the purpose of the interview was for the defense to hear from you what you observed on that date. You were also advised by the court that although you are not required to speak to the defense you have a right to speak to the defense without any adverse consequences from the government or your precinct. You still refused to speak to defense lawyers in this case didn't you. You spoke to the prosecutors in this case before you testified today didn't you.*

The officer may still say, "I just don't trust defense lawyers", but if the presiding judge and jury see that the court made the admonitions and that there was no real reason for not speaking, it can give the appearance of not being a neutral witness and of trying to sabotage the defense in favor of the prosecution.

Interviewing Witnesses

Both counsels should interview witnesses as soon as possible. Ideally, the defense should interview witnesses before the prosecutor has had a chance to speak with them since witnesses may become more reluctant to speak with the defense after speaking with the prosecution. In cases where there has been ongoing investigation, many of the witnesses will already have been interviewed by the prosecutor before the charges were filed, but in some cases there are witnesses who have yet to be interviewed.

As with interviewing police officers, it is important to have an observer present when interviewing any witness in the event the witness changes his or her testimony on the stand. If the differing testimony goes to a non-collateral issue in the case, a party is entitled to call the observer to impeach the witness as to what was said previously.

One issue which often arises when interviewing witnesses is whether the investigator or witness to the interview for the attorney should take notes of the interview. The main concern is that if the investigator or witness is called to the stand to impeach the person interviewed, if the investigator's notes are related to the upcoming testimony the opposing party would be entitled to review the notes before cross examining the investigator under 18 USC § 3500 (so-called *Jencks* material) in the federal system.

There are pros and cons to the issue of whether notes should be taken. Something bad for the party doing the interviewing could be encapsulated for the other side to use. On the other hand, if the investigator or agent needs to refresh recollection or to bolster what was actually said, a relatively verbatim set of notes including the necessary statement could be useful. Witnesses should ordinarily be advised to takes notes sparingly but to make sure that important information is set down for future reference. A student at a criminal clinic seemed to have it both ways by simply writing her notes out in Mandarin.

Much of what was said about interviewing police officers also goes for interviewing lay witnesses. Counsel must clearly identify who they are and their purpose. Multiple witnesses should be interviewed separately; the argument for the other side being that the witnesses heard each other's versions and crafted their testimony to conform to one version after hearing what the first guy said.

The defendant should never be present at any of the interviews done by defense counsel. Not only is it likely to impact how freely the witness is willing to speak, but the interviewee could also become a witness to anything said by the defendant to his lawyer which might otherwise be confidential. Witness tampering accusations may also ensue regardless of what was actually said to the witness if the defendant is present.

Moreover, if the defendant is present during the interview it opens both the defendant's and the witnesses' testimonies to allegations that the two put their heads together to make sure their stories were consistent. Typically the case agent will be present for most of the interviews for the prosecution who can then be called to impeach the witness if he or she says something different on the stand.

Choose the location of the interview wisely. If the witness' testimony relates to where the arrest took place or where the search was conducted, if possible interview the witness at that place. Witnesses are often more comfortable on their own "turf" and will be more likely to speak with a lawyer or investigator if the lawyer or investigator comes to them rather than in some stuffy lawyer's office.

Sometimes it is better to have only the investigator or paralegal interview a witness, particularly at the outset to determine the relevancy of the person's testimony. Lay people are often intimidated by lawyers and might be less forthcoming out of nerves. Before any witness is put on the stand, however, the attorney must interview him and prepare him to testify. No matter how wonderful or reliable an investigator or paralegal is, ultimately it is the attorney who is responsible for providing effective assistance of counsel and deciding who should be called and why. *See also, Chapter Twenty-Five: Trial and Post Trial Proceedings.*

Use of Subpoenas in Pretrial Investigation

Both parties to a criminal case have subpoena power. A subpoena is an order to give testimony or compel the production of documents or evidence. In federal court, subpeonas are governed by Rule 17 FRCrP, and most state jurisdictions have similar provisions. A subpoena duces tecum is the normal mechanism for securing documents. A subpoena testificandum is the mechanism for obtaining witness testimony.

Defense counsel may require a subpoena in either of two situations: to obtain documents that are relevant and material to the hearing or trial while preparing its case, or to compel the production of documents and/or the testimony of witnesses at a hearing or trial. The defense may issue subpoenas without court order or seal. Certain agencies could require a court-ordered subpoena before responding; this is the usual procedure when serving subpoenas on any police department.

Rule 17(c) allows for obtaining certain materials in advance of trial and provides a practical procedure by which material can be inspected at a reasonable time before the date of trial. This procedure avoids delay during the trial and allows for effective trial preparation.

Material in the possession of the government and third-parties is subject to subpoena. The Supreme Court made this clear in *Bowman Dairy Corp. v. United States*, 341 U.S. 214, 71 S. Ct. 675, 95 L. Ed. 879 (1951):

[T]he plain words of the Rule are not to be ignored. They must be given their ordinary meaning to carry out the purpose of establishing a more liberal policy for the production, inspection and use of materials at the trial. There was no intention to exclude from the reach of process of the defendant any material that had been used before the grand jury or could be used at trial. In short, any documents or other materials, admissible as evidence, obtained by the Government by solicitation or voluntarily from third persons [are] subject to subpoena.

Id. at 221-222, 71 S. Ct at 679, 95 L. Ed. at 885. The primary restriction on this provision is Rule 16(a)(2) FRCrP, which bars the disclosure of reports pertaining to the prosecution's criminal investigation. *See Chapter Twenty One: Fourth Amendment and Discovery Issues.*

Pretrial subpoenas can take a long time, especially if the subject of the subpoena moves to quash the subpoena and there is litigation on the issue which can delay obtaining the information. One of the first things an attorney in a criminal case should do is sit down and figure out what information needs to be obtained by subpoenas well in advance of trial.

The following is a preliminary list for defense counsel in particular to think about in terms of issuing subpoenas early on in the case:

• Are there **education records** that need to be obtained? They could also help to establish that the defendant had limited education or a very low I.Q. and was unable to voluntarily consent to the search.

• Are there **housing records**, leases, etc., that need to be obtained? Housing records are often critical in Fourth Amendment issues to show or dispute standing—who owned the apartment, house, mobile home, etc.

• Are there **911 tapes**? If there was a 911 call it might contain valuable information regarding the information known to the officer at the time of the arrest. Typically these tapes are taped over after a certain number of days. As a matter of course the defense should always request at the outset that any 911 case in a tape be preserved and serve a subpoena immediately for its production.

• Are there **police inventory procedures** including memoranda and manuals to determine whether there was indeed a standardized procedure for inventory searches?

• Are there **telephone records** to show that the defendant did or did not make a certain call? Pen Registers, which show the incoming as well as the outgoing local calls rather than just long distance, are often extremely useful in a case, but typically take a long time to produce although in the age of improved computer technology, the process has shortened.

• Are there **DMV (Department of Motor Vehicle) records** such as car titles or registration to show ownership for standing purposes?

• Are there **medical records** of the defendant or a witness that need to be obtained (such as medical records showing the defendant received treatment for wounds where the case is self defense). If medical records are needed, defense counsel should have the defendant sign medical releases for the information which expedites the process considerably. Make sure to include in the subpoena as much information as possible including the name of the treating physician and the dates of the treatment.

• Are there **bank records**? Like medical records, if the records are the defendant's, defense counsel should obtain a release from the client to expedite the process.

• Are there **personnel records** of prosecution witnesses or of the defendant which need to be obtained? Has the officer been reprimanded for failing to obtain warrants in the past? Has the officer been sued for civil rights violations for unlawful arrest? As discussed in more detail in *Chapter Twenty One: Fourth Amendment and Discovery Issues*, there is a detailed showing required to get police personnel records, but the defendant's records may also be useful particularly in negotiations or to show alibi.

For more information on subpoenas, *See Chapter Twenty One: Fourth Amendment and Discovery Issues.*

CHAPTER TWENTY-ONE
FOURTH AMENDMENT AND
DISCOVERY ISSUES

Discovery in General

When starting a class on discovery, law students are asked what information they would want to know in advance of trial if they were defending someone accused of a crime. The two replies at the top of list are always the same: names of witnesses who will be called against the defendant, and any police reports that were filed in the case. These students are amazed when told that under the Federal Rules of Criminal Procedure in a non-capital case the defense is not entitled to pretrial disclosure of the witnesses or police reports. (Many states have similar rules, although some prosecutors have a more open file policy.)

The absurd federal discovery rules were adopted ostensibly to protect the safety of witnesses and to prevent the defendant from "tailoring" his story to match the police version. But the reality is that very few cases involve such violence or tailoring, yet the delay in discovery works to the detriment of the entire administration of justice. When a United States Attorney for one of the New York districts was asked whether the real concern was witness safety, he candidly replied that it was strategic; the less time the defense knew about witnesses and police reports the less time the defense lawyers would have to conduct an effective cross-examination. The federal rules and those states with similar statutes have made the discovery of vital trial information a game of hide and seek.

Without the names of witnesses and police reports in advance of trial, the defense is hampered in its ability to interview witnesses and to do its own investigation on witness credibility, which compromises the truth seeking function of the system. (Incidentally, the defense is required to disclose nearly every possible witness it could call under alibi theory, insanity theory, or public authority defense.)

Although Rule 16 FRCrP does not require the prosecution to provide witness names and reports, many prosecutors do. Indeed, with respect to discovery in general, often the best source of information is the prosecutor. Before filing anything formal, it is a good idea for the defense to speak to the prosecutor who might be more than happy to disclose the full case to facilitate a speedy resolution. There is no reason to prepare a formal, adversarial motion for discovery if the prosecutor has every intention of showing the defense the entire file.

The wise prosecutor appreciates that when the defense is able to obtain information from witnesses and officers' reports pretrial, it assists the defense attorney in counseling a client on whether to file a motion, accept a plea offer, or take the case to trial.

Often defendants are skeptical of attorneys who are pushing a plea offer, with the clients frequently believing that their lawyers are doing it for their own reasons rather than their client's best interests. When damaging information in the case is presented to a defendant in black and white in the form of a police report, the lawyer's assessment of the defendant's chances at trial can be supported. Both the system and the prosecution are benefited because only cases that really should go to trial go. Instead, when prosecutors resist providing the information in advance, cases are needlessly prepared and often tried when the defendant could very well have decided to accept a plea offer had he had all of the information before him to make an intelligent, well-informed decision.

Although Rule 16 FRCrP does not require the prosecution to disclose police reports or other reports of witnesses pretrial except expert witnesses as set forth in the rule, the defense should request the reports from the prosecution and provide reasons why pretrial disclosure would assist in the resolution of the case. If the case is particularly complex or complicated, disclosure close to trial is likely to require a delay, which will irritate the judge. Defense counsel should also emphasize when a case does not involve violence or any allegations of witness tampering.

If the defense is able, it should provide an individualized reason for why officer reports should be provided well in advance of trial. Even though the judge cannot order the disclosure, a paper trail showing the defense efforts to try to obtain the information pretrial will assist in obtaining an adjournment at trial if needed. Again, there are prosecutors who recognize the value in providing the reports in advance redacting any information that could compromise safety. Prosecutors who adopt a "close to the vest" approach end up preparing for trial for weeks only to have the defendant plead guilty the morning of the trial after he has reviewed the "3500 material" the night before. Prosecutors who provide the information sufficiently in advance, understand as well that defense counsel is likely to be more forthcoming with its information when the prosecution has been forthcoming and cooperative.

Although witnesses and reports are not discoverable pretrial under the federal rules, and many analogous state rules, in general, the defense is entitled to be informed of statements made by the defendant, the defendant's prior record, expert witnesses and reports of examinations and tests, and documents and objects the prosecution intends to use in its case-in-chief that are material to the defense or were obtained from the defendant. There are also discovery needs specific to wire taps, which are discussed in *Chapter Sixteen: Wiretaps and Electronic Surveillance.*

The obligation to provide information to the defense to which it is entitled technically requires a defense request. (The defense request for discovery triggers reciprocal defense discovery obligations as set forth in Rule 16(b) FRCrP.) In some jurisdictions there is a standing rule that the defense has automatically requested all materials. Even so, it is good practice for the defense attorney to serve a pro forma discovery letter to the prosecutor at the outset of a case requesting the standard information in the event there are discovery disputes later on.

A more detailed letter should be sent if the case is expected to be litigated, which should be tailored based on the specifics of the case and acknowledging what information has already been turned over. Information that is material to the defense which the prosecution is not intending to offer in its case-in-chief should be particularized in a discovery request. For example, the prosecution might not intend to introduce breathalyzer manuals but the defense would need them. (The defense might want to hold off on requesting expert witness information under Rule 16(a)(1)(G) FRCrP unless it is clear that an expert will be called by the prosecution, as such a request requires the person calling an expert to create a detailed summary of the testimony which the defense might not want to disclose until it is certain that the expert will, in fact, be called.)

For Fourth Amendment purposes it is essential that the defense be aware of any physical or tangible objects taken from the defendant. The rules allow the defense to inspect the physical objects. The defense should also ask the prosecution which of the items recovered it will introduce at trial. The prosecution may advise the defense of what items will be used pursuant to FRCrP 12(b)(4) but is not required to do so. As discussed in more detail in *Chapter Twenty: Fourth Amendment Issues and Investigation*, defense counsel must go and look at the evidence and any bag or container in order to assess potential Fourth Amendment motions. Defense counsel also needs to be aware of any statements made by the defendant that might be fruits of the poisonous tree from a Fourth Amendment violation, such as an unlawful arrest that led to incriminating statements.

The defense should consider what information would be in the prosecution's custody or control that would be material to the defense and request that information under discovery rules. For example, if the search is an inventory search the policies and practices of the law enforcement officers are essential to determine whether the administrative procedures used to justify the search were in place before the search of the defendant's car. These requests to the prosecution should be made in writing, dated and provide the reason why the defense needs them for the suppression issue. Then there will be a record of that request in the event the defense needs to ask for an adjournment if the information is not disclosed in time. Administrative manuals and the like tend to take a long time to procure.

Production of Witness Statements

Rule 26.2 FRCrP and 18 USC § 3500 (also known as the *Jencks Act*) require the production of witness statements after a witness has been called to testify in federal court. Rule 26.2 requires production of the statement only after the witness has testified and the other party moves for production of the statements. Rule 26.2 specifically applies to suppression hearings.

Rule 26.2 permits the judge to recess the proceedings to allow time for a party to "examine the statement and prepare for its use." 26.2(d) FRCrP. To avoid delay and incurring the wrath of a judge who does not want to prolong the proceedings, especially when witnesses and juries must wait, most prosecutors will give the statements to the defense at least the night before the proceeding.

If the reports are voluminous and the contents unknown to the defense, the judge is more likely to give the defense additional time to review the information if it is given to them close to the hearing. However, because the statutory rule is specific as to disclosure only after the witness has testified on direct examination, a judge cannot require the prosecution to provide the statements in advance of hearing or trial. *See, e.g., United States v. Gluzman*, 154 F.3d 49, 51 (2d Cir. 1998) (defense not entitled to impeachment material regarding cooperating witness prior to opening statement).

Most prosecutors do provide the materials in advance, but some do so within a ridiculously short period of time before the proceedings (the night before or the morning of), often to gain a strategic advantage. Experienced prosecutors learn, however, that providing these materials in advance assists defense attorneys in advising their clients as to whether to go to trial or proceed on the motion to suppress.

To qualify for production under Rule 26.2, the statement must "relate to the subject matter of the witness's testimony." A statement is defined as (1) a written statement that the witness makes and signs, or otherwise adopts or approves; (2) a substantially verbatim, contemporaneously recorded recital of the witness's oral statement that is contained in any recording or any transcription of a record; or (3) the witness's statement to a grand jury, however taken or recorded, or a transcription of such a statement.

Counsel should also ask for notes from any interview, although it will depend on the circumstances of the note taking whether they would qualify under Rule 26.2. Most officers have a "policy" of destroying notes after a report is completed. More fruitful for the defense in a Fourth Amendment situation are the field notes of the officer (usually preserved and still in the notebook) which are taken at the scene and often include statements by the defendant and other observations on site.

When the defense is subpoenaing the officer to testify at the suppression hearing, it is important to include in the subpoena that the officer bring any reports, notes, etc. If the witness is not the officer but someone who gave statements to the officer, the opposing party might want to inquire when the officer is on the stand whether the officer took any notes during that interview of the lay person. If so, those notes should be requested as "3500 material."

Police reports could be crucial at the hearing on a motion to suppress and an opportunity to review them in advance of trial. Both counsels should review the reports carefully for what is contained and also for what is not contained. If the officer claims that consent was given but there is no mention of that in the report, the defense will want to confront the officer with that omission at the hearing since it is the crux of the Fourth Amendment claim and will bolster the defendant's version. To do so, it is critical that an "air tight" impeachment trap be laid as described in *Chapter Twenty Four: Fourth Amendment Hearings.*

It should be emphasized that the obligation to turn over statements by witnesses does not apply to statements made by the defendant. Even if the defendant takes the stand at a hearing or trial, defense counsel is not required to turn over interview notes of the client even if they relate verbatim to what he said on the stand. Rule 26.2 specifically provides that "after a witness *other than the defendant* has testified..." statements must be provided. (Emphasis added).

Subpoenas

Subpoenas are generally thought of in terms of obtaining information for trial. Documents and manuals, however, are often needed for hearings on motions to suppress. Information that cannot be obtained under Rule 16 can usually be procured through subpoena, with the exception of witness statements and reports as set out in Rules 16 and 26.2 FRCrP discussed above.

Defense counsel should consider what information is needed for the motion hearing or any potential Fourth Amendment issue as soon as possible since that hearing is usually held well before trial and it often takes some time for compliance with a subpoena.

Subpoenas in General. A subpoena is an order to give testimony or to compel the production of documents or evidence. In federal court, subpoenas are governed by Rule 17 FRCrP, and most state jurisdictions have corresponding provisions.

The defendant has subpoena power and may usually issue subpoenas without court order. Since Rule 17(c) does not specifically require that a party invoke the court's discretion by motion before the subpoena is made returnable, *see, e.g., United States v. Urlacher,* 136 F.R.D. 550, 554 (W.D.N.Y. 1991), certain material unrelated to the prosecution's criminal investigation or not otherwise subject to the discovery limitations imposed by Rule 16(a)(2) of the Federal Rules of Criminal Procedure may be subpoenaed without a motion and corresponding court order. Clerk's offices have blank pre-signed and sealed subpoenas for that purpose as required under Rule 17(a) FRCrP: "[t]he clerk must issue a blank subpoena—signed and sealed—to the party requesting it, and that party must fill in the blanks before the subpoena is served."

Certain agencies may require a court-ordered subpoena before responding or if an indigent defendant is seeking the payment of the subpoena on the same terms as the prosecution; this is the standard procedure when serving subpoenas on most police departments. A subpoena *duces tecum* is the normal mechanism for securing documents not in the possession of the prosecution. (A subpoena *testificandum* is the mechanism for obtaining witness testimony.) The defense can often include in the subpoena that it may be complied with by sending the information to defense counsel rather than awaiting it to be brought to a hearing or trial by a witness, particularly if the witness is not going to be called at the proceeding.

Defense counsel may require a subpoena in either of two situations: to obtain documents that are relevant and material to the hearing or trial while preparing its case, or to compel the production of documents and/or the testimony of witnesses at a hearing or trial. Rule 17(c) allows for obtaining certain materials in advance of trial and provides a practical procedure by which material can be inspected at a reasonable time before the date of trial. The primary restriction on this provision is Rule 16(a)(2) FRCrP which bars the disclosure of reports pertaining to the prosecution's criminal investigation.

Counsel should invoke Rule 17 for materials necessary for the suppression hearing. This procedure avoids delay during the hearing and allows for effective preparation. For example, a 911 call is likely to contain valuable information regarding what was known by the officer at the time of the arrest. Typically tapes of 911 calls are taped over after a certain period of time unless specifically preserved. As a matter of course the defense should always request in writing immediately that any 911 tape in a case be preserved and issue a subpoena for its production. If the prosecution has refused to provide information requested by the defense, such as a 911 tape or manuals, the defense should seek such information in a subpoena.

The defense will usually want to make subpoenas ex parte, without notice to the prosecution. This ex parte procedure is usually permissible. *See, e.g., United States v. Reyes*, 162 F.R.D. 468, 471 (S.D.N.Y. 1995) (holding that parties may apply for ex parte subpoenas and stating that "[T]he Court is mindful that it is often defendants who seek a subpoena duces tecum on an ex parte basis in order to avoid disclosing their trial strategy to the Government").

To obtain more sensitive materials, such as police personnel or investigation records, or if the defendant is indigent and needs payment on the same terms as the prosecution, a court order is generally required. When the subpoena is being served on a law enforcement agency, judges will generally require that the defense seek the information through Rule 16 or at least provide notice to the prosecution of any subpoena. (Even if the defense is not required to provide notice, invariably the agency will contact the prosecution anyway and the defense could have more cooperation from the agency if the prosecution is contacted in advance).

If the prosecution refuses to provide the information, a subpoena is appropriate. When the defense is requesting a court order for a subpoena, it should include in the request the fact that the defense is unable to procure the information through other means—refusal by the prosecution to provide such information, for example, usually suffices.

When the defense is required to give notice to the prosecution, in no case should the defense allow the declaration or affidavit supporting the subpoena to be given to the prosecution. These sworn statements necessarily contain the basis for the subpoena and typically include attorney work product and case theory. The prosecution never provides the defense with notice of its subpoenas or orders unless they are served directly on the defendant, such as a subpoena for handwriting exemplars, and even then it usually contains only the subpoena itself and not the supporting affidavit.

Elements of a Court Ordered Pretrial Subpoena. To ensure pretrial production, counsel usually must make the following showings in the ex parte attorney declaration:

(a) that the material sought is evidentiary and relevant;

(b) that the material is not otherwise procurable reasonably in advance of trial by exercise of due diligence;

(c) that the party cannot properly prepare for trial without such production and inspection in advance of trial and that the failure to obtain such inspection might tend unreasonably to delay the trial;

(d) that the application is made in good faith and is not intended as a general "fishing expedition."

The prosecution will cite ample authority that it was not the intention of Rule 17 to swallow the limitations on discovery imposed by Rule 16. There are a number of cases helpful to the defense to counter that argument and attempt to broaden the materials available by defense subpoena: cf., *United States v. Berrios*, 501 F.2d 1207, 1212 (2d Cir. 1974) (affirming trial court's discretion after an *in camera* review to require production of materials relevant and probative to the defenses raised, even though the documents ordinarily would be exempt from disclosure under Rule 16(a)(2) and prosecution refused to return certain documents to court for review); *United States v. La Rouche Campaign*, 841 F.2d 1176 (1st Cir. 1988) (refusing to quash defendant's subpoena despite NBC's qualified privilege as materials were relevant, admissible and requested with specificity); *United States v. Arditti*, 955 F.2d 331, 345 (5th Cir. 1992) (holding that Rule 17 extends to material that might not be the subject of Rule 16).

Subpoenas for Impeachment Materials. The prosecution will usually claim that impeachment evidence is not properly procured by subpoena citing *United States v. Nixon*, 418 U.S.683, 701, 94 S. Ct. 3090, 3104, 41 L. Ed. 2d 1039, 1060 (1974). In *United States v. Giampa*, 1992 WL 296440, at 3 (S.D.N.Y. Oct. 7, 1992) (Leisure, J), the district court explained why traditional impeachment material is not properly the subject of a Rule 17(c) subpoena:

> The Court finds that the rationale behind the well-established rule that impeachment materials are generally not subject to pretrial production applies with equal force to a request that such documents be produced on the first day of trial. Impeachment statements are generally not subject to pretrial production under Rule 17(c) because such statements ripen into evidentiary material for purposes of impeachment only if and when the witness testifies at trial.

Id. (emphasis added) (internal citation and quotes omitted).

Often the direct purpose of the material for the defense is to obtain impeachment documents to use against prosecution witnesses. In order to make the requisite showing, counsel must demonstrate to the court that the material is necessary to the preparation of the defense. The material must be more than just impeachment with a prior inconsistent statement—it must be admissible in the defense case-in-chief usually to present an affirmative defense, for example, mistake, inadvertence, self-defense, necessity or entrapment.

In essence, counsel must provide the court with a basis on which the subpoenaed evidence can stand on its own "fours" as admissible and not just as only for the purpose of impeaching the other party's witnesses. If defense counsel can make this showing, then the subpoenaed material is not merely impeachment material, but rather has "other valid potential evidentiary uses," then the materials are properly the subject of a Rule 17(c) subpoena. *See Nixon*, 418 U.S. at 702, 94 S. Ct at 3104, 41 L. Ed. 2d at 1060. The materials are then properly the subject of a Rule 17(c) subpoena.

Subpoenas for Bias. Bias is a possible ground for seeking disclosure of information relevant to a Fourth Amendment issue. If documents are sought for impeachment purposes only, the court will review the disputed documents for relevancy and materiality. If counsel can make a showing that the material sought might be used to demonstrate an officer's bias against a particular defendant, disclosure is more likely. *See e.g., United States v. Blackwood*, 456 F.2d 526, 530 (2d Cir. 1972) ("A defendant's major weapon when faced with inculpatory testimony of an accusing witness often is to discredit such testimony by proof of bias or motive to falsify. Evidence of such matters is never collateral ... for if believed it colors every bit of testimony given by the witness whose motives are biased")

Subpoenas for Personnel Records of Law Enforcement. Courts will typically require substantial support for the subpoena for personnel records or any records that are sensitive in nature, as well as require that they be returned to the court for *in camera* inspection provided there is a specific showing and not just a general request. The defense will need a declaration explaining the materiality of the documents requested and the basis of belief that they exist. Typically such a request requires notice to the prosecution if it involves law enforcement. With these more sensitive materials, it is preferable to invoke the court's aid at the earliest stage, because production of this material is discretionary and could involve protracted litigation.

It is always difficult to persuade a judge to allow the defense access to personnel records of law enforcement or other sensitive documents. To be successful the request should be made through the court for an *in camera* review (meaning the judge herself will review the information before any disclosure). For the court to grant an *in camera* review the defense has to show some basis other than "we hope there is something in there." For example, where the defense is arguing that this officer's violation of the Fourth Amendment is his modus operandi and that the defense is aware of other complaints detailed in the affidavit, a judge could be persuaded to at least look at the records.

The prosecution will often assure the court that it has reviewed the records and there is nothing relevant. Defense counsel should object that it must be the court who reviews the records, not the adversary. The case of *United States v. Kiszewski*, 877 F.2d 210 (2d Cir. 1989), is instructive. In that case, defense counsel made a *Brady* request for "any and all records and information revealing prior misconduct ... attributed to the witness." *Id.* at 215. The defense never received a response to this request and elected to serve a subpoena on the FBI for "[t]he complete personnel files maintained by the Federal Bureau of Investigation for Bureau agents Dean Naum and John Culhane, including any and all records pertaining to any complaint, investigation, or other internal administrative or disciplinary proceeding concerning either Naum or Culhane." *Id.* In an *in camera* discussion with counsel, the prosecutor informed the court that there was no *Brady* material in one agent's file and the other agent's file contained an unsubstantiated complaint and a letter of reprimand. The district court declined to compel the prosecution to produce the files for *in camera* inspection or disclose the files to the defense and the Second Circuit overruled. *Id.* at 215-216 (citations omitted). The *Kiszewski* court remanded the case for an *in camera* inspection and a determination as to whether disclosure of the information. *Id.*

Motions to Quash Subpoenas. As a threshold matter, the language of Rule 17(c) states that a motion to quash must be made "promptly." The Advisory Committee Notes to Rule 17(c) state that this rule is substantially the same as Rule 45(b) of the Federal Rules of Civil Procedure. The rule dealing with civil subpoenas says the motion to quash must be made promptly and, in any event, *before* the date on which the subpoenaed material is made returnable to the requesting party or the court. *See* FRCrP 45(b) (emphasis added).

To move to quash or challenge a subpoena requires standing which is some proprietary interest in the documents. With respect to government documents, the courts have permitted an extremely minimal showing that the prosecution must make to have standing even if the subpoena is issued to a third-party. In *Giampa*, 1992 WL 296440, at *1, for example, the district court described the showing for standing and quoted the Third, Seventh and Second Circuits as embracing a broad understanding of standing for the prosecution in a criminal case:

> A party to a criminal case has standing to move to quash a subpoena addressed to another if the subpoena infringes upon the movant's legitimate interests. The prosecution has standing to quash a defendant's subpoena based upon its interest in preventing undue lengthening of the trial, undue harassment of its witness, and prejudicial over-emphasis on the witness's credibility.

Id. (citations omitted). Similarly, law enforcement agencies, even if independent from the federal government, may forward any material responsive to the subpoena to the U.S. Attorney's Office. In so doing, the agency, in effect, is requesting that the prosecutor represent it and any government interest implicated by the Rule 17(c) subpoena and confers standing on the prosecution to quash the subpoena.

Although there are virtually no limitations on a grand jury subpoena, *see United States v. R. Enters., Inc.*, 498 U.S. 292, 297-298, 111 S. Ct. 722, 726-27, 112 L. Ed. 2d 795, 805-06 (1991) (quashing grand jury subpoena requires party to meet heavy burden and demonstrate that there is no reasonable possibility that the category of materials grand jury seeks will produce information relevant to the general subject of the investigation or that the subpoena is indefinite and compliance would be overly burdensome), Rule 17(c) provides that the court upon motion made promptly may quash or modify a subpoena if compliance would be either "unreasonable or oppressive." FRCrP 17(c).

Even though courts have declined to specifically state what is unreasonable or oppressive, it is clear that a subpoena must request documents with reasonable specificity and may not be overly broad or indefinite. Similarly, a valid claim of privilege or proprietary interest in the documents sought could cause the document request to be unreasonable and/or oppressive such as where compliance would reveal the names or addresses of law enforcement officers, identify undercover surveillance vehicles or disclose law enforcement techniques and procedures.

Service of Subpoenas. Most prosecuting agencies and public institutions do not insist on personal service of subpoenas for documents. They will usually accept service by fax or mail. If an agency refuses to cooperate in this way, the subpoena must be served in person. When a party or agency is reluctant or unwilling to respond to inquiries concerning documents or testimony, a court-ordered subpoena might be required even if the documents involve the defendant, such as medical records or employment records. The specifics of service are set out in Rule 17(d)&(e) FRCrP and generally provide that a federal subpoena may be served anywhere in the United States by a nonparty or marshal who is at least 18 years old. Fees and costs are also described in Rule 17 FRCrP as well.

CHAPTER TWENTY-TWO
FOURTH AMENDMENT ISSUES AND NEGOTIATIONS

Most criminal cases are resolved through plea negotiations and not by trial. In the federal system, for example, over ninety percent of all cases are resolved without trial; this is a lot of negotiation. As with discovery issues, usually the first and best strategic step in a case is for the defense attorney to speak to the prosecutor as a start to effective negotiation. A flow of communication between the parties can lead to the discovery of information, a sense of how the prosecution sees the case in terms of seriousness, etc., and is essential to the negotiation process.

Despite the importance of negotiations in the criminal justice system and the expectation that most cases will be resolved without trial, Fourth Amendment issues must be carefully assessed before defense counsel can properly advise a defendant to accept an offer to plead guilty in a case. If the prosecution could not prove its case because it lacks sufficient evidence that is not tainted by Fourth Amendment violations, the prosecution would have to dismiss the case rather than proceed. Thus, advising a defendant to plead guilty where the prosecution could not otherwise convict the defendant would not be effective assistance of counsel.

Indeed, defense counsel should be wary when receiving an offer at the outset that seems "too good to be true" if the Fourth Amendment issues have not been properly assessed. While prosecutors have been known to make such offers to protect the identity of a confidential informant or because of the equities of the case, it could also signal a concern about the lawfulness of the evidence recovered.

Although the prosecutor might be unlikely to reveal the reason for the great offer, defense counsel should make inquiries whether it is due to the fact that there were Fourth Amendment violations. (A prosecutor only has an ethical responsibility to reveal information that negates guilt or mitigates the offense.

Because a Fourth Amendment violation usually does not affect whether the defendant is guilty—indeed recovery of evidence often proves guilt—the prosecutor need not reveal the existence of Fourth Amendment violations. *See, e.g., Model Rule 3.8(d)* (a prosecutor shall "make timely disclosure to the defense of all evidence or information known to the prosecutor that tends to negate the guilt of the accused or mitigates the offense....").

A forthcoming prosecutor might be candid and concede that the search is suspect. Rather than rely on the generosity of information from the prosecution, the defense should investigate the case as soon as practicable and employ Rule 12 FRCrP to request as much information from the prosecution at the outset to assess what evidence will be used and the source of that evidence. *See* FRCrP 12(d)(1) ("At the arraignment or as soon thereafter as is practicable, the government may give notice to the defendant of its intention to use specified evidence at trial in order to afford the defendant an opportunity to raise objections to such evidence prior to trial....") For example, did the officers have a warrant? If they lacked a warrant, was there an exception to the warrant requirement? Knowing potential problems with the prosecution's proof when assessing early plea offers is one of the reasons it is imperative to discuss potential Fourth Amendment issues with the client as soon as possible. *See Chapter Seventeen: Fourth Amendment Issues and Client/Agent Interviews.*

There is a flipside to the Fourth Amendment issue in terms of negotiations. Defense counsel should consider whether the existence of a potential Fourth Amendment issue could entice the prosecution to make a good plea offer where the untainted evidence would still be sufficient to convict a defendant, but would make the prosecution's case weaker. The prosecution may not be aware of potential problems early on in the case. To determine the strength of the prosecution's case without the evidence often requires additional discovery and investigation, which should be conducted as early as possible to allow informed decision making on the part of the defendant and the prosecution.

In some cases, prosecutors will offer the defendant a good plea on the condition that the offer is accepted before any motions are filed. In other words, provided the prosecution does not have to respond to motions or put a police officer on the stand at a hearing the prosecutor might be more willing to bargain. Indeed, certain prosecutors have been known to "punish" the defendant for filing a motion to suppress where there are allegations that the police acted unlawfully, especially where the prosecution doubts the veracity of a defendant's affidavit. Prosecutors often file perjury charges or seek sentencing enhancements for obstruction of justice or object to acceptance of responsibility points under the Federal Sentencing Guidelines because of an affidavit made by the defendant conflicting with officer testimony. If affidavits are going to be filed in support of any motion to suppress, they should be carefully crafted to minimize the conflict with police testimony but still meet the defendants' burden of going forward. *See Chapter Twenty Three: Motion Practice Under the Fourth Amendment.*

Once a motion is filed, many prosecutors will withdraw the offer or advise the defense counsel that the offer expires on the date motions are due. After filing motions, it can be harder to bargain with the prosecutor who might become less accommodating having committed time, resources and police officer testimony to the case. Both sides often become more invested in the case and more adversarial once the case begins to be litigated through formal proceedings like motions to suppress.

Before filing motions, it is important that defense counsel understand the prosecutor's position with respect to whether a particular offer or any offer will be affected by the filing of motions to suppress. Sometimes that position is particular to a certain prosecutor or the policy or culture of the prosecutorial office or district. If counsel is unfamiliar with the prosecutor's individual policy or the standard procedure in the prosecutor's office, if there is one, it is crucial to find out just how level the playing field is. Institutional defenders are an ideal resource as they are repeat players in the system and usually know the idiosyncrasies of the various prosecutors and the prosecutor's office as a whole. Although it might be the best strategy to file a motion given the facts of the search, the key is to have an informed counsel and client to assess the risks of filing motions and the likelihood of success on the motion.

Of course, when there is a serious dispute as to the legality of a search or seizure, filing motions could provide a means of leverage in extracting a dismissal or more lenient plea offer. Should it become clear to the prosecutor that the evidence might be suppressed or that the officer made some misstatements on the stand that might affect the officer's credibility at trial, the motion to suppress litigation could enhance the defense's bargaining position.

There are also the possible discovery benefits from having the prosecution respond to defense allegations and the opportunity for defense counsel to discover information during the hearing by observing and cross examining the police officer. These discovery benefits should not be discounted, particularly in federal court or jurisdictions where access to information is very limited. In particular, witness statements including police reports are often provided at the hearing, which are then available for trial preparation. *See Chapter Twenty One: Fourth Amendment and Discovery Issues* and *Chapter Twenty Four: Fourth Amendment Hearings.*

Defense counsel should also assess as soon as possible whether there is any room for negotiation. If the prosecutor is inflexible and insists that the defendant plead to everything anyway, there is little to lose in filing a motion to suppress if the case is going to go to trial no matter what. Moreover, the client might insist on going to trial and filing the motions notwithstanding the risks of prosecutorial retaliation including any risk that the prosecutor will claim that the defendant's affidavit contained falsehoods or perjury.

Ultimately it is the defendant's decision whether to plead guilty or go to trial. An important role of defense counsel is to ensure that the defendant makes an informed decision based on the strength of the prosecution's case, including consideration of all Fourth Amendment issues regarding the recovery of evidence in the case.

CHAPTER TWENTY-THREE
MOTION PRACTICE UNDER THE
FOURTH AMENDMENT

Motions to Suppress Generally

Many of the pretrial motions made in a criminal case involve Fourth Amendment issues. Because the remedy for a Fourth Amendment violation is exclusion of evidence from trial, these matters are inherently pretrial (although motions to suppress can sometimes arise during trial if information is recently discovered). Moreover, motions to suppress evidence in federal court are governed by FRCrP 12, which specifically requires that a motion to suppress be raised before trial. See FRCrP 12(b)(3)(C).

The federal rules also insist that a judge rule on the motion pretrial unless there is "good cause" to defer a ruling. FRCrP 12(d). A judge may not defer ruling if it would "adversely affect a party's right to appeal." *Id.* It would be the rare occasion when deferral beyond the start of the trial would be appropriate on a motion to suppress, given that the point of suppression is to preclude the use of the evidence at trial and both parties would need to know its admissibility well in advance of trial to make strategic and litigative decisions.

Timing of Motions

Federal courts are permitted under Rule 12(c) FRCrP to set deadlines for motions. Some judges will set the date at the initial appearance before there has been any discovery. Defense counsel in particular should ensure that the court provides adequate time for investigation and to write a comprehensive motion. If discovery has not been provided, defense counsel should make that clear to the judge especially if counsel is requesting additional time to file motions. A party waives any objection to the evidence if it fails to file a motion by the court date unless the court grants an extension or permits relief from the waiver. See FRCrP 12(e).

A motion to suppress is moot if the prosecution does not intend to use the evidence at trial. Before writing the 20-page memorandum of law on search and seizure of a vehicle, for example, defense counsel should speak to the prosecutor at the outset to determine whether the prosecutor is going to introduce the evidence. If the prosecution is unsure, the motion can be filed and later withdrawn should the prosecutor decide not to go forward. Indeed, sometimes filing the motion will persuade the prosecution that the evidence is problematic and the motion could convince the prosecution not to introduce the evidence.

When a motion would require a lengthy response in opposition, the prosecution might also choose not to introduce the evidence, particularly if there is other damaging evidence in the case so that the prosecution can afford to exclude some of the evidence voluntarily. Filing of the motion by the defense also alerts the court to unlawful conduct by the officers which could impact the judge's view of the case, especially if the prosecution later agrees not to introduce the offending evidence. Finally, a hearing on the issue, even if unsuccessful, could provide valuable discovery for the defense.

FRCrP 12(b)(4) provides that the defense may request notice of the prosecution's intent to use specified evidence as early as the arraignment, and the prosecution, in its discretion, may give notice of that intent. There is little to be lost by the defense submitting a detailed request for evidence under FRCrP 12(d) at the outset. Although many jurisdictions have standing rules regarding discovery such as a presumption that the defense requested discovery triggering prosecutorial response, it is a good idea for the defense to have a paper trail of the request for evidence in the event there is any dispute that the information was requested—particularly if it is likely that the case will go to trial. *See also Chapter Twenty One: Fourth Amendment and Discovery Issues.*

There is little to be gained by the prosecution not informing the defense of the evidence it intends to use in its case in chief as soon as possible. A delay in providing that information will ultimately delay any hearing, trial or sentencing (the dated request can come in handy if there is any dispute about what was requested and when). Most of the evidence requested under

FRCrP 12 is ultimately discoverable by the defense under FRCrP
16 anyway. *See Practice Commentaries Federal Rules of Criminal
Procedure, Natali, Parsons, Statsinger & Wolfe, Commentary to
Fed. R. Crim. P. Commentary to Rule 16* (2002-2003).

Burden of Persuasion and Proof

In the absence of a warrant, many judges will consider the
burden to be initially on the prosecution to show lawful procurement of evidence without requiring much from the defense. The
rationale being that without a warrant, the search and seizure
was presumptively unreasonable and the prosecution must show
it was obtained reasonably under the Fourth Amendment.

Even if the judge requires the defendant to meet her burden
at the outset to show she has standing to make a claim, the burden then shifts to the prosecution to show that the evidence was
obtained lawfully. The burden of proof to establish that the evidence was lawfully obtained is by a preponderance of evidence.
See Bourjaily v. United States, 483 U.S. 171, 175-76, 107 S. Ct.
2775, 2778-79, 97 L. Ed. 2d 144, 152-53 (1986).

Format

When making an application to a district court for an order requesting suppression of the evidence due to a Fourth Amendment
violation, the request is generally made by written motion. See
FRCrP 47. Oral motions are more appropriately brought at trial or
hearing or as the court permits. In some cases judges will accept
a motion in letter form and "so order" the letter. Each district
has local rules which often specify the form of motion papers and
the formality of those filings. *See Practice Commentaries Federal
Rules of Criminal Procedure, Natali, Parsons, Statsinger & Wolfe,
Commentary to Fed. R. Crim. P. 57* (2002-2003).

Judges frequently have individual standing orders that describe
their particular requirements for motions, such as maximum number of pages and whether a table of contents is required. Before
filing a motion with the judge, an attorney must review the local
rules, administrative orders and standing orders of the particular

judge. *See* FRCrP 49 for the service and filing of motions. Pretrial motions are governed by FRCrP 12. *See also, Practice Commentaries Federal Rules of Criminal Procedure, Natali, Parsons, Statsinger & Wolfe, Commentary to Fed. R. Crim. P.* 12, 47, and 57 (2002-2003)

Although the formality of motions varies from district to district, a typical formal motion consists of a notice of motion, a motion supported by affidavit or declaration and a memorandum of law, as follows:

Notice of Motion. The notice of motion informs the court and opposing counsel of the nature of the issues and the anticipated date for submissions and any hearing. The notice typically apprises the court and the opposing party that a motion will be heard on a date certain or one to be established by the court, depending on whether the court has set a motion schedule in advance.

The Motion. The motion states the specific relief requested and a summary of the grounds for relief. The grounds need be nothing more than conclusory "Mr. Smith moves to suppress any and all evidence obtained as a result of the search of Mr. Smith on the grounds that the officers conducted a search without probable cause in violation of Mr. Smith's Fourth Amendment rights." The motion is usually supported by an averment either by affidavit or declaration typically by the defense attorney and/or the defendant. In some jurisdictions, motion and notice of motion are combined in one document entitled simply notice of motion.

Affidavit. A motion to suppress ordinarily must be supported by an affidavit or other sworn statements usually provided by the defendant, defense counsel or both. The affidavit sets forth the factual basis for why the motion should be granted. Affidavits ordinarily should not contain argument but only the facts in support of the argument, although in some jurisdictions where the law is not the basis of the dispute but only the application of the facts to that law, a joint affidavit and motion are often filed.

Memorandum of Law. The memorandum of law is the legal analysis of the case setting for the legal standards and case law and applying them to the facts of the case. A memorandum of law typically contains a preliminary statement setting forth the procedural posture of the case, a factual background and the legal arguments raised by the motion. In some case in certain districts, the memorandum of law is combined with the attorney's affidavit for expediency. Counsel should also determine if such a combination is permitted especially where the resolution of the motions depends on the factual determinations and not analysis of the law per se. If counsel is unsure whether to use a combined motion, counsel should error on the most formal of motions and memoranda. Memoranda of Law are discussed in more detail below.

Affidavit Considerations in Motions to Suppress

Rule 47 governs motions to suppress in federal court. Most states have comparable rules. Rule 47 does not require that a motion be supported by an affidavit, only that it "may" be supported by affidavit. *See* FRCrP 47. Some circuits insist that in order to put a fact in issue the party with the burden of going forward must do so through personal knowledge sworn to under the penalties of perjury. *See, e.g., United States v. Gillette*, 383 F.2d 843, 848 (2d Cir. 1967). An attorney's affidavit based on information and belief that the defendant had a reasonable expectation of privacy is usually insufficient, where the personal knowledge rests with the client or agent. The attorney's declarations are not based on personal knowledge that would subject the lawyer to perjury charges.

Some case issues may proceed by information and belief and not direct personal knowledge particularly if the necessary facts are set out in an arresting officer's complaint. However, when it is a threshold issue to meet the burden of going forward, an affiant with personal knowledge must ordinarily swear to the truth of the information. Where the opposing party fails to place a fact in issue through sworn testimony, litigants should insist on the filing of sworn affidavits or declarations or request that the judge deny the request for a hearing and/or dismiss the motion outright.

There are important strategic considerations when the defendant or the case agent must swear to facts to support or counter a motion. The inexperienced attorney is often tempted to include all of the facts in the case in the affidavit or declaration. That is a usually a mistake, particularly at the outset of the matter when certain facts will not be known and many of the known facts will be in dispute or uncertain.

Both sides should be cautious in committing an agent or client to a detailed account unnecessarily, which can later be used to impeach the affiant should she take the stand and misstate a detail. For the defendant, the stakes are even higher since sworn statements by the defendant contradicted by law enforcement officers could be used to support obstruction of justice and perjury enhancements. *See also Practice Commentaries Federal Rules of Criminal Procedure, Natali, Parsons, Statsinger & Wolfe, Commentary to Fed. R. Crim. P. 47 (2002-2003).*

Counsel should craft any declaration carefully to ensure that only the minimal information needed to support or oppose the motion is asserted. Moreover, detailed affidavits are not ordinarily necessary because the facts the judge will rely on in assessing the motion to suppress usually will be those brought out under oath and subject to cross examination at the hearing. Indeed, counsel must be vigilant that all the necessary facts included in the affidavits and declarations are elicited at the hearing through testimony since the affidavits are not ordinarily considered testimony. In some cases there will be no factual dispute because the facts are not contested or are stipulated to for the purposes of the motion.

Word choice when setting forth facts is critical, particularly where there could be a conflict between what the officer says happened and what the defendant says happened. For example, there is quite a difference when considering a perjury count between "I do not recall the officer ever reading me my rights" and "the officer did not read me my rights." If possible, it is better to allow for the possibility that the defendant might have been mistaken rather than taking on the officer as a liar if that is consistent with the facts. It is also a good idea to add to the declaration that it was prepared by counsel and does not include every fact known but only those determined by counsel to be necessary for the purposes of the motion.

Affidavits technically should not contain argument, but only the facts in support of the argument. A person cannot affirm under the penalties of perjury that a particular argument is true. A person can affirm that he owns a car, carried a wallet, refused to agree to let the officers search without a warrant, etc. These facts could constitute a Fourth Amendment violation, but neither counsel nor a defendant is in a position to "affirm" that there was a Fourth Amendment violation.

Sometimes the attorney will include his or her own affidavit affirming statements made by the prosecution to defense counsel or based on counsel's own investigation, regarding the use of the evidence at trial, or the facts known from an affidavit for a search warrant, etc. that would not be in the purview of the defendant, but should be sworn to as facts to support a Fourth Amendment claim.

Memorandum of Law Issues

The initial memorandum of law contains the legal argument applied to the facts set out in the affidavits, or to the facts elicited at a hearing in a post-hearing memorandum of law. It is here where the argument is made that there was a Fourth Amendment violation.

In preparing the memorandum of law many judges will admonish lawyers that a "brief" should be just that—short and to the point. It is good advice. Much of the verbiage in motions is "lawyerese" and attorneys should strive for plain English and short sentences.

Make sure the law is good and the arguments sound. Too often parties rely on exaggerated language such as "clearly" "undeniably" "without a doubt" in an attempt to make their point. If the issues were so clear the case would be settled and there would be no need for motions.

Judges are human and are affected by visual professionalism. Just as one would not wear a crumpled suit and loose tie to an interview for a judicial clerkship, a motion should be neat and clean. The memorandum of law should be easy to read and well organized. A list of citations included in appellate briefs is not ordinarily required in district court motions although many practitioners include a table of contents particularly for lengthy motions, and some jurisdictions require a table of cases depending on the length of the motion. Check the local rules and the judge's particular rules if she has them. Most of the rules are found on the court websites.

Pages should be numbered and citations checked. In a word... proofread. Spelling and grammatical errors are distracting and suggest sloppiness which could color a judge's view of the quality of the attorney and the attorney's argument. A judge who used to sit in the Central District of California would consider a split infinitive a personal affront and view the lawyer's arguments with much greater skepticism. In the computer age of automatic spell check programs and grammar check programs errors are avoidable. If nothing else, make sure the judge's name is spelled correctly.

Preliminary Statement. The preliminary statement typically sets forth the procedural posture of the case as well as the basic ground for the motion. The basis is essentially a summary of the motion; a headnote, if you will.

Factual Statement. Some lawyers will not include a statement of facts in the memorandum of law relying solely on the affidavits that were attached to the motion or notice of motion. Law clerks usually hate it when there is no statement of facts and the clerk has to flip between two separate documents to get the facts from the affidavit to apply to the law. The better practice is to include a brief statement of facts taken from the various affidavits and citing to those affidavits in a separate background or fact section of the memorandum of law and attaching the affidavits to the memorandum of law as well. This saves the judge (or her law clerk) from having to go back and forth from the memorandum of law to the attached affidavits. For example, *Mr. Jones is the registered owner of the 1996 black Camaro, see Jones. Aff. at ¶ 3 attached hereto as Exhibit A.*

A factual statement also allows the attorney to choose the important facts and put them in a desirable order in a persuasive narrative. The factual statement is like an opening statement at trial—it should not be waived. However, the factual should still contain facts and not argument. The facts should mirror what was affirmed in the corresponding affidavits. In other words, the factual statements should look like the factual statements courts include in their written orders. "Mr. Jones told the officer he did not want his car searched" is a neutral fact statement. "The officers searched Mr. Jones' car without permission in violation of the Fourth Amendment" is an argument and should be reserved for that section.

In some cases where the facts are not well known it might be better to submit a cursory memorandum of law and seek leave to file a post-hearing memorandum of law applying the law to the facts established at the hearing.

Argument. The argument is the meat of the memorandum of law. It is where the attorney applies the facts and analyzes them within the governing case law. Typically the argument is broken down into subheadings. Conceptually it makes sense to provide the standards for review for the judge at the outset. Judges think something along these lines:

- Do I have to decide?

- Is there a way to get the parties to settle or withdraw or change their position?

- If I have to decide what are the factors and standards that I must consider?

- Who has the burden of persuasion or proof?

- How do these facts stack up against the law?

- Is the Circuit going to overrule me if I find for the defense?

- Is the Circuit going to overrule me if I find for the prosecution?

The argument in the memorandum of law should be persuasive and forceful but not histrionic. Inexperienced attorneys will be tempted to attack opposing counsel personally for whatever claims are contained in their papers and to respond with indignation and righteousness. This is unprofessional and distracts from the quality of the argument. Counsel should be careful not to misstate the facts. If it appears an intentional misstatement or "stretch" a judge is likely to discredit the entire motion.

One thing to always keep in mind when making an argument to the judge is that judges do not like to decide things. They prefer to have counsel withdraw their position or consent to a particular outcome so that nobody gets overruled on appeal. Some judges will bully weaker counsel away from their position to avoid having to make a decision that could subject the judge to review. The memorandum of law should be written to give the judge confidence to rule in your favor. Do not hide the bad law; deal with it as a judge must when writing a decision in your favor.

Judges will often use one side's papers as a starting point to write their opinions. Counsel should strive to have it be their memorandum of law. Even though the prosecution's submission are often the judge's starting point, particularly where the judge is denying a motion to suppress, judges will still use defense papers that are "judicial"—well written, well researched and carefully analyzed. Ideally, the memorandum of law should read as if it were the judge's written opinion. Neutrally stated facts and fair and reasonable application of law and facts is more likely to result in the use of your papers by the judge than hyperbole and pounding on the table. Read the judge's published opinions and the opinions of judge's known for their writing style to get a sense for how to write the memorandum of law.

Post Hearing Memorandum of Law. In some cases the facts will be unclear and undetermined at the time the motion is filed so that it is impossible to argue that the bag should be suppressed as a result of an unlawful search and seizure until after the hearing. In such cases typically there will be little factual statement in either the affidavits or memorandum and counsel should seek leave in the motion to file a post-hearing memorandum of law responsive to the facts actually elicited during the hearing. *See Chapter Twenty Four: Fourth Amendment Hearings.*

Research Tips

When researching case law know which cases control in your jurisdiction. In federal court it is the Supreme Court and the federal circuit court within which the case is being litigated which control. District court cases, even in the same district, can be persuasive but are not controlling precedent.

Keep your searches narrow. There are tens of thousands of cases involving the Fourth Amendment. Use your warrant exception terms that apply, *e.g.*,: incident to arrest, grabbable space, etc.

ALWAYS look up cases decided by the judge you are before particularly if they relate to the issue. In other words, if the judge in your case has previously ruled on what constitutes a search incident to arrest, if you have the same issue, you want to know what the judge wrote and what was important to her.

Reading through opinions written by the judge you are litigating before will help you construct a memorandum of law that is in a similar style and manner as the judge. One can also learn how the judge thinks and decides cases. Remember, it is not about "zinging" it to your adversary; it is about getting the judge to rule in your favor.

CHAPTER TWENTY-FOUR
FOURTH AMENDMENT HEARINGS

Hearings in General

Where there is a factual dispute as to a search and seizure the judge ordinarily grants a hearing to resolve the factual issues. In some cases the prosecution will concede that a hearing is required.

The suppression hearing is not a trial on the issue of guilt. It is a hearing on the issue of the lawfulness of the search or seizure. Such a hearing is held before a judge not a jury; the ultimate issue is whether the jury will hear the evidence at trial. Hearsay is admissible at a suppression hearing, and the standard of proof is preponderance of the evidence considering a totality of the circumstances.

Because motions to suppress are inherently factual, it is rare that a hearing would not be required unless the parties stipulated to the facts. Defense counsel should avoid stipulating to facts in most cases since the hearing itself will be valuable to the defense apart from the motion to suppress by providing discovery of the prosecution's case.

There may be situations, however, when the facts alleged in a complaint or officer's report are sufficient to make a legal argument by the defense that the search or seizure was unlawful. In such cases, there may be some risk to the defense in having the officer expand on those facts at a hearing rather than stipulate to the facts. For example, the police report or complaint may detail the location of the drugs and the argument would be strictly legal: was there sufficient nexus between the location and the defendant. However, in most cases a stipulated hearing is usually not as beneficial to the defense because of the lost opportunity to hear more about the prosecution's case and to cross examine the arresting officer.

Timing of Hearings

Motions to suppress are inherently pretrial since the remedy for any Fourth Amendment violation is preclusion of the evidence from use by the prosecution at trial. Ideally the judge will allow the issue to be resolved well in advance of trial so that the parties can adjust their litigation strategies and witnesses depending on the outcome of any motion to suppress. There are judges, however, who insist on hearing the motion immediately before the trial to conserve the use of witnesses.

Neither side is benefited by back to back hearing and trial. Both counsels should object to the lack of any meaningful time between the motion to suppress hearing and the trial since this time is necessary to give the parties an opportunity to negotiate depending on the outcome of the motion. If the case continues to trial, both counsels will need to adjust and accommodate the court's ruling in trial strategies and witness preparation.

Counsel should try to work together to provide a suggested motion schedule to ensure that there is sufficient time to prepare the motions, hold a hearing, give the judge an opportunity to rule, and get transcripts of the hearing—all before trial. Some judges will set motions schedules automatically and a hearing date at the first opportunity so as not to delay a trial to accommodate speedy trial requirements.

Practically speaking, the statements made by the witnesses at trial will need to be transcribed and available for possible impeachment at trial. When there is no meaningful interval between the two proceedings, counsel might not have the transcript in time to use against the witness or to refresh a witness' recollection. For this reason alone, counsel should request at least enough time to get the transcripts of the one proceeding for use in the following proceeding.

In order to convince a judge not to combine the two proceedings, counsel must couch the arguments in terms of efficiency, because efficiency is clearly paramount for this type of judge. The argument will be along the lines that allowing for at least one week between the two proceedings will permit both counsels to streamline their presentations making them more efficient at trial.

Further argument to this judge should be that, depending on the court's ruling and what is actually elicited at the hearing, the parties could determine that a trial is not necessary and resolve the case through plea bargaining. The opportunity to negotiate or renegotiate could save everyone, including the judge, the parties and the witnesses, from an unnecessary trial and unnecessary preparation. In some cases the outcome of the hearing will be dispositive of the outcome of the case; meaning if the evidence comes in the defendant will plead, but if the evidence is suppressed the prosecution will dismiss the case.

Hearing Procedure in General

Who goes first? Ordinarily the defendant has the burden of going forward in terms of a motion to suppress in the sense that the defendant must have standing: a reasonable expectation of privacy in order to make a Fourth Amendment claim. *See Chapter Five: Issues of Standing.* Some judges might require that the defendant get on the stand first and assert her standing rights under oath subject to cross examination in order to shift the burden to the prosecution to show that the evidence was obtained lawfully. In most districts, however, the defendant's affidavit suffices to meet the burden of going forward and the hearing begins with the prosecution's burden to show that the evidence was obtained lawfully.

Prosecutors should insist that the defendant take the stand first. The defense should avoid putting the client on the stand to meet the burden of going forward countering that the defendant's affidavit is sufficient to shift the burden. If the prosecution has essentially conceded in its motion papers that the defendant had a reasonable expectation of privacy, defense should argue that there is no need to have the defendant take the stand on that point since it is not disputed. If the prosecution disputes standing but not with sworn facts, the defense should object on that basis as well arguing that the prosecution as failed to put a fact in issue

given the lack of sworn facts. Ultimately, who has the initial burden at the hearing will depend on whether standing is contested
as well as local practice and the individual judge's custom.

Although affidavits are submitted with the motion papers, the
actual facts the judge relies on at the hearing are ordinarily only
those elicited from witnesses during the hearing. Sometimes a
judge will consider affidavit evidence, but most courts require
that the information come from witnesses subject to cross examination.

Counsel must be vigilant to ensure that all the necessary facts
included in the affidavits and declarations relied on to make their
arguments are elicited at the hearing through testimony since the
affidavits are not ordinarily used by the judge. It is a common mistake, particularly by inexperienced lawyers, to assume that the all
of the facts are out there for the judge to assess, only to find that
a critical fact, *e.g.*, that the defendant did not have a key on him,
was included in the affidavit of the defendant, but not elicited
from the arresting agent who did the personal property inventory
and was the only witness who testified at the hearing.

Some judges will come to the hearing very well prepared and
know exactly what the issues are. Statements made by the judge
at the outset will clue counsel in as to how informed the judge
really is.

Defining the issues. Typically, the judge will initially inquire
of the prosecutor or the defense the basis of the motion. Although
the defense is the moving party, judges, as former prosecutors,
tend to look to the prosecution to provide such information. In
many cases the judge throws out a general question, such as,
"What is this hearing about?" (unless the judge has personally
read the parties' papers before the hearing). This situation should
be thought of as the "jump ball" of the hearing. Who gets the ball
often gets to define the issues for the court at the outset. Defense
counsel should not defer to the prosecution if it is at all possible.
Rather, counsel should take control of the hearing and set out the
important factual disputes for the judge. Compare:

JUDGE: What is this hearing about?

PROSECUTOR: The defendant claims his arrest was illegal. We are prepared to show that the officers had sufficient probable cause to arrest and search incident to that arrest where the officers discovered two kilos of cocaine in the defendant's coat pocket which are properly admitted against the defendant at trial.

VERSUS

JUDGE: What is this hearing about?

DEFENSE COUNSEL: Mr. Jones was walking through the train station when he was approached by four officers who surrounded him and searched him. At the time, the officer had no objective basis to support either reasonable suspicion or probable cause to believe he had committed a crime. As a result, any evidence recovered from this illegal stop and arrest must be suppressed as having been obtained in violation of Mr. Jones' Fourth Amendment rights to be free from unreasonable searches and seizures.

Opening statements. The judge may or may not ask for a statement from counsel before hearing testimony. Counsel should be prepared to give a brief summary of the issues for the judge, not dissimilar to what is contained in the motion or preliminary statement to orient the judge as to the important testimony. Consider it a mini opening statement. Remember it is a judge not a jury—it should be brief and to the point. Included in that statement should be what is not at issue, *e.g.*: Your Honor Mr. Jones had a reasonable expectation of privacy in his home where he lived with his wife and two young children. The prosecution concedes that the officers did not have a warrant to search Mr. Jones' house. There was no exigency justifying an exception to the warrant requirement, therefore the defense moves for suppression of all evidence taken from the house on the grounds that the evidence was procured in violation of Mr. Jones' Fourth Amendment rights.

Clues from the judge. Sometimes the judge will tell the parties her impression of the case before the hearing based on a reading of the parties' papers. (Be aware that not all judges read the papers in advance, particularly if the issue is a factual one where the judge's decision will depend on the facts elicited at the hearing rather than some unusual application of law.) The judge might also inform the parties of specific issues on which she wants the parties to concentrate, such as why the officers did not get a telephonic warrant before entering the house.

It is crucial for counsel to listen closely to the judge. She is the decision maker and her initial impressions will provide counsel with invaluable insight into the arguments that are especially important to her. Listen to the judge and heed her statements. If she says that she is convinced that the defendant had standing to make out a Fourth Amendment violation, defense counsel need not spend twenty minutes cross examining the officer on who was on the lease of the apartment, who had a key, who was a guest, etc., unless the prosecution makes clear to the judge that they are still contesting standing or the defense attorney is pinning down the officer on statements that will be used at trial.

Testimony. After any preliminary statements by the judge or counsel, the prosecution ordinarily puts on an officer or two. The defense cross examines those witnesses. The defense may put on witnesses as well and the defendant would have the right to testify. *See Strategies at the Hearing* discussed below.

Oral argument and post-hearing memoranda. Once all of the testimony is completed, the judge will usually ask for oral argument. In some cases the issues will require more briefing and counsel might want to request the opportunity to file post-hearing memoranda. Post-hearing memoranda are essential if there were facts elicited at the hearing that were not known to the parties at the time of the filing of the motions and could require further research. In cases where the judge believes the officers and the legal argument is straightforward, counsel should be prepared for the judge to deny the request for post-hearing briefing and for the judge to simply rule from the bench. Some judges will ask for oral argument and then reserve decision either to issue a decision from the bench after a recess or to issue a written opinion at a later time.

Strategies at the Hearing

Prosecutor strategies. In terms of putting on their own witnesses, prosecutors ordinarily try to avoid having more than one witness testify to the facts if possible to minimize inconsistencies with other evidence or witnesses. Putting an officer on the stand creates "impeachment material" that could be used by the defense at trial if the officer should misstate something at the hearing or say something different at trial. Because hearsay is admissible at these proceedings, prosecutors have been known to call officers who will not be testifying at trial who were told about the facts so as not to create impeachment material for the main witness.

A prosecutor's goal is usually to meet the minimum standard to show that the evidence was obtained lawfully. The prosecutor will object to any defense efforts to use the hearing to discover evidence beyond the scope of the lawfulness of any search or seizure. Judges are particularly receptive to such objections because it speeds up the proceeding.

Defense strategies. When the officer and any other officers on site. Some judges will not require other officers to testify if their testimony would be merely cumulative, but frequently officers have different recollections as to the same event and these differences may induce a judge to suppress or indicate reasonable doubts should the case go to trial. Ideally counsel will have had the opportunity to interview the officers in advance of the hearing (*see Chapter Twenty: Fourth Amendment Issues and Investigation*), but even if she has not had that opportunity, it is still often a useful strategy to call the other officers, particularly if one of the goals of the hearing is discovery of information.

Defense counsel's strategies at a hearing on a motion to suppress will depend on the goal or goals of the proceeding. If this is a case where there is little to counter the officer's version of events as to the exigency of the situation, the goal may be less to win the hearing (often an impossibility) than to discover additional information about the case and to pin the officer down on the facts that are needed at trial. The cross examination may be more accrediting than adversarial.

Prosecutors should be vigilant and object to questions by defense counsel that do not call for information related to the issue of the validity of obtaining the evidence. Judges dislike the use of these hearings for discovery purposes or "fishing expeditions" and are likely to side with the prosecution unless the prosecutor has opened the door by having the officer testify about the investigations. Defense counsel should keep an ear out for broad questions from the prosecution on direct examination such as "why did you decide to arrest Mr. Jones that day," which can open the scope of the cross to nearly everything that happened in the case.

Although it is wise to pin down the agents as to certain testimony, most of the cross examination of the officers should be open-ended questions to find out what happened unless it relates directly to an issue of suppression. If the officer says something that is inconsistent with his report, unless the issue relates directly to the Fourth Amendment violation, it is often better not to bring out the inconsistency at the hearing if the case is going to go to trial. Bringing out the devastating impeachment of the officer by prior inconsistent statements during this hearing will usually be a waste; the judge is very unlikely to discredit the officer's testimony unless there is objective evidence of fabrication, and confronting the officer with the inconsistency at this pretrial stage will give him an opportunity to prepare for the inconsistency when he takes the stand at trial.

Unless the hearing is in essence the trial where, if the evidence comes in the defendant will plead and there will be no trial or the inconsistency in the report relates directly to the Fourth Amendment issue, defense counsel should think of the suppression hearing as an opportunity to learn more about the case and to see how the officer testifies. It is also useful to pin the officer down on crucial facts so that he does not have a "better recollection" at trial. *See also Practice Commentaries Federal Rules of Criminal Procedure, Natali, Parsons, Statsinger & Wolfe, Commentary to Fed. R. Crim. P. 12 (2002-2003).*

Use of Statements at a Suppression Hearing

The defense is entitled to reports of witnesses at a suppression hearing. *See Rule 26.2* FRCrP. When an omission or error in a report relates to the Fourth Amendment violation it should be exploited at the hearing since the issue will probably be irrelevant at the trial, *e.g.*, whether the officers had consent to enter the house is not relevant as to his guilt at trial.

It is critical once a police report is obtained by the defense to review it carefully for any information that could contradict or undermine the officer's testimony regarding the basis for the search. One issue that often arises and requires a great deal of litigation skill on defense counsel's part is when the report does not contain a fact which was relied on by the officers for the search, such as the fact that the defendant consented. The failure to include such a fact in the report is often a goldmine for the defense. Exploiting that error could mean the difference between winning and losing the hearing.

Use of an omission necessitates a very disciplined and detailed impeachment during cross examination. It involves the 5Cs of omission impeachment: Commit; Credit; Context; Confront and Conclusion. In deciding how to set an impeachment trap or foundation, the best way to begin is to set out a list of what the prosecutor is likely to ask on redirect: did you personally type the report (no, but he signed it before he read it); you have a lot of cases and can't look for every detail (yes, but this detail is important and he could have filed a supplement), etc., which will help you in closing off all reasonable avenues of escape.

Commit the Witness. As with any impeachment it is important to commit the officer to his original position. When the officer and the prosecution have relied on consent as the basis for the search, this aspect of impeachment is usually quite easy to accomplish but still important for a clean examination. "Officer, you claimed on direct that Mr. Jones told you to search his house." Notice how the examiner distances herself from what the officer said. If the questioner said, "Mr. Jones told you to search his house," the attorney has defeated her entire purpose and argument which is to say that Mr. Jones never gave consent. The following is a brief example:

Q: Officer, you claim that Mr. Jones told you to search his house.

A: That's correct.

Q: In fact, you claim that he invited you into the house and told you to look anywhere you wanted.

A: Yes, he did.

Q: Held the door open wide for you and your six partners to enter his home and search it.(Skeptical voice)

A: Yes, that is what he did.

Credit the Report. The next part deals with crediting the report itself. Sometimes it is problematic to credit the report if certain things in there are not good for the defense. Counsel must weigh the benefits and whether the part that is credited can still accommodate sloppy or inaccurate testimony. If at the end of the day the claim is this officer cannot be trusted, the defense can argue the same about the report. Crediting of the report is broken into subchapters (these are for example purposes and are not exhaustive) to assist the lawyer in mapping out the questioning:

• **Report is thorough and accurate.**

Q: Officer, you filed a report in this case?

A: Yes.

Q: And you have been trained to fill out those reports?

A: Yes.

Q: And you have been trained to be accurate and thorough in those reports?

(He's not going to say no)

A: Yes.

Q: And you include in that report important information?

(Again, he's not going to say no)

A: Yes.

- **Reviews and signs report.**

Q: You signed this report.

A: Yes.

Q: Before you signed, it you read it over?

A: I believe so.

Q: Officer, before you signed your report, you read it over?

A: Yes.

Q: Your supervisor signed this report.

A: Yes.

Q: And your supervisor reads it over before signing it.

A: Yes.

(They usually won't say no).

- **Accuracy is important because others rely on the report.**

Q: You are the case agent?

A: Yes.

Q: This is the only 302 report that was filled out in this case?

A: That's right.

Q: If you were unavailable and someone in your department needed to find out what happened in the case, they would read your report?

A: Yes.

Q: Others rely on your report?

A: They might.

Q: Your supervisor reads the report?

A: That's right.

Q: In fact he signed the report as you've stated.

A: Yes.

Q: The prosecutor relies on your report.

A: Yes.

Q: And sometimes the judge relies on your report.

A: Sometimes.

• Timing of report.

Q: The report you filed in this case was prepared on May 24th.

A: I believe that's right.

Q: May 24th was the same day as the arrest?

A: Yes.

Q: You claimed on the stand today that there was consent to search?

A: Yes.

Q: And today is three months after the arrest of Mr. Jones.

A: About.

• Could file a supplemental report.

Q: Officer you can file a supplemental report in a case, can't you?

A: Yes.

Q: If you discovered additional information you would add that to a supplemental report?

A: Yes.

Q: You could file a supplemental report at any time, can't you?

A: Yes.

Q: You never filed a supplemental report in this case, did you?

A: No.

Q: The only report filed is the 302 dated May 24th.

A: That's right.

Contextualize the Report. It is important to put the statement or lack of statement in the context of the report. The argument ultimately is that if it had happened as the officer claims, it would be in the report. One of the counter arguments is that not every fact is included. The defense needs to make sure that the officer agrees that how they entered the house is an important fact. It is also useful to show how other information, perhaps even less important, was included in the report to show how it is unlikely that if consent had been given it would have been left out.

Q: Officer you've stated that you include important information in your report?

A: That's right.

Q: You included the fact that Mr. Jones told you that the narcotics belonged to his cousin.

A: That's right.

Q: And you put that statement in quotation marks.

A: Yes.

Q: And you also put in quotations the statement that "he and his cousin lived in the house?"

A: Yes.

Q: You included the fact that all of the shades were down in the house?

A: I believe so.

Q: And you included the fact that Mr. Jones had a skull tattoo on his left bicep.

A: Yes.

Q: You would agree that statements made by a suspect are important?

A: They can be.

Q: Officer, you would agree that permission to enter a house is important information?

A: It can be.

Q: Not only can it be officer, it is important, isn't it?

A: It can be.

Q: In fact, it can be the only lawful way to get into a house with a warrant?

P: Objection, calls for legal conclusion?

J: I'll allow it.

A: That's right.

Q: You indicated on the report that there had been no warrant?

A: That's right.

Q: And you've been trained about lawful entries, haven't you officer.

(He's not going to say no.)

A: Yes.

Q: And you understand that ordinarily officers need a warrant to enter someone's home.

A: That's right, but there are exceptions.

Q: And one of those exceptions is consent.

A: Yes.

Q: And it is your claim that Mr. Jones gave consent.

A: That's right.

Confrontation. There are a number of ways to confront the witness with the inconsistency or omission. One is to simply ask the question: you didn't include the consent in your report did you? How far you go with it will depend on whether you are before a judge or jury. Motions to suppress are before a judge who is less impressed with theatrical confrontations, but often it is better to have the officer admit it himself than to ask him out right.

Q: Could you show the court where in your accurate and thorough report that Mr. Jones gave you consent to search his house?

A: I'd have to look at my report.

Q: May I approach, your honor?

J: You may.

Q: Showing you what has been marked as Defendant's Exhibit A for identification, that's your report, isn't it?

A: Yes.

Q: That's your signature?

A: Yes.

Q: That's your supervisor's signature?

A: Yes.

Q: That's the date, May 24th (indicating), the same day as the arrest?

A: Yes.

Q: Please show the court where you put in the report of this case, that others will rely on, that you prepared the day after Mr. Jones' arrest that he gave consent.

(Looking through document)

A: I guess it's not in there.

Q: It's not even a guess, is it officer. Nowhere in your three page single-spaced report does it say that Mr. Jones gave consent?

A: No, it doesn't.

Conclusion. Depending on the demeanor of the officer and the judge you are appearing before (a good lawyer knows the law a great lawyer knows the judge), you may want to suggest a reason for why the officer would lie about the consent issue as a conclusion to the impeachment. You do not necessarily need to do a conclusion and some judges will not make the leap that the prosecutor had any hand in tailoring the testimony, but it does provide a reason for why the officer may have altered his story once he figured out or was told that the search might be problematic.

Q: Officer, between the time you wrote the report on May 24th and came to court and said it was consent, you met with the prosecution, didn't you?

A: Yes.

Q: How many times?

A: Two or three.

Q: And you discussed with the prosecutor why you searched the house without a warrant?

A: Somewhat.

Q: And these discussions took place after you had written the 302?

A: Yes.

Q: And before you testified today you talked to the prosecutor about what you would say when asked about not including that fact?

A: We might have, I don't recall.

Q: Officer, you had a battering ram in your car that day didn't you?

A: It's standard equipment.

Q: You had standard equipment in your car on May 24th, didn't you?

A: Yes.

Q: That standard equipment included a battering ram, didn't it?

A: Yes.

Defense counsel needs to be prepared for the prosecutor to come up and ask the officer on re-direct why the information is not in the report. It is going to happen. Also, if there are other documents that show consent—the complaint, witness interviews, etc. the prosecutor will bring those out to rebut a charge of recent fabrication. The key for the defense is to make sure that any explanation is going to sound pretty lame given the concessions the officer has made on cross examination.

A good prosecutor will have realized that there is an omission and will have prepared the officer for that possibility. It is surprising, however, how often the officers are not prepared for omissions and inconsistencies. The defense questioning anticipates this and suggests that any excuse will have been concocted or at least "massaged" in readiness for the defense argument. If the impeachment trap is well set, it will be hard for the officer to explain using such excuses as: I didn't read it over, we don't usually put that in reports, it's not important, people don't use the reports, etc. The supplemental report question is critical to this trap because it shows that the report was never supplemented and could have been supplemented.

Should the Defendant Testify?

One of the biggest issues for the defense is whether the defendant should testify at the hearing. The answer will depend on the goals of the hearing, and of course, whether the defendant wishes to testify. If there is absolutely no way the judge is going to disbelieve the officer's version even if the defendant says it happened differently, there is little to be gained and much to be lost in putting the defendant on the stand. When defendants contradict officers, prosecutors often bring perjury charges against the defendant and the defendant may also receive enhancement points at sentencing for obstruction of justice. The prosecution is also likely to object to the defendant receiving acceptance of responsibility under the Federal Sentencing Guidelines.

In some cases the motion to suppress will be the trial in the sense that if the evidence is allowed to be introduced, the defendant would absolutely be convicted and thus is likely to plead. For example, say the defendant had been accused of being a felon in possession of a firearm where the gun was recovered in a security sweep of the defendant's home where he lived alone. The police claim the gun was in plain view during their security sweep of a closet in the defendant's bedroom. The defendant claims the gun was in a closed bureau drawer. If the gun is introduced at trial the defendant is very likely to be convicted; however, if the gun is suppressed the prosecution would have to dismiss the felon on the possession charge. Putting the defendant on the stand could be the whole case.

The goal of the hearing in the above example is not necessarily to get more information but to win the case at the motion stage since it is unlikely that the case would go to trial unless there was some defense that the defendant did not "possess" the gun. If the case is not going to go to trial no matter what happens at the hearing, it is less risky to put the defendant on the stand, although the charges of perjury and obstruction of justice are always a possibility if the judge does not credit the testimony of the defendant. The decision is made easier if there is objective evidence, photographs, other officers, eye witnesses, etc., to corroborate the defendant's version.

One of the prosecutor's goals should be to compel the defendant to take the stand. As discussed above, prosecutors should insist that the defendant take the stand in order to meet his burden of going forward. Although the defendant has an absolute right not to testify given his Fifth Amendment privilege against self-incrimination, the Supreme Court permits the defendant to make such statements at a suppression hearing, but precludes the use of those statements by the prosecution in its case in chief. *See Simmons v. United States*, 390 U.S. 377, 394, 88 S. Ct. 967, 976, 19 L. Ed. 2d 1247, 1259 (1968). The prosecution would be allowed to use the statements to impeach the defendant if the defendant took the stand at trial and said something different from what was said at the hearing. Also, it may be the only time the defendant is heard by the prosecution since the defendant has an absolute right not to testify at trial under the Fifth Amendment.

Should the defendant testify at the suppression hearing, the prosecution should try to use the opportunity to obtain as much information as possible and to pin the defendant down on facts just as the defense attorney tries with the police officer. Prosecutors should ask questions about criminal history and the crime itself if the judge permits it. Although the defense should argue that this is not relevant to the determination of Fourth Amendment rights, the prosecutor can argue that the questions relate to the credibility of the defendant which is always an issue when he takes the stand. It will be up to the individual judge as to the scope of the cross examination with respect to the defendant's criminal history and involvement in the crime at a suppression hearing.

Defense counsel should be vigilant to object to the use of the cross examination of the defendant as a fishing expedition that is beyond the scope of the direct testimony or that goes beyond areas that are the concern of the trial not the hearing. (This objection will be made easier if the defense was limited by the judge with respect to the scope of the defense's cross examination of the prosecution's witnesses). For example, if the only reason the defendant was called was to establish standing, defense counsel should limit the testimony to just that, and then attempt to limit the cross examination to the scope of the direct testimony. Because the hearing is before a judge and not a jury, and the judge is probably curious as to what the defendant has to say, the judge is likely to give the prosecution quite a bit of leeway in terms of asking questions. Defense counsel must consider this in advising a client whether to take the stand at a suppression hearing.

Appeals Issues Based on the Hearing

In cases where the only issue is whether the evidence can be introduced, the prosecution will sometimes consent to a "conditional plea" in that if the defendant loses the motion to suppress, he can plead guilty with the condition that should he win the motion to suppress on appeal, he can withdraw his plea of guilty. Sometimes a prosecutor will not agree to a conditional plea and in that case the trial would go forward or there could be a trial on stipulated facts. Prosecutors should have a very good reason for conducting a trial where the defense has agreed to plead guilty provided the Fourth Amendment issue can be appealed.

If the court grants a motion to suppress, the prosecutor has a right to an interlocutory appeal, meaning an appeal before the conclusion of the case, provided it certifies to the district court that the appeal is not taken for "purpose of delay and that the evidence is a substantial proof of a material fact in the proceeding." 18 USC § 3731. The appeal must be taken within 30 days from the suppression order and must be diligently pursued. *Id.*

The defendant, on the other hand, does not have a right to an interlocutory appeal but can appeal a conviction on the basis that his Fourth Amendment rights were violated and the evidence wrongfully admitted at trial. The remedy for such a violation is usually a retrial without the evidence. The primary reason for allowing the prosecution to appeal immediately the granting of a motion to suppress that involves a substantial proof of a material fact, is that the prosecution is not entitled to appeal an acquittal, which could be based on the fact that the incriminating evidence had been improperly suppressed.

CHAPTER TWENTY-FIVE
TRIAL AND POST-TRIAL PROCEEDINGS

At trial, most Fourth Amendment issues will have been litigated, usually at a pretrial suppression hearing to determine whether the evidence was lawfully obtained. The role of counsel at trial with respect to the Fourth Amendment is basically one of gatekeeper. For the defense, if the evidence was precluded, counsel must ensure that it is not introduced and that doors are not opened allowing use of evidence precluded in a motion to suppress. For the prosecution, counsel must look for openings by the defense that might permit the use of the otherwise precluded evidence.

Gatekeeping

If the evidence was suppressed, meaning excluded from use at trial, defense counsel must ensure that the evidence is not improperly introduced. Such gatekeeping requires contemporaneous objections to any question or answer that suggests the evidence. Rather than popping up to make ten objections to questions directed to the arresting officer surrounding the arrest of the defendant, it is a better idea for defense counsel to speak to the judge outside the presence of the witness either before trial starts or before the witness testifies and request the court to admonish the witness not to "blurt out" anything about the suppressed evidence. At a minimum, the defense should request that the prosecution inform the witness that the two kilograms found in the defendant's home are not admissible and cannot be "accidentally blurted out."

In addition to the actual evidence precluded from use at trial, the Supreme Court compromise in *Simmons v. United States,* 390 U.S. 377, 88 S. Ct. 967, 19 L. Ed. 2d 1247 (1968) allows the defendant to make the incriminating assertions necessary to establish her right to bring a motion, but prevents the prosecution from using that information in its case-in-chief to establish guilt. Proper use of these statements must be guarded by the defense. If information is related by the officers but was not included in the

305

police report, complaint, etc., but could only have been known to the officer as a result of an affidavit by the defendant or if the defendant took the stand at the suppression hearing, defense counsel must seek to have the testimony stricken from the record and possibly seek a mistrial, see discussion below.

Defense counsel must also strive to keep gates closed; meaning avoid eliciting testimony or making arguments that would open the door to the prosecution bringing in the otherwise precluded evidence. For example, it is problematic for the defense to elicit statements from the defendant that would suggest that he never knew anything about drugs when two kilograms were recovered from his house. Prosecutors, on the other hand, should listen carefully for defense arguments or elicited testimony that contradicts suppressed evidence. For example, questioning that suggests that the defendant had no contact with drugs or would not have known what narcotics looked like, etc., should prompt the prosecution to ask for a sidebar and seek to introduce the suppressed narcotics to counter the otherwise unfair representation by the defense.

When the motion to suppress is denied and the evidence will be admitted, defense counsel should still object when the evidence is being offered. To avoid looking obstructionist before the jury, defense counsel should seek a ruling from the judge that the evidence is received over defense objection without requesting that counsel physically stand up and voice an objection in the presence of the jury. Put bluntly, juries do not like objections.

Some judges will not allow "continuing objections" and will require defense counsel to object at the time the evidence is introduced. Counsel should not assume that the motion to suppress is the only objection needed, although in most jurisdictions usually the pretrial motion preserves the objection. If in doubt, defense counsel must object to preserve the issue for appeal; otherwise the issue will be deemed waived. Once waived, the burden for appellate review becomes the nearly impossible plain error standard rather than harmless error.

Remedies

The issue arises as to the remedy when otherwise precluded testimony is presented to the jury The judge will often look to defense counsel to craft an appropriate instruction hoping to cure any taint through the instruction. Plainly stated, there really is no appropriate remedy other than mistrial (which the judge and prosecutor are likely to resist unless the prosecutor was trying to compel a mistrial by deliberately introducing the evidence). One cannot "unring" the bell, as they say. Defense counsel ordinarily should seek a mistrial and object to any instruction on the basis that no instruction will cure the error. When the judge asks whether any instruction shall be given, the defense must make clear that it is obvious that without some instruction the jury will consider the precluded testimony, but that even with the instruction the prejudice is too great to be overcome by instruction and a mistrial must be granted. *See Practice Commentaries Federal Rules of Criminal Procedure, Natali, Parsons, Statsinger & Wolfe, Commentary to Fed. R. Crim. P.* 26.3 (2002-2003).

Judges will typically craft an instruction rather than grant a mistrial. The instruction follows along these lines: Ladies and gentlemen, you have heard testimony as to two kilograms of cocaine that were found in the defendant's home. I advise you that you are not to consider the two kilograms of cocaine as evidence against the defendant. The testimony of the two kilograms was improperly presented and is stricken from the record. Yeah right. One federal defender describes this as the "don't think about the white bear" admonition. Surely it is impossible for the jury to think about anything else except that the police officer blurted out "inadvertently" that they recovered two kilograms from the defendant's home. Having the judge repeat the offensive two kilograms makes the cure worse than the disease.

If the judge refuses to grant a mistrial defense counsel must ensure that it has not consented to the instruction and await the eventual appeal on the issue. At a minimum, the defense should request that any mention of the drugs in the instruction should not repeat two kilograms of cocaine and that it should be a very brief instruction, although the defense argument is that no instruction could cure the taint and a mistrial must be granted.

Permissible Uses at Trial

Even if the evidence is suppressed, there are permissible uses at trial. If the defendant takes the stand at trial evidence obtained even in violation of the Fourth Amendment can be used to impeach his testimony. Defense counsel must be very careful to limit the testimony so that it does not open the door to the impeachment. Counsel should seek a preliminary ruling from the judge on what the defendant will testify about and whether that would open the door to the precluded evidence. The prosecution, on the other hand, should seek to introduce the evidence if at all possible. The information does not come in automatically if the defendant testifies, only if it is proper impeachment such as where the defendant denies that he ever had the drugs in his house or that he knew what drugs looked like.

Testimony from witnesses other than the defendant cannot be impeached with tainted evidence. *See James v. Illinois*, 493 U.S. 307, 313, 110 S. Ct. 648, 652, 107 L. Ed. 2d 676, 684 (1990). However, some circuits will allow illegally-obtained evidence to refresh a recollection, *see, e.g., United States v. Kusek*, 844 F.2d 942, 949 (2d Cir. 1988) (allowing prosecution to refresh defense witness' memory with tape procured outside scope of warrant). If the witnesses testify that the defendant never had drugs in his apartment, the prosecution should seek to introduce the evidence. The defense should be careful not to open the door through other witnesses.

Motions In Limine

In cases that are scheduled to go to trial, a motion *in limine* is frequently brought requesting the judge to exclude or allow the introduction of certain evidence. *In limine* means at the threshold and often the motions are made before or near the beginning of trial to determine what evidence will be allowed.

There is a difference between motions *in limine* and motions to suppress even if the outcome of winning either is effectively the same for the defense: inability to use the evidence at trial. A motion to suppress precludes the use of the evidence at trial because the evidence is obtained in violation of the law and is precluded to deter police misconduct. A motion *in limine* does not involve the suppression of evidence under the Exclusionary Rule; the evidence was permissibly obtained but is inadmissible for other reason such as unduly prejudicial. Although motions *in limine* are often brought against evidence that was challenged in a motion to suppress, many motions *in limine* are never challenged through a suppression motion.

It is helpful to think of a motion *in limine* as a motion in limbo—how does one prepare the case until the attorney knows if the evidence will be permitted at trial? The sooner the issue is resolved, the more time each side will have to prepare its case, although some issues will not ripen until trial. Until the issues are resolved the parties often are unable to prepare opening statements or even develop a full case theory. A request to the judge to rule on the issue will make trial preparations easier and more efficient. Waiting until the first day of trial for the judge to decide if a prior criminal act will be admitted is not advised. There will not be sufficient time to adapt. Moreover, judges are reluctant to take a lot of time with preliminary issues when jurors are waiting.

Most of the issues surrounding a motion in limine involve the Federal Rules of Evidence such as whether the prosecution can offer statements made by the alleged child victim to a psychiatrist, whether the shocking autopsy photos can be shown to the jury or whether a letter from the defendant to his wife can be admitted. The most common basis used by the defense to preclude introduction at trial is that the probative value of the evidence is outweighed by its prejudicial effect pursuant to Rule 403 F.R.E. and corresponding state rules. The evidence in these situations is known as "unduly prejudicial." (Counsel should avoid claiming that the evidence is simply prejudicial; judges will often respond—quite often sarcastically—that the reason the other side wants it in is because it prejudices the other side's case. The test is not whether the evidence is prejudicial "of course it is counsel" but whether it is "unduly" prejudicial.)

Motions *in limine* are frequently made in letter form and even orally. Whether to make a formal motion *in limine* will depend on the judge, the local rules of the jurisdiction and also the complexity of the argument. If the analysis is whether the probative value of the autopsy photos to show defensive wounds outweighs the prejudice from the gory emotional impact, a lengthy memorandum of law is probably unnecessary. But if the issue is whether the testimony of a child complainant in a sexual assault case can be introduced through her psychiatrist rather than having the child take the stand, the issue will need to be thoroughly briefed well in advance of trial. Counsel may also want to request an opportunity to give oral argument on the issue.

When a judge rules against the defense on a motion to suppress, the next level of strategy should be whether there are other reasons for precluding the evidence, such as the prejudice outweighing any probative value. For example, say there were very explicit pornographic adult video tapes found in the defendant's apartment during a search that was contested by the defendant. Although the judge refuses to suppress the evidence, the defense should still move to preclude the tapes in that the pornographic video tapes are not unlawful or probative of child pornography and any conceivable probative value would be outweighed by the prejudice to the defendant. Stipulations may also achieve the same result, in that the parties can stipulate that there were videotapes of pornography involving adults without having to show the films to the jury which, the defense should argue, would be done solely to inflame the jurors' passions and emotions against the defendant.

Fourth Amendment Issues and the Jury

Bottom line, juries want to know everything that happened in a case. They do not like to have evidence kept from them and they could not care less about so-called "technicalities." Judges typically will give an instruction when a motion to suppress has been denied that the evidence was properly obtained in the case and the jury is not to speculate on the propriety of the evidence. Defense counsel should object to the instruction as unnecessary unless the defendant has made some argument questioning the propriety of obtaining the evidence.

Defense counsel is certainly permitted to impeach an officer with a prior statement including testimony at a suppression hearing. Use of the testimony must be done so that the prior "proceeding" is not described as a suppression hearing which would clue the jury in that not all the evidence might have been admitted even if the motion had been denied. "Prior proceeding" is commonly used. Witnesses should be admonished not to refer to the prior proceeding as a motion to suppress evidence by the defense.

Fourth Amendment Issues and Sentencing

Suppressed evidence can be used at the defendant's sentencing and in certain civil proceedings. Evidence that was obtained in violation of the Fourth Amendment may be used to enhance a sentence by including the weight of the drugs that were unlawfully seized from the home, for example. If the agents obtained the evidence specifically to enhance the defendant's sentence by increasing the weight of the drugs, however, in most circuits the additional weight will not be added to increase the defendant's base offense level. In addition, the recent Supreme Court decision *Blakely v. Washington*, 2004 WL 1402697 has called into question what can be used to enhance a sentence where the issue was not found by a jury.

Fourth Amendment and Post-Trial Proceedings

If a defendant is convicted after a motion to suppress when the evidence was permitted into his trial, he should file a timely notice of appeal. There is a wrinkle in time calculation when it comes to filing a notice of appeal. A notice of appeal must be filed within 10 days from the date of the judgment. The problem is that exclusion of holidays under the Federal Appellate Rules is different than exclusions under the Federal Rules of Criminal Procedure. As discussed, FRCrP 45(a) excludes interim holidays and weekends for time periods of less than *11 days*. FRAP 26(a) excludes interim holidays and weekends when the time period is less than *7 days*. Because appellate rules govern the filing of a notice of appeal, defense counsel has fewer days to file a notice of appeal than would be available under FRCrP 45. *See also Practice Commentaries Federal Rules of Criminal Procedure, Natali, Parsons, Statsinger & Wolfe, Commentary to Fed. R. Crim. P. 45 (2002-2003).*

Appellate courts will review probable cause determinations under a *de novo* standard, unless the officers obtained a warrant. *See Ornelas v. United States,* 517 U.S. 690, 699, 116 S. Ct. 1657, 1663, 134 L. Ed. 2d 911, 920 (1996). In cases where there is a warrant the reviewing courts will give great deference to the issuing judge in order to provide an incentive for the use of warrants. *Id.* In considering a district court's denial of a motion to suppress, appellate courts ordinarily review the court's factual findings under a clearly erroneous standard, construing all evidence in the light most favorable to the prosecution.

A person who is "aggrieved" by an unlawful search and seizure can move for return of the property if they may lawfully possess the property. *See* FRCrP 41(e) for the procedures on return of property. Much of the evidence seized, though, will be subject to the forfeiture laws and will not be returned. *See, e.g., FRCrP 32.2, see also Practice Commentaries Federal Rules of Criminal Procedure, Natali, Parsons, Statsinger & Wolfe, Commentary to Fed. R. Crim. P. 32.2 and 41 (2002-2003).*